GOETHEANISM

GOETHEANISM
AN IMPULSE OF TRANSFORMATION AND RESURRECTION

SCIENCE OF THE HUMAN BEING AND SOCIAL SCIENCE

Twelve lectures given in Dornach between 3 January
and 2 February 1919

TRANSLATED AND INTRODUCED BY
CHRISTIAN VON ARNIM

RUDOLF STEINER

RUDOLF STEINER PRESS

CW 188

The publishers gratefully acknowledge the generous funding of the translation of these lectures by the Rudolf Steiner Charitable Trust

Rudolf Steiner Press
Hillside House, The Square
Forest Row, RH18 5ES

www.rudolfsteinerpress.com

Published by Rudolf Steiner Press 2024

Originally published in German under the title *Der Goetheanismus, ein Umwandlungsimpuls und Auferstehungsgedanke. Menschenwissenschaft und Sozialwissenschaft* (volume 188 in the *Rudolf Steiner Gesamtausgabe* or Collected Works) by Rudolf Steiner Verlag, Dornach. Based on shorthand notes that were not reviewed or revised by the speaker. This authorized translation is based on the third revised German edition (1982), edited by Johann Waeger and Robert Friedenthal

Published by permission of the Rudolf Steiner Nachlassverwaltung, Dornach

A catalogue record for this book is available from the British Library

ISBN 978 1 85584 667 8

Cover by Morgan Creative
Typeset by Symbiosys Technologies, Visakhapatnam, India
Printed and bound by 4Edge Ltd., Essex

Contents

FIRST LECTURE
DORNACH, 3 JANUARY 1919
The response of spiritual science to the most important questions of the time
Rejection of spirituality as a characteristic of our time. Formation of abstract concepts. Materialism as a product of Church teachings. The animal lives in abstract concepts. Difference in sensory perception between animals and humans. 'Human and animal soul' by Wasmann. Passing the Guardian of the Threshold in the age of the consciousness soul. Abstraction of concepts leads the human being down to the animal, a regression in advancement. Fear in animals because the earthly world is alien to them. Future state of fear of people who cannot take in the spiritual world.

SECOND LECTURE
Dornach, 4 JANUARY 1919
The place of the human being in the age of the consciousness soul—John of the Cross on contemplation and the modern path to spirit cognition
Modern spiritual science and ancient spiritual currents. For the Church, the endeavour to penetrate the supersensory world through special abilities is heretical, as is the view that human beings partake of the divine spirit. John of the Cross on contemplation. His teaching distorted by the clergy. Spiritual science is the continuation of the union of the human and the divine-spiritual taught by John of the Cross. The path of mystical contemplation in John of the Cross. The necessity of supersensory cognition in order to understand the processes in the human subconscious.

THIRD LECTURE

DORNACH, 5 JANUARY 1919

The decisive aspect of the present epoch

Old impulses until the fifteenth century. The catastrophic events of our time are a consequence of the rise of the spirits of personality. Thanks to spiritual training, the view of the mineral, plant, animal and human realms is transformed. No perception of our own being in our conceptual faculty: our own I as a hole in consciousness. Spectral conception and incomplete volition. The actual being of a person in the middle between conception and volition. Beings banished from the spiritual world are in the mineral and plant kingdoms. The human being remains a child, the animal has dried out. People who do not ascend to a grasp of the spiritual world will lose their connection with the world in their conception and consciousness after death, but not in their longing. This is what makes the present sick. Something living in the sphere of the will that cannot be managed with a person's conceptual capacity brings about rage. If people only give themselves over to their heads, they will soon have no thoughts at all. The necessity of active thinking through spiritual science to fertilize social life.

Pages 39-66

FOURTH LECTURE

DORNACH, 10 JANUARY 1919

The relationship between the soul-spiritual and the bodily-physical

Experience of the I and the astral body in sleep; weakening of this experience in the waking state. This makes it possible to understand the external side of nature, but not to bring order to the social structure. Increased courage is necessary. Lack of interest in the spiritual life. Being lulled to sleep when people face each other with reference to our deeper human nature. On entering the spiritual world, that which is put to sleep awakens. The solutions to the social question lie only beyond the threshold of sensory consciousness. Sentiments which are necessary in order to avoid exploring the social impulses without substance are like maternal love on the physical plane. The solution to the social question lies in recognizing the divine-spiritual nature of the human being. European logic and science are convinced that humans are actually bad; an expansion of the spiritual horizon is necessary in order to talk fruitfully about the social problem.

Pages 67-85

Fifth Lecture
Dornach, 11 January 1919
The infusion with the spirit of modern history—paganism, Judaism and Christianity—Goethe's Fairy Tale

Elevating the understanding of the Mystery of Golgotha through spiritual science. The thought of resurrection. Conception of the living only by ascending to imagination, inspiration, intuition. Paganism: view of nature; Judaism: moral impulse—Job. Entry of the Christ impulse when pagan and Jewish culture had reached their peak and their power was exhausted, the external symbol was the dying representative of humanity. Christianity had to take on the form of the pagan mystery in order to spread throughout the Roman Empire; hence the Mass. The acceptance of Christianity by the Nordic barbarians was much more primitive due to their personal relationship of the heart with Jesus Christ. In the primitive peoples of the north, that which was previously developed in the south at an earlier stage is developed for a later time. What was Platonism in Greek civilisation is Goetheanism in the fifth cultural epoch. Goethe points to an expectation. Goethe's prose hymn 'To Nature'.

Pages 86-103

Sixth Lecture
Dornach, 12 January 1919
Goetheanism as a mood of expectation

Crisis of humanity at the time of the Mystery of Golgotha; weakening of the atavistic forces of the body; strengthening of the soul and spiritual forces through the Christ impulse. Inner resurrection of the ancient mysteries as a historical fact, incomprehensible to ordinary reason. Goethe's position in relation to the understanding of the Christ impulse. Radiating out of cultures from the middle of Europe. The will to destroy the middle of Europe. Goetheanism as a mood of expectation. The threefold structure of the social organization of humanity. The pagan Isis mood, the *Fairy Tale of the Green Snake and the Beautiful Lily*. The development of Goethe's personality. The influence of Shakespeare, Spinoza and Linné. Goethe's unfinished works (*Mysteries, Pandora*). Goetheanism still rests in the grave as far as external culture is concerned, but it must rise again and bring about a new understanding of Christ.

Pages 104-122

economic value from the concept of human labour. Unrealistic definitions of the concept of value. Economic value: state of tension between commodity (natural basis) and need (spiritual).

Pages 155-174

TENTH LECTURE
DORNACH, 31 JANUARY 1919
What form can social demands take in the present?

Economic system of the sixteenth and seventeenth centuries: crafts, guilds, etc. The shattering of these contexts with the unfolding of the consciousness soul. Development of economic individualism through the capitalist mode of production. Current situation in the West: Bourgeois-democratic impulses without understanding for the proletarian movement; Centre and East: dilapidated state structures, destroyed economy. The 'Erfurt Programmes' of social democracy: transferring scientific conceptions to the social organism. Karl Kautsky. Jaffé. Machine output in relation to human labour.

Pages 175-190

ELEVENTH LECTURE
DORNACH, 1 FEBRUARY 1919
*The detachment of the economic process from the personal—The detachment of the moral
and spiritual life from the external realities of existence*

Socialist idea of the transition from capitalism to socialism. The scientific view of social processes. No social judgement without a spiritual-scientific view. The development of capitalism. The influence of morality on medieval craftsmen. The capitalist economic order: working for profit. Detachment of the economic process from the personal. The four socialist ideals (socialization of the means of production, production only for needs, democratic wage and labour relations, surplus value to the community). The moral side of the social question. The awakening of animal instincts as a result of a lack of spiritual interest. Economy: imagination; spirit: inspiration; political organism: intuition.

Pages 191-203

TWELFTH LECTURE
DORNACH, 2 FEBRUARY 1919
*The three preconditions in the human being's position towards the world, towards other
human beings and towards spirituality*

The four components of the socialist programme: socialization of the means of production; production only by need; democratic living and working conditions; added value to the community. The proletariat has no confidence in the morality of the ruling class. The pursuit of knowledge of nature, free of morality. The spiritual is the most important aspect of the social question today. Necessity of a free system of ideals. Risk of the emergence of angry instincts. Spiritual science leads to a spiritual view instead of faith, to a genuine appreciation of human beings instead of indifference, to the correct valuation of all things.

THIS volume was preceded by the important lectures contained in volume 187 of the Complete Works entitled *How Can Mankind Find the Christ Again? The Threefold Shadow-Existence of Our Time and the New Light of Christ.*

In the first dark winter after the war, Rudolf Steiner appealed in the lectures in this volume to the spirit of Central Europe that had been forgotten since the middle of the nineteenth century, as it can be summarized under the term Goetheanism. A new constellation had emerged in the world: East and West faced each other in hostile opposition; in the centre, with no task in the world and no hope of a better future, in material hardship, the defeated Central Europe. In Russia, Bolshevism arose violently and threatened the world. The victorious West, exhausted and also spiritually and physically drained, wanted to convert the whole world to 'democracy'. Dejection and confusion prevailed in Germany, endowed with the new, unfamiliar 'democracy' that was unwelcome in large parts of the population.

These facts must be borne in mind in order to fully understand the deep seriousness and urgency with which Rudolf Steiner speaks here of the forces that could have helped Central Europe regain self-confidence and a meaningful future: the great minds of the late eighteenth and early nineteenth century and the task of seeking a solution to the pressing social and national questions on a spiritual basis through a threefold organization of the social organism. For immediately after the lectures printed here, the so-called 'threefolding period' begins, in which Rudolf Steiner endeavoured for almost two years to promote this idea for a modern reorganization of Central Europe to the public and made a superhuman effort to achieve an immediate effect on external events, but this was unsuccessful and ultimately had to be abandoned (see also Note 102).

Introduction

RUDOLF Steiner was nothing if not engaged with the issues of his time. So also in these wide-ranging lectures, given barely two months after the First World War had come to an end in November 1918, he addresses from the perspective of spiritual science the social and political upheavals convulsing society, highlighting the limits of a purely materialistic outlook in trying to solve them.

But even before starting on the substantive issues, and while seeking to argue that these times urgently needed spiritual science in order to shed a deeper light on how a solution to the questions of the time might be found, he sees himself compelled to issue an appeal for an openness to engage in two directions. In his very first words he criticizes, on the one hand, the blinkered attitude of a materialistic thinking that, on the basis of its own ignorance of a spiritual world, dismisses out of hand that anyone else might have knowledge of it as a reality. On the other hand, addressing the people sitting in front of him, he appeals to those in the anthroposophical movement equally not to indulge in the 'snootiness' to think that all they need to do is study anthroposophy in a bubble to have the answer to everything—without properly trying to look outwards and understand what the serious issues of the time are in order to engage with them.

In these lectures, Steiner discusses in a very wide historical sweep the various influences and currents of thought, both progressive and regressive, that have led humanity to the point it has reached at the start of the twentieth century. But he also looks at the development of the human being as a spiritual being and the development of consciousness, in order then to draw parallels between the threefold organization of the human being and how society might be structured in a new way through the threefold organization of the social organism into independent, but interrelated spheres of economic life, political life, and cultural and intellectual life. This would respond to the demands of the proletariat in a way that is not abstract but accords with reality. And here spiritual science plays a crucial role, Steiner argues, because without an understanding of the underlying reality of a spiritual world, the material world and the influences that shape it, human endeavour cannot be understood.

It is in this context that he sees the particular role of Central Europe, where the old order had been destroyed as a result of the war and which appeared to be without any hope for the future. Building on the holistic phenomenological approach and spiritual and intellectual tradition of a Goethe, what Steiner called Goetheanism and saw as representing the spirit of Central Europe, his hope was that in the ferment of the disintegration of the old order, and of the states that represented it, there would be an opportunity for a new kind of thinking to arise in the centre between East and West. In his view neither Marxism nor socialism, with their flawed analyses of the aspirations of the working class, had the answers as to how to bring about such change, and western capitalism, which had separated production from human aspiration, was no better.

In looking at the social and economic conditions, Steiner also puts forward an idea that in its modern form was a long way ahead of its time. Nowadays everyone is familiar with the term globalization as the concept of an interconnected world in which supply chains, goods, capital, people, but also ideas and culture move between countries around the globe at an unprecedented pace. Particularly in the economic sphere, globalization is not always viewed as a force for good because of the way it can become exploitative. Think of the Bangladeshi workers producing garments for a pittance in unsafe working conditions so that they can be sold at rock-bottom prices in the rich Global North. Or transnational corporations moving factories around the world to where labour happens to be the cheapest. A multinational doesn't look at individual countries or regions as isolated economic units but rather sees them in a global context.

That the earth needs to be looked at as an interconnected organism, although not necessarily in the way that a multinational might, is exactly the point that Steiner makes in discussing his ideas for societal change and renewal with the threefold division of the social organism—with the three distinct spheres of economic life, the life of politics and law, and cultural life, each with their own inherent ways of functioning. People in his day, he says, are still unable to think properly in terms of the social organism, in other words, cannot come to the right answers to the social problems that need solving, because they proceed from the 'grotesque' idea that a single state or a single national territory is an organism in itself.

Rather, when looking at the coexistence of people across the earth, the whole earth has to be looked at as a single organism. A single state is only one component of that organism. 'This is how it is', he says, 'that everyone who is familiar with the social organism in its inner living conditions—and this is something that must proceed from this threefold structure—knows how to place themselves in the right relations, be it that they have to assess the social conditions in Russia or England or in Germany or anywhere else.' His hope was, that Central Europe would become the cradle for such a new and holistic way of thinking.

Christian von Arnim,
September 2024

First Lecture

DORNACH, 3 JANUARY 1919

How often have we had to emphasize here that the truths of spiritual science, when they are spoken, are easily misunderstood in one direction or another. And I have also spoken to you about the most varied reasons why it is certainly easy to fail to grasp, to misunderstand these spiritual-scientific views and insights. It must be said again and again that it is of course incredibly easy, when a person has had little opportunity to delve into spiritual matters, to find here or there that the things that come to light spiritually are not fully justified or the like. It is also incredibly easy to say, how does a person who communicates something through spiritual science know that, how do they know that, if we are not willing to consider what the person themselves has often stated about how they know these things, and we merely form our judgement according to what we ourselves know. It is not hard to say, how can they know that? It is not something I know!—and then to declare confidently, that which I do not know, no one else knows either; at most they can only believe it! But such a judgement only comes about because people do not even bother to go into the sources from which spiritual-scientific knowledge must be drawn, especially in this day and age.

Now one of the misunderstandings that can arise in this way can include the belief that spiritual science wishes the wholesale condemnation and annihilation of everything the times strive for, insofar as this striving emanates from personalities who stand outside spiritual science. But here, too, it is just a misunderstanding. The spiritual scientist who in a serious and dignified way examines the present state of the world will certainly consider the state of mind, the mood of their contemporaries and will ask themselves the question: What is going on in the souls of serious contemporaries in the present with regard to the direction in which an improvement of many things worthy of improvement or in need of improvement must be sought?

What must, however, be considered here above all as an extraordinarily striking fact, especially in the present day, is that the thing which is rejected, sometimes by the hardest striving contemporaries, is precisely the concrete engagement with the knowledge of the spiritual world, with the cognition of the spiritual world, which can present itself to a person as a reality and not merely as something that can be developed through a sum of concepts. Most people today wish only to remain in the world of the senses with their experiences and at most admit a spiritual world as being accessible through concepts, through ideas. They do not want to associate themselves with research that speaks of methods to truly penetrate the spiritual world in an experiential way. This rejection of real spirituality is, however, a characteristic trait of our time; it is a trait of our time that we, in particular, who are trying to place ourselves on the ground of spiritual science, must take into account. Otherwise we will remain outside this spiritual science, only engaging with it as with something that should also be taken into account alongside other things that emerge in the present.

I have recently shown here, by presenting to you the thoughts of Walther Rathenau,[1] that the spiritual scientist is already in a position—within the limits in which present schools of thought are to be appreciated—to really appreciate these schools of thought. But what is striking is particularly this rejection of the real spiritual impact that is to come in our time. This rejection can be experienced at every turn if we are attentive to what people think today.

Certainly, many people in the present have been confronted with the current disturbing situation in the world; there are people who are able to appreciate the full seriousness of the present time and have indeed been able to appreciate it for some time. Here, too, I would ask you not to indulge in the snootiness of some anthroposophists and to think that anthroposophy as such already provides instruction as to how better to appreciate the seriousness of the times than people outside the anthroposophical movement appreciate it. For it would also be desirable that within this anthroposophical movement some people would be moved in their minds to a greater extent by what is decisive in our present world situation. We find all too often, especially within our ranks, people who today, despite the seriousness of the times, do not like to look at this seriousness and prefer to occupy themselves with their own worthy person instead of arousing some interest within themselves for the great questions pulsating through humanity.

In today's reflections, I want to start from an example that came into my hands, we might say by chance—if we do not misunderstand the word, and we do not need to misunderstand it. An essay[2] which, however, is now out of date insofar as it was written while the so-called War was still in full swing. So the essay is out of date today. It is not very penetrating in other respects either, as it treats most of the things it discusses in a very one-sided way. But it comes from a person—we can see that from the whole attitude, from the whole way of writing—who gives the most serious thought to what should actually happen now, what the world should expect from events. It shows, this essay, how the Western powers, the Central powers, the Eastern powers have progressively behaved within the catastrophe of the last few years. It presents the great dangers—albeit in a one-sided way, but it does so nevertheless—that lurk within this catastrophe today and will lurk into the future. The author has a certain farsightedness. He does not only look at the world purely from the point of view of national borders; even this is said to still happen among people today, that they only look at the world from the point of view of their national borders, and if they can then reassure themselves that within their country this or that is not yet taking place, then they are unconcerned.

Indeed, the author of this essay not only sees the parish pump but he does also see something from a world perspective. And summing up his thoughts, he arrives at some very strange words. He says:

> That a terrible fate beckons white humanity, this seems to me certain under all circumstances, unless a period of the supreme rule of

wisdom very soon replaces that of passion and delusion. We have indeed been living for a long time in the period that bears much resemblance to the time of the migration of peoples. The pace is accelerated tremendously by the World War. What corresponds to the Germanic tribes migrating at that time from the outside into ancient civilized lands are the considerable, ascending lower social classes which, both in blood and in cultural heritage, are very different from the hitherto ruling ones. The fact that this migration of peoples

—it is indeed much better to speak of a migration of peoples than of a war—

is taking place at all is good insofar as it brings about a spread, a spread of the cultural base and a raising of the overall level. But it is very dangerous if it goes too fast. And this danger is magnified the longer the World War lasts.

The essay is out of date today. The danger has not become any less great, but since it derives all its arguments from the still ongoing raging war, its arguments are outdated. But we should be particularly interested here in the first sentence I read out: 'That a terrible fate beckons white humanity,* this seems to me certain under all circumstances, unless a period of the supreme rule of wisdom very soon replaces that of passion and delusion.' For this is indeed absolutely true as an abstract truth. And when someone says that the only salvation of humanity lies in turning to the supreme rule of wisdom, and not to any other political or social quackery, then we must recognize such a fact, such a line of thought. But we must not forget here that it is just such people, of whom we must admit that they are touched in all the depths of their being by the seriousness of the situation of the times, that just such people, when it is a question of saying what the ideas of wisdom consist of which are to replace the old delusions, that they then immediately fall back again on some old delusions which have turned into fine words. For that is precisely the tragedy, that is the terrible fate of our time, that people do indeed become aware of this: it is necessary to turn to the spirit—but that they are always overcome by fear and

---

*Whilst the author of this quotation is unknown, it is clear that Rudolf Steiner is referencing 'white humanity' in the sense of 'Western humanity'.

anxiety when they are supposed to turn to the spirit; that they are then immediately ready to reach for the old delusions that have driven humanity into the present terrible fate. After all, we only need to take the example of a very widespread school of thought.

Do you think that if you asked a fully-fledged, to put it crudely, representative of the Roman Catholic creed whether he would be inclined to believe that the old ideas had led us into this catastrophic time, that they must be replaced by new ones; do you think that he would really be inclined to believe in the necessity of renewing those ideas which could not save humanity from this terrible catastrophe? No, he would say: If people only become properly Roman Catholic again, then they will no doubt become happy. And it will not even occur to him to say to himself that they have had time to be Roman Catholics for one thousand nine hundred years and have still ended up in the catastrophe; that at the very least the catastrophe must teach us that we need new impulses. This is just one example of many. It is necessary in general to show up the interrelationships that exist with regard to this point without any hesitation.

It is easy today, even for a genuine-seeming follower of this or that Church, to say: Haeckelism or materialism, they are the work of the devil; they must be eradicated root and branch. This is the opposite of what can lead people into a beneficial state of mind. Yes, we can speak in this way, but if we stick to this statement and do not examine the connections that come into consideration here, then it is impossible to arrive at something that can be beneficial for the present and even less so for the immediate future. Because if you take in any worldview coloured with a materialistic sentiment and ask yourself, where does it come from historically?—then you will not, if you really want to obtain an insight, be able to avoid saying to yourself in the end after all: it basically comes precisely from the way Christianity has been represented by the various denominations for one thousand nine hundred years. The person with a deeper insight knows that Haeckelism would not have been possible at all without the Christianity of the Church that preceded it. There are people who remain stuck in the Church's point of view, let's say, as it was in the Middle Ages; who today still represent the thoughts that the Church had in the Middle Ages. Others have developed these thoughts further. And among those who have developed them further is Ernst Haeckel, for example.[3] He is a straight descendant of the ideas cultivated by the various Churches for centuries. This did not originate outside the Church; in a deeper sense, this is definitely truth that originated within the doctrines of the Church. However, we will only really recognize the connections if we fertilize ourselves a little with insights from spiritual science in order to consider these things.

Therefore, today—although some of you may say that the matter is too difficult, but nothing must be too difficult for us, we should acquire insight—I would like to start by explaining one point in particular to you today.

If you read the philosophically inclined writings of well-trained scholars today, for example Catholic scholars, you will find a very specific view formed everywhere with reference to a certain point. And we can say: you will find this view formed in the very best of these Catholic-trained scholars. I would like to remark right away in this context that I am not at all inclined to underestimate the formal training of the Catholic clergy, for example. I am very well aware—I have also expressed this in my book *Vom Menschenrätsel [The Riddle of Man]*—of the better training that especially some Catholic theologians have when they write philosophically, compared to the scribblings of philosophical scholars who have not gone through Catholic theology, for example. In this respect, it must be said, the scholarly literature, the theological literature of the Protestant, the Reformed clergy lags far behind the good philosophical training of the Catholic theologians. These people, through their rigorous training, have a certain ability to form their concepts in a truly contoured way; they have—something, for example, of which people who are famous today in the non-Catholic philosophical literature do not even have an inkling—a certain ability to discern what a concept is, what an idea is and the like; in short, these people have a certain training.

It is not even necessary to take a book by Haeckel; we can take a book by Eucken[4] in order to notice this conceptual awkwardness, this awful, merely feuilletonistic harping on about the most important concepts; or we can take, for example, a book by Bergson[5] where you always have the feeling: he catches the concepts without being able to handle them, like the familiar Chinese man who wants to turn around and always catches his pigtail. You will not find this absolute floundering about in the world of concepts, which is the case with these untrained people, if you get involved in the philosophical literature originating from the Catholic clergy. In this respect, for example, a book like the three-volume *History of Idealism* by Otto Willmann,[6] a genuine Catholic, who displays his Catholicism on every page, ranks far higher than most of what is written by non-Catholics in the philosophical field today in particular. It is perfectly possible to know all this and still take the standpoint that one must take as a spiritual scientist. Inferiority of the spirit may decide differently in this area, may, for example, be of the opinion, because there is good training, it is worth more in general. Well, that may be so; but it is also possible to exercise objectivity even when we are forced to adopt a certain point of view in life.

One point will always confront you in this well-schooled Catholic philosophical literature, a point that also has immense fascination for the thinker of today. This is the one that always crops up for consideration when people talk about the difference between humans and animals. You see, the ordinary readers of Haeckel and admirers of Haeckel will always aim to blur the difference between humans and animals as much as possible, to make people believe that humans are, on the whole, only animals with a higher level of education. Catholic scholars do not do that, but they always emphasize something that seems to them to be a radical difference between the human being and the animal. They emphasize that the animal stays with the ordinary perception it gains of the object it is smelling now, of the next object it then smells or looks at, and so on; that the animal, in a sense, always remains only in single individual ideas, while the human being has the ability to form deduced, abstract concepts for themselves, to combine things. This is indeed a radical difference, because if you take the matter in this way, it makes the human being really radically different from the animal. The animal that only looks at things individually cannot develop spirituality in itself, because abstract concepts must live in spirituality. And this must lead us to recognize that this particular soul lives in the human being, which forms the abstract concepts, whereas the animal with its particular kind of inner life cannot form these abstract concepts.

Anyone who looks at the corresponding Catholic arguments on this point will say to themselves: this is something tremendously significant, that through good philosophical training this decisive, radically decisive point in the difference between humans and animals can be correctly pointed out. People today do not even appreciate the significance of such a thing. For example, when the fuss started that Drews[7] created, this argument about whether Jesus lived or not, when a big assembly was held in Berlin at that time, where all kinds of possible and impossible people spoke about the problem: Did Jesus live?—there the Catholic theologian Wasmann[8] also spoke about it, and of course he could only say things that the others regarded as very backward. But even though the luminaries, especially of Berlin Protestant theology, were speaking at that time, basically two statements, or rather the documentation of these statements, appeared to me to be on a somewhat better level—not on the level of the present, but on a somewhat better level—in the speeches of that time.

One of them was a presentation by a—I don't mean to say anything bad, but actually to praise the man—learned dawdler of the very highest order. I do not think I can praise him better than by calling him a learned dawdler[9] of the very highest order. For the man could have achieved much through his astuteness and through his unique knowledge in the most diverse fields, through a great deal of knowledge. Even then, when I was in contact with him—that was eighteen, nineteen years ago—he had already been working on a revision of logic for fifteen years I believe it was, and I think he must still be working on it since then, because this revision of logic has not in the meantime come to my attention. He already said then what is quite correct: people were actually quite terrible in the present time; they were quite terrible when they started to think, because you only needed to hear two or three sentences, be it in a scientific or in an unscientific conversation today, to observe how the most terrible lack of logic immediately sets in. What people needed to observe, he said, so that they did not fall into the most horrible delusions that are common today, that could be written down on a quarto page, it was only necessary to really take this quarto page into account. Now I don't know if he wants to produce this quarto page as a revision of logic; as I said, it was already fifteen years at that time, since then another eighteen, nineteen years have passed, I don't know how far he is now with this revision of logic. But so I want to praise him by calling him a witty, spirited dawdler, because I want to suggest that if he were not a witty dawdler, he could accomplish an awful lot.

He said something very nice at that time, namely he said, well, the Catholic Church had to hear one day that comets, which consist of a nucleus and a tail, are celestial bodies like the others and move according to laws, just like the other celestial bodies. When it could no longer be denied, according to the things that were known, that comets were also such celestial bodies as the others, the Catholic Church decided to admit that the other celestial laws should also be applied to comets; but it admitted it at first only with reference to the nucleus, not yet with reference to the tail. Well, he only wanted to symbolically express that the Catholic Church is generally only inclined to admit what is absolutely necessary, in the same way that it was not until 1827 that it allowed the Copernican worldview for its faithful; but that even when it has to admit what is absolutely necessary, it at least still holds back the tail end of the matter! That is a remark that I thought actually characterized the situation quite well.

The other remark, however, was made specifically by the Catholic ant researcher Wasmann—he is an excellent ant researcher, but he is also a well-trained philosopher—who said: 'Actually, gentlemen, you cannot understand me at all, because in reality none of you know how to think philosophically; the person who thinks philosophically just doesn't talk like you!' And indeed, he was right in this, there is no doubt that he hit the nail on the head. Now there is a nice little paper by Wasmann on the difference between humans and animals which sharply emphasizes what I have just indicated: this ability of humans to really think in abstract terms, which animals are not supposed to have. This is something that is extraordinarily dazzling because it is convincing in a certain direction for those who have only trained their thinking to such an extent that they can grasp the full force of such an assertion.

But now let's take a look at the matter from a spiritual-scientific point of view, and only then will you see the significance of the whole business. If we start from the insights and experiences that can be gained about this in the spiritual world on the basis of spiritual science, then we understand on the one hand how, without the spiritual-scientific considerations, this dazzling assertion of which I have just spoken can arise; that it must indeed apply to everyone who does not want to become a spiritual scientist, especially if they are well trained philosophically. That can be accepted on the one hand. But on the other hand you see the following, you see it simply by looking at things in the world: if we compare the human being with the animal on the basis of spiritual-scientific assumptions, then we see that the human being confronts the things of the world in individual observations and then forms abstract concepts through all kinds of thought operations in which they combine what they see in isolation. It can also be admitted that the animal does not have this abstraction, that the animal does not carry out this activity of abstraction.

But the curious thing is that the animal does not lack abstract concepts, that the animal lives with its soul precisely in the most abstract concepts that we humans painstakingly form, and that the animal does not have the individual perception as we do. The advantage we have is precisely that we have a much freer use of the senses, a very specific kind of interaction between the senses and inner emotions and impulses of will. That is the advantage we have over the animal. But the certainty of instinct that animals have is based precisely on the fact that the animal lives from the outset with such abstract concepts that we must first form. What distinguishes us from the animal is that our senses become emancipated and freer in their use towards the outside world, and that we can also pour into our senses the will that the animal cannot pour into them.

But that which we humans do not have, but must first acquire, the abstract concepts, that is precisely what the animal has, as strange as it may seem. Certainly, each animal has only a certain field, but in this field the animal has such abstract concepts, strange as it may seem to us. Humans depend on seeing one, two, three dogs; they form the abstract term 'dog' from it. The animal has the same abstract concept of 'dog' in this field, and in quite a precise way, that we have; it does not need to form it. We have to form it first, the animal doesn't need to do that. But the animal does not have the ability precisely to distinguish one dog from another, precisely to individualize it through sensory perception.

If we do not acquire the ability to address the true facts of reality through spiritual science, we are deceiving ourselves in a certain respect about the most essential things. We believe that because we humans must develop the ability to form abstract concepts, it is through abstract concepts that we differ from the animal, which does not possess this ability. But the animal does not need this ability at all because it has the abstract concepts from the start. The animal has a completely different kind of sensory perception than we humans do. It is precisely the external sensory perception that is quite different.

In this respect there is even a need for a very profound transformation in human ideas. After all, people have learned about all kinds of scientific concepts that have already become popular today. Either they were able to learn about them in some school, through direct instruction, or they taught themselves through the dishwater—I meant to say through reading the newspapers—by means of which scientific ideas are now flowing out into the world. But people are dominated by these scientific ideas. With reference to what I have just indicated to you, people are very deeply dominated by an, one could almost say, instinctive inclination to believe that animals really do see the same things in the environment as humans do.

When they walk their dog, they have the instinctive belief that the dog sees the world as they see it, that it see the grass coloured, the wheat coloured, the stones coloured just as they themselves do. And then, if they can think to some extent, they also have the belief that they themselves can make abstractions and therefore have abstract concepts, but their dog does not abstract, and so on. And yet it is not so. This dog walking next to us lives just as much in abstract concepts as we do. Indeed, it lives in them more intensely than we do. Neither does it even need to acquire them, but it lives intensively in them from the very beginning. But it doesn't have the same external perception, this gives it a completely different picture; you just need to be attentive to certain observations that you can make in life.

However, people don't always take things seriously enough. I could give you a whole number of examples from which you would see how people think wrongly in this regard purely by instinct. For example, once, I think it was in Zurich, I went out into the street from a lecture that had been given at a branch evening. There was a coachman waiting, and the horse didn't quite want to go, gave the impression of shying away a little. The coachman said: It's afraid of its own shadow. Of course he saw the shadow of the horse cast by the lantern on the wall, and therefore he assumed that the horse saw this shadow just as he did. He, of course, had no idea, if I may say so, of what was going on in the horse's soul and what was going on in his soul. He sees the shadow of the horse, but the horse has a living sense of being in that part of the etheric body where the shadow is formed. That is a completely different process, a completely different process in relation to the inner perception.

There you have the clash of the previous way of thinking, right down to the most elementary, instinctive views of naive people, with that which must enter people in a new way through spiritual science. However, you will first have to appreciate with all seriousness what actually lies at the heart of this. For with reference to such things the worst materialism of a Vogt[10] or Moleschott[11] or Clifford[12] or Spencer[13] and so on differs much less from the traditional confessional concepts of the individual denominations than that which must differ from these confessions as a new way of thinking underlying spiritual science. Because today, certain materialists actually think: humans are not very different from animals. They may also at some point have heard it said, even if they only picked up half of it, that human beings can form abstract concepts which are different from the ordinary, merely sensory conceptions; but they say to themselves: abstract concepts, that is perhaps not such an important thing after all, such an intrinsic thing, so basically the human being is no different from the animal. The whole materialism of the present is actually a creation of the creeds of the Church. You only have to consider this in all seriousness, then you will see that a renewal of the way human souls conceive of things must be considered here if you don't want to stop at saying, well, back again to the old conceptions, then everything will be all right!

What you cannot say is that people could simply refrain from turning to real spiritual life now and things would continue as they are! No, those are right who say: 'That a terrible fate beckons white humanity seems certain to me under all circumstances, unless a period of the supreme rule of wisdom very soon replaces that of passion and delusion'. Such people should also realize, however, that the delusions include most of the scientific ideas about the world today. That is something that should be recognized. Humanity has reached the point in its evolutionary current that we often characterize by saying: since the fifteenth century, humanity has been in the age of the consciousness soul. And this development of the consciousness soul takes place in the way I have often characterized. Let us look at a very important characteristic with regard to the development of the consciousness soul.

I already indicated to you last time that everything which the spiritual researcher learns, that is, raises into consciousness, particularly of those things which lie in the development of humanity, goes on in people's subconscious, even if it is not recognized. Humanity, in developing towards the future, passes through certain experiences. It passes through these experiences unconsciously, unless it prefers to raise them to consciousness, which is precisely what should happen in the age of the development of the consciousness soul. But precisely in this age of the development of the consciousness soul, many things that approach the human being in the subconscious are still being rejected today.

Among other things, a certain part of the experience which may be called the encounter with the 'Guardian of the Threshold' approaches the human being to an increasing extent.[14] Certainly, if we really want to enter the spiritual world fully consciously, to develop imaginations, inspirations, intuitions, we must enter the realm of the supersensory world to a much greater extent, with more abundant experiences, with quite different experiences. We must pass more thoroughly—if I may use the expression—by the Guardian of the Threshold than the rest of humanity must in the course of the age of the consciousness soul. But to a certain extent the human being must simply have passed by the Guardian of the Threshold by the end of the development of the consciousness soul. They can now choose the convenience of leaving this passage entirely in the subconscious. But that this does not happen, that is precisely what spiritual science is there for. It is intended to draw attention to the fact that this is now one of the events that are taking place in the development of humanity. And those who today keep people away from spiritual science actually want nothing less than to force people to pass by the Guardian of the Threshold—who simply steps into people's horizon in this age—not consciously but unconsciously.

In other words, humanity must pass by the Guardian of the Threshold in some incarnation during the 2160 years that the age of consciousness soul evolution lasts, from about 1413 onwards, and experience some of the experiences that can be had with the Guardian of the Threshold. People can let themselves be forced by materialistically minded people to pass by unconsciously; or they can take the decision in freedom to be attentive to spiritual science and, either through introspection or through common sense, to learn something about this passing by the Guardian of the Threshold. And in passing by the Guardian of the Threshold in this way, that very thing is heard which enables the human being to form correct, accurate conceptions of the concrete supersensory world, conceptions first of all which are able, above all, to bring conception itself, thinking, into a certain free, unbiased direction amenable to reality.

I have often described this as the greatest achievement of spiritual science, that thinking becomes more amenable to reality, that it can really enter into the impulses that lie in the events and not merely know something about the processes in an abstract way, as natural science does externally. Knowing certain things about the spiritual world is what becomes necessary for people. This must enable human beings to learn to judge their position in the world from the point of view of a spiritual horizon, whereas today they are only able to judge their position in the world from the point of view of the sensory horizon. You are already judging something in a new and correct way when, for example, you make such a thought fruitful in yourself that animals do not for instance have no abstract ideas, but that they live precisely in the most abstract ideas, and that what distinguishes humans from animals is a certain development of their senses, which emancipate themselves from the close connection with bodily life. This is how you actually come to accurate conceptions about the difference between humans and animals. Outwardly this is expressed in such a way that the organization of the senses in animals is connected in a very pronounced vital way with the whole organization of the body. The organization of the body in animals extends very significantly into the senses.

Take the eye. It is well known to natural scientists that the eyes of lower animals have organs in them, for example the fan or the xiphoid process, which are filled with blood, which establish a living connection between the interior of the eye and the whole organization, while the human eye does not have this organization, but is much more independent. This greater independence of the senses, this emancipation of the senses from the overall organization, is something that first occurs in the human being. In this way, however, the whole world of the senses is much more connected with the will in humans than in animals. I once expressed this morphologically in a different way. I drew your attention to the same thing from another point of view,[15] by saying, if you take the threefold organism, organs of the extremities, chest, head, then, if I draw it schematically, in the animal it is like this: here the organism of the head [drawing on the left, p. 22], here the organism of the chest, here the organism of the extremities. The head is directly above the ground. The earth is under the head organism—approximately of course, but in essence—with all animals. The spine is perpendicular to the earth's axis or radius. In humans, it is the case that the head rests on its own chest organism and organism of the extremities. In humans, the chest organism is under the head organism in the same way that in animals the earth is under the head organism. The human being stands with their head on their own earth. Thus in the animal there is a separation between the will organism, especially the organism of the extremities, the rear extremities, and the head. In the human being, the will, the will organism is directly involved in the head organism and the whole in the earth's radius. In this way the senses are, as it were, suffused with the will and that is the characteristic of the human being. This is how they differ in reality from the animal, that the senses are suffused by the will. In the animal, the senses are not suffused by the will, but by a deeper element; hence also the more intimate connection of the sense organization with the organism as a whole. The human being lives much more in the outside world, the animal lives much more in its own inner world. By using their sensory tools, human beings live much more in the outside world.

So consider, now we are living in the age of the consciousness soul. What does that mean? This means, as I have now explained to you several times, that we are currently advancing towards a situation where the consciousness only contains reflections, only mirror images, because the age of the consciousness soul is also the age of intellectualism. To train the faculty of abstraction in such a pure way as an art is actually not done until the age of intellectualism. In this age of intellectualism and materialism, the most abstract concepts were formed.

Now let us think of two people; one is a well-trained philosopher, as well-trained as Catholic theologians are. The latter should actually say something from his point of view, but he will not say it because he sees the mess that has come about as a result of materialism arising out of the centuries-old development of Christianity, and that is uncomfortable for him; but he should actually say, the human being in the age of the consciousness soul can best form abstract concepts, they have therefore risen most above the animal.

But alternatively the spiritual scientist can come and say, in this age of the development of the consciousness soul, the characteristic feature of the human being is precisely that they can develop the ability to form abstract concepts to a particularly strong degree. Where does this take them as a result? It is precisely through this that they return to animality! And that explains an awful lot. This explains to you why the human inclination to approach the animal as closely as possible arises precisely from the fact that people enter into the abstractions of concepts. But this also explains to you something that often occurs in practical life and in the way we lead our lives today. The sciences become more and more abstract, and in social life the human being comes more and more to want to live as our good livestock actually lives, namely to provide only for the most mundane needs arising from hunger and other necessities.

The inner connection between the capacity for abstraction and animality is shown by spiritual science. This inner connection is what human beings go through under all circumstances as an experience in the age in which the consciousness soul develops. If they are impeded in the way described previously, they go through it unconsciously. Many people go through what the depths of their soul tells them: you are becoming more and more like the animal, precisely by advancing, you become more and more like the animal. This is what makes people frightened of advancing along their trajectory. This is also what makes people so fond of dwelling conservatively on old concepts.

Can that be? Can this unconscious manifestation of animality at the Guardian of the Threshold keep people from moving forward? No, that must not happen; but something else must occur. By striding backwards in the apparent move forwards, the stride backwards must take place in such a way that it does not simply take place back and forth, as it would necessarily do if only the faculty of abstraction were developed: we would arrive at earlier stages in the development of humanity, indeed, we would arrive at animalization as such. No, we must stride backwards, but back and forth in such a way [drawing on the right, p. 22] that an elevation takes place, and this elevation must lead into the spiritual.

That which we lose by stepping into abstraction we must paralyse by filling our abstract mirror images with the spiritual, by absorbing the spiritual into the abstraction. This is how we progress. Before the Guardian of the Threshold, the human being is confronted, be it consciously or unconsciously, with a terrible decision: either 'more animal to be than any beast'[16] through abstract concepts and to sniff out 'any old baloney',[17] in the words of Goethe's Faust, or else, at the moment when they enter into abstraction, to pour into these abstract concepts that which flows out of spiritual worlds, as we have characterized it in these days.[18] Then the human being begins to appreciate their position within the world correctly, for then they perceive themselves as being in the process of development, then they know why at a certain point in this development they are in danger of sinking down into animality precisely because of the abstractions. When humans were on the animal level in primitive cultural periods, they were distinguished from animals by their senses, not by their abstract concepts. The animals were better at the abstract concepts. Humans can only develop these abstract concepts today at a pinch. The animals are much better at it. I once explained it[19] with another example by saying to you, how long ago is it, that humans tried to make paper in the course of historical development? The wasp makes its nest out of paper; it's been doing it for millions of years! And just look at what is revealed by the animals in terms of cleverness in active, prevailing reason, in terms of intellectuality, in terms of the capacity for abstraction, even if it is in a one-sided way through the various animals. It is foolishly called instinct. But if you see through the matter, you know that by far the fewest people today are so far advanced with what they possess in terms of their capacity for abstraction that they would be, for instance, more advanced than the one-sidedness of the animal classes of today in what they produce from out of their capacity for abstraction.

The human being is thus confronted with this important choice: either to return to the animal state to a very great extent, more animal to be than any beast, to use the Mephistophelean expression in *Faust*—Ahriman-Mephistopheles would like to achieve this in the human being, with the human being—or alternatively to embrace the spiritual.

A certain intensity in conception is necessary, however, if we want to know today what is actually mapped out for human beings in the progression of time, in the necessities of our time. We have to dig very, very deep into cosmic development, and we must not shy away from preparing ourselves through spiritual-scientific concepts for the more difficult concepts that underlie reality. Because of course, when someone hears something like I said today for the first time, they will say, that's pure madness! That is understandable. But we could also imagine that someone considers a great deal of what the 'clever' people have been doing for years to be great madness, and they could consider very large majorities to be mad; but then they might also find it understandable why these very large majorities consider them, the dissenter, to be mad. For in a society of mad people, it is usually not the mad person who is thought to be mad, but the sane person.

But the human being learns through this to fertilize their entire view of the world. And they learn to fertilize precisely that which in reality has always distinguished them from the animal. After all, humans are basically quite inattentive to their own abilities, and they will become more and more inattentive if they only train their intellect in the age of the consciousness soul. If you go back to earlier times, you very often find that clever people also had a certain sense of their surroundings. If you take the conceptions that earlier people formed about certain animals, for example, they are often penetrating. The conceptions in today's zoology books are sometimes very respectable and quite commendable from the point of view of creating abstractions, but penetrating they are not. First and foremost, I would like to ask you whether among the ideas that you absorb in school today are really those that can lead you to penetrate, let's say, the lives of animals? Do people today, surveying a large number of animals, still see the fearful gaze with which whole flocks, whole groups of animals look into the world, the timid, fearful gaze? There is no doubt that we will learn to see it again once we have advanced so far through the faculty of abstraction that it has driven us to the Guardian of the Threshold, that it enables us once again to develop compassion for the animal! Not the compassion that is often artificially instilled today, but one that corresponds to an elementary inner experience. It can be said that a particular fearfulness, a fearful looking into the world, is spread over all the higher animals, all the warm-blooded animals. I was once walking with a man who was academically educated, and at a certain point on the path we saw deer, stags that were running away from everything. So this man said to me: It must somehow lie at the root of this, that in ancient times people tormented the animals, shot them or something like that, and as a result the animal souls got used to being afraid of people. But animals are also afraid of other things, not just of people.

So people are trying to explore why certain animals are afraid. There is no need to explore that. Fear is in fact a very general, universal characteristic of animals. If some animals are not afraid, it is due to training and habituation in some way. Fear is quite specific to the animal for the reason that the animal has to a great extent the ability of abstraction, abstract concepts. The animal lives in them. The world you acquire when you study for a long time, when you have engaged in abstraction for a long time, that is the world in which the animal lives; and the world in which humans live here on earth through their senses is much more unknown to the animal than to humans, even though the animal has senses, and we fear the unknown. This is absolutely in accordance with a profound truth. The animal looks fearfully into the world. That has certain implications. I recently stated it in an essay [20] I wrote about the ahrimanic and luciferic in human life in the last issue of the magazine *Das Reich*: people are afraid of the spiritual life.

How is it, then, that they become so caught up in fear? It comes from the fact that now they have to approach the Guardian of the Threshold in the subconscious. There they are faced with this decision that I spoke about. There they come closer to the animal. The animal is afraid. Animals pass through the region of fear. That's the context. And the state of fear will become greater and greater if people will not make a serious effort to really get to know, to really absorb, that world which must approach them, the spiritual world.

There are only a few, very few people in more recent times in whom something of earlier, atavistic conceptions of world reality has penetrated through the general delusions. If you look at the animal in the whole context of the development of nature, if you look at its organization in the whole context of the natural order, what is actually happening with the animal? When the old moon evolution existed, there was no differentiation between the higher animals and today's human beings as far as the outer organization was concerned. This is only a result of earth evolution. Human beings have participated in the normal development of the earth, animals have not. The animal has dried out, as it were, in moon evolution. Its organization does not match earth evolution. Whoever sees through this—in more recent times just a few have instinctively understood it, Hegel among others—can answer the question, What actually is the animal in relation to its form of organization?, by saying, nature becomes sick,[21] and the sickness of nature is the animal, namely the higher animal. The sickness of nature, the sickness of the whole earth, prevails in the animal organization. The earth's becoming sick, sinking back into the old moon development in sickness, is the higher animals; not so much the lower animals but the higher animals. But this is also something which unconsciously confronts the human being at the decisive moment when they pass the Guardian of the Threshold, if they do not consciously want to do so.

And if you take what I have told you now together with how I presented to you some time ago the spread of the encounter with the Guardian of the Threshold in its different forms in the American west, in the European centre, in the east,[22] if you take this together, then you will see how we can inform ourselves about what is happening in humanity on earth, if we only engage with these things. And if you engage with these things, then you will understand that human beings would really come to think differently at last about themselves and also about their relationship with their fellow human beings. The question should be raised by all more serious people at the present time, the question which may follow such a sentence as the one mentioned: 'That a terrible fate beckons white humanity seems certain to me under all circumstances, unless a period of the supreme rule of wisdom very soon replaces that of passion and delusion.' Where these ideas of wisdom are to be found, how they can be obtained, that is what spiritual science wants to answer. But in doing so, it wants to answer the most important questions of the present day. And if someone comes who feels so thoroughly what is necessary for the present as such a man, then it can be said to him: If you do not want to continue to fear that a terrible fate beckons white humanity, then engage with a spiritual-scientific observation of the world and its phenomena!

We will talk more about that tomorrow.

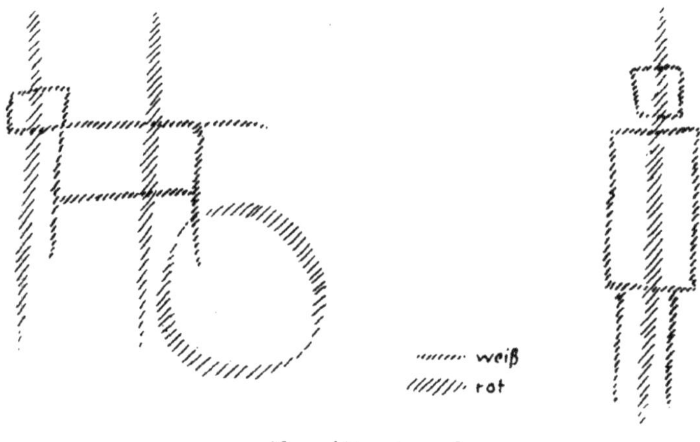

weiß = white; rot = red

Second Lecture

DORNACH, 4 JANUARY 1919

It is perhaps relevant, especially on the occasion of such reflections as we are now in the habit of doing, to look back at some of the things that were connected with this or that spiritual current in earlier times. For as you have seen, it is a question of the spiritual events which underlie the physical world making it necessary in the present time for the human being themselves to arrive at a new attitude, so to speak, with regard to the whole conception of their relationship to the world and to the rest of humanity. Yesterday we already pointed out a number of things in this regard, pointed out how many things must be understood anew which, apparently well-founded, shine into the spiritual life of humanity from one place or another. You must be clear that if impulses of this kind are taken seriously, then—in the way life happens to proceed today—opposition will arise against such seriousness and against these impulses in general, opposition of hatred, opposition of envy, opposition of fear, which comes from the pettiness of people, and so on. Only the thorough understanding of things can help overcome the many obstacles that the proponent of such spiritual change faces. For such a thorough understanding is also capable of giving strength to the soul, so that the soul is a match for many things that have always asserted themselves against the most serious endeavours in the world's affairs. And so today we would like to supplement what was said yesterday with a few more things.

Yesterday I pointed out how it is possible—especially when standing on spiritual-scientific ground—to be objective in the face of all other intellectual currents, and how it is not necessary to misjudge other intellectual currents. From this point of view I said that, with regard to certain points, the representatives of the Catholic clergy are superior to the non-Catholics in some current philosophical, theological disputes outside the Church because of their training. Right now in particular, we are living in a time when anyone who wants to get serious about matters of worldview should be addressing such things. Both the currents in the view of the world and the social currents of the present demand this. The temptations that emanate especially from the well-trained side could at times become great, and what is put forward could then not be understood, not be recognized in its actual insignificance in relation to the greater demands of the present, if we do not engage in a very thorough contemplation. The temptation to succumb to the objections of well-trained opponents of spiritual-scientific endeavours are indeed not small in the present. However, if people were sufficiently discerning, if they would endeavour to enter into the fact that this spiritual science is well-founded, broadly founded, they would be little exposed to such temptations. But such discernment is rare. What spiritual science wants to integrate into the cosmic stream, as we understand it, explains many attacks, and also explains attacks specifically from the point of view of the Catholic confession, for example. But it is nevertheless necessary to deal with such things for the reason that in the chaos that will ensue, and which unfortunately people appreciate far too little, pay far too little attention to, because in this chaos there will also be many confusing things that emanate from the content of Catholic faith.

Now I would like to acquaint you today with the thrust of the judgement which such a proper Catholic believer can indeed advance against one thing or another in spiritual science, if they can presuppose that they will find uninformed readers or listeners. One of the most common objections to spiritual science as it is meant here is that it is pantheism. One of the main objections made, for example, in the essays by the Jesuit Zimmermann in *Stimmen der Zeit*,[23] is that this spiritual science is pantheism.

As you know, I have often spoken about this point; you know, as I have set out, that the banal pantheism in particular which dominates so many circles in the present day can only seriously be overcome by entering into the concrete spiritual world of which spiritual science speaks. It is, of course, not intended on the side from which the above-mentioned objections arise to get to the bottom of the real truth; rather, it is their endeavour, calculating everything that lives as prejudices within a certain confessional following, to put forward such things as have a certain suggestive and hypnotic effect. Pantheism would be the view that the divine lives in everything that extends as nature, in everything that extends as the world of appearances, that nature itself is to be regarded as a direct revelation of the divine. It is precisely against such wishy-washy pantheism, which only ever speaks of the world of appearances spreading out and behind it being spirit, spirit, spirit, that I have always turned. I have always pointed out how this is the same as someone on the physical plane not wanting to discuss the fact that there are tulips and roses and lilies, but only plants, plants, plants! Spiritual science on the other hand deals with the individual concrete spiritual entities and does not speak of the spirit in general in a pantheistic way.

Another characteristic of pantheism is that people say, pantheism does not want to separate the outer world of nature from the divine-spiritual, it wants to mix the two together. Well, it takes a Jesuit to give oneself the appearance of believing that where there is such mention of the concrete position of the beings of the higher hierarchies—individualized in themselves, existing in themselves personally and supra-personally—there can be talk of a mixing together this whole world of hierarchies with external nature. Anyone who can really think will not be able to make anything at all of the allegation of pantheism against such a characterization of the world of the hierarchies and its individual beings in relation to nature.

The only thing that remains, which is now particularly emphasized in those essays in *Stimmen der Zeit*, is that reference is made in my spiritual science—which is deemed to be heretical in the Catholic Church—that the divine lives in the soul of the human being, that the soul of the human being itself is a drop in the ocean of the divine. Such and similar statements are compiled there, and they are presented as heresies within the Catholic confession.

So it is indicated that the teaching that something divine is said to live directly in the soul is heretical and to be condemned. A sensible person could certainly say, it is not necessary that you should draw my attention to such foolishness. But that is not what matters; that is not what it is about. But it must be about the fact that these things play a real role in the world, that these things will play a huge role where the intention is to deceive, and that one must indeed be alert to these things. But they are connected with something else.

And now let us leave aside this or that attack which has really happened, and place before our souls someone who either lives in Jesuitism and who has been dulled with regard to their own thinking, or who consciously lives in it, that is, who knows that they do not need to reflect on things for themselves, but that they only have to judge the faithful in the sense of the officially recognized confession, be it one way or the other; and let us consider how such a person's arguments can be with regard to the spiritual-scientific path itself. So I am not telling you anything other than—I don't want to say the average opinion, because opinion is out of place here—the average statement of an official representative of the Roman Catholic Church in relation to the path of spiritual science as it is taken by one who professes it today.

He would say, for instance, well, the Catholic Christian must not take such a path as is recommended by spiritual science for the attainment of supersensory insights. For all the Fathers and Doctors of the Church—so the present cleric will say—condemn such a way. Such a path leads to the human being evoking special abilities in themselves in order to ascend to the supersensory world. But that is heretical, that must not be sought at all. All that may be sought by a faithful Catholic is that which the Doctors of the Church allow to be considered as 'rightful contemplation'. This rightful contemplation is something that the present Rome-approved cleric is prepared to accept. What does he understand by that?

You will be able to get an idea of what he understands by this if you distinguish between two kinds of gifts which a person, a believing Catholic, can have in the sense of the orthodox Catholic Church. One of the gifts are the so-called *gratiae gratis datae*, the supernatural gifts of grace, we could say the charismata. The other gifts are those which can be called the general human gifts. The extraordinary gifts, the charismata, are given as a special gift of grace to extraordinary people, but must not be sought either, the Church commands. One example would be the Maid of Orleans. On the other hand, a certain elevation of the general life of the soul may be sought, which, however, does not lead the human being to extraordinary abilities but only to an enhancement of the general human abilities. Such an increase in the general human abilities, however, puts every human being—so says today's Roman Catholic Church—in a position of being able to be infused by the Holy Spirit.

So let's put it this way: the ordinary mortal thinks something, or feels something, or does something. They are obliged by the commandment of the Church, by the commandment of the State, to do these things in such and such a way; they can endeavour, with their ordinary mortal thinking, to perform their action in accordance with the Church, in accordance with the State—which in the Church's sense then means in accordance with God. But they can also notice, if they are otherwise decent as a Catholic Christian, that the Holy Spirit intervenes more often in their actions, thoughts and feelings, and that they then perform certain virtues, which otherwise cause them difficulties, more easily because the Holy Spirit is working in them. But this must not be sought as if a person wanted to go beyond the ordinary status of human striving and develop special abilities in order to penetrate the supersensory world. All such striving is reprehensible.

Now, with this I have characterized for you what a properly approved Roman Catholic cleric would object to with regard to what is written, for example, in *Knowledge of the Higher Worlds. How is it Achieved?* [24]. He would say, special abilities are sought here which are intended to put him in a position to unite with the spiritual world in a certain way. But he is not allowed to do that. He must only behave passively until he notices that the impulses of the Holy Spirit enter his mind and do not bring about a qualitative change in his behaviour, but only an enhancement, as it were, an easing in being virtuous, an easing in the other faculties which the human being exercises on the outer physical plane.

You can read this today not only in opposition to our spiritual science, but you can read it in opposition to all endeavours which amount to a person striving to produce from within themselves someone who sees a spiritual world around them in the same way as the physical person sees a physical world around them with their physical senses. This is also familiar to all those who believe that they stand on the very firm ground of the Christian faith dictated from Rome. And in the widest circles today, anyone is considered a heretic who thinks differently about these things from the way I have just characterized for you. You always have to realize, when you discuss something like this, that these things play a real role in the world, that these things still have a tremendous influence on millions of people today. You don't have to be so selfish as to think that because you think you're done with these things—but only think you're done with them—you don't have to worry about them. This is the great harm of the present time, especially with regard to the social movement, that people are so egoistic that they only look at the needs of their own souls and do not want to look at what connects people with people, at what moves millions and millions of people as a driving impulse, and which, when it bursts forth at the right time, can flood one thing or another which appears in this or that form as things appear now in the world. It is necessary today to educate ourselves also about the sources of these things and about the necessary position on these things.

Now, as a rule, the Rome-approved clerics refer to the Doctors of the Church. They go back to the Doctors of the Church of earlier centuries and derive from their statements what they believe to be in accordance with what I have just characterized for you. Now, of course, I cannot lecture you for hours on the teachings of the Doctors of the Church, but I would like to draw your attention to a few things in this direction, namely what position the person of the consciousness age, which began in the fifteenth century, can adopt on these things.

Firstly, then, we must take into account that the path to the spiritual world, as it is understood by spiritual science, is considered heretical. This is what the clerics, who are today approved by Rome as legitimate, say. Secondly, we must note that the accusation is levelled that spiritual science speaks of human beings being able to partake of the divine in their own souls, and that this is heretical, as once again the clerics of Catholicism, who are approved by Rome, say today.

Let us take a closer look at what an outwardly—but not inwardly, as we will see in a moment—very respected Doctor of the Church, outwardly also very respected by Rome, says about something like contemplation, of which I have just given you some characteristics. John of the Cross,[25] for example, speaks of that which is to become contemplation for the rightful Christian Catholic believer who, through such contemplation, is to go beyond mere, general faith in the Church to a kind of higher contemplation of the divine which pulses through the world. The Catholic Church, too, allows this today, that through contemplation a person can go beyond what is merely common belief. But it forbids the human being to attain supersensory faculties, faculties which lead into the supersensory world in the same way as the outer senses lead into the world of the senses. Now St John of the Cross says, the time has come—he means the time of contemplation when the reflection and observation which the soul previously undertook with its own powers virtually ceases and the soul finds itself deprived of former pleasures and palpable joys.

So St John of the Cross admits this state—that the ordinary reflection is silenced by which we deal with the things of the physical plane which we perceive through the senses and comprehend through the intellect; that we therefore abstain from the ordinary observation which the soul undertakes with its own powers, that also the pleasures which the soul has in such observations and in such a relationship with external nature, cease. This he admits.

Condemned to a state of aridity and dryness—he then goes on to say—the soul can no longer deliberate with its intellect. So by closing the senses, by letting the intellect stand still—that is what he demands to bring about contemplation—we enter into a kind of aridity and dryness with the soul. This, then, is the way we arrive at that participation with the divine essence which St John of the Cross considers permissible. So when the soul no longer deliberates with its intellect, nor finds any sensory support, then the senses no longer enrich themselves; the spirit gets the benefit without receiving anything from the senses. From this it follows that in this state God is the principal actor.

So be very clear about this. St John of the Cross says, the human being can cease reflecting, the reception of external perceptions through the senses can also cease, the soul can become passive, the soul no longer does anything of its own accord. As a result, God becomes the main actor in the soul. He himself instructs the soul and infuses it with knowledge. In contemplation, he bestows upon it entirely spiritual goods, especially the knowledge and love of God, without the soul practising reflection or other exercises which it can no longer perform as before.

Take these words of a Father of the Church who is also recognized as legitimate in Rome today, John of the Cross, who has even been canonized; take these words and contrast them with the accusation of pantheism that has just recently been levelled against spiritual science because spiritual science speaks, for example, of the life of the soul behaving like a drop in the ocean of the divine, that is, itself being of divine essence, which is heretical according to the faithful clerics preaching today. But St John of the Cross describes the possibility of arriving at a passive state of the soul, where reflection and sense perception are excluded, and where God is the principal actor in the soul, where God, according to the words of St John of the Cross, bestows entirely spiritual goods on the soul in contemplation, where he himself instructs the soul and imparts to it instilled knowledge.

Now I ask you, what is the meaning of these words if it is then claimed that the human soul is never to be brought into a real connection with the divine being? What is the point of John of the Cross saying, God is the principal actor in the soul—and yet it is supposed to be heretical to speak of bringing the human soul into a direct knowing connection with God? If you say that the soul relates to the totality of the divine-spiritual as the drop does to the ocean, being of the same essence as all the water of the ocean, being a drop from the ocean—should that be taken as illicit pantheism, if truth prevailed, when at the same time it is acknowledged that a legitimate Father of the Church, St John of the Cross, admits the possibility of God becoming the principal actor in the human soul!

You must set this fact before your soul in order to recognize how far truth prevails in the official currents today: that people simultaneously invoke such teachers as St John of the Cross, who truly teaches a 'pantheism'—if you want to call it pantheism—in much clearer words, namely in order to speak in popular terms to the people, than spiritual science. But the latter is considered heretical, and what do they do? They allow St John of the Cross to be the authoritative Father of the Church, and deceive people by telling them that pantheism is not allowed. But this means that no one may claim that it is heretical to say that God is directly present in the soul, so that the human soul can know this.

No, today people should not be unthinking; they must not be unthinking if even greater misfortune is not to befall humanity. People today should be conscious that such a distortion of the truth can be officially channelled through the world.

And another saying of St John of the Cross is, the inner goods that such silent contemplation impresses on the soul, unconscious of itself, are inestimable. In short, they are nothing other than the supremely mysterious and immensely delicate anointing of the Holy Spirit, who, being God, acts as God: the Holy Spirit acts as God in the soul directly—says St John of the Cross. That was Catholic at the time of John of the Cross, that is, before the beginning of the consciousness soul age—and secretly acts in and floods the soul with riches and gifts and graces to such an extent that it cannot be described. In contemplation—this is another saying of St. John of the Cross—we are receivers. And another saying of St John is the following: in contemplation it is God who is at work—namely within the soul.

And now I ask you, what does it mean when any of those who write about heresy today say that it is heretical to claim that God is consubstantial with the human soul!

That's just the way things are. But people are so sleepy today that they do not even pay attention to how truth is managed. But that such a terrible catastrophe has come into the world is ultimately because so little attention is paid to those things which are channelled through the world as truth. This is also the reason why truth can be hated as much as it is still hated by certain people today.

In particular, the cleric approved by Rome today is at pains to emphasize again and again that there should be no difference between the ordinary faculties as developed by the believer in their faith and that enhancement of faith which is expressed in contemplation. There should be no difference, or at most a difference of degree, for if a real difference were sought, it would be heretical. But St John of the Cross says, the difference is that in faith we see only darkly, but in spiritual contemplation we see him—he means God—unveiled.

That was Catholic back then, when St John of the Cross wrote these things down before the emergence of the age of the consciousness soul. But what prevails today of these things as Catholicism, that is their shadow, that is no longer the light. Actually, John of the Cross describes the mystical path of knowledge, the path into the supersensory, very beautifully for that time when he says that the narrow portal is the night of the senses. In order to pass through it, the soul must free itself from itself and detach itself. This is spoken for that time as we speak today, not from Rome, but in spiritual science. Spiritual science is the real continuation of such noble aspirations out into the spiritual world as appear in John of the Cross. But it is the continuation for the present time. It takes the progress of humanity into account.

The narrow portal is the night of the senses. In order to pass through it, the soul must free itself from itself and detach itself. And then, taking faith, which has nothing to do with the senses, as its guide, it walks along the narrow path of the second night to the night of the spirits. And St John of the Cross describes this union with the divine-spiritual very beautifully: the union takes place when the two wills, that of the soul and the divine will, take the same form.

It cannot be expressed more clearly that there is a divine will which rules throughout the world, and an individual will of the soul, and both merge into one another in contemplation. But that is supposed to be heretical today. The truth would be honestly represented if people said, St John of the Cross is no longer a saint today, he is a heretic. This is what the Roman cleric would be obliged to say if he wanted to maintain his assertions.

St John of the Cross says, union takes place when the two wills, that of the soul and the divine will, take the same form, that is, when there is nothing in the one that is contrary to the other. Now, however, in the section of the rightful Roman Catholic clergy they are very eager to block the way for the mere so-called faithful and also for the lower clergy to have their own knowledge. That is why today, although such a person as John of the Cross is actually denied, they point again and again to such people as John of the Cross. They point out that John of the Cross would only have allowed people to turn to contemplation if they were prompted to do so by three signs.

The first sign by which the soul might feel called upon to turn to contemplation, that is, to mystical contemplation, would be the inability to behold and to make use of the imagination, the aversion to outer beholding. So when the soul feels a reluctance to receive sense perceptions and to reflect, then the time has come when it may passively surrender itself to the will of God.

The second sign would be the observation that a person no longer has any desire to keep the imagination of the senses occupied with particular external and internal impressions. So the first one is that you've become tired, the second one is that you're fed up. The third inner sign would be the sensation of the innermost joy that the soul has with being alone—that is, without sensory perception and reflection—and with pure attention to the divine.

Well, you will not be able to read and understand what is written in the book *Knowledge of the Higher Worlds. How is it Achieved?* if you do not say to yourself, albeit adapted to our time, I can only be in complete agreement with those three signs. There is nothing at all to object to in these three signs. You only have to understand them in the sense of the immediate present. Let us look at these three signs, which St John of the Cross considers to be the signs that allow the soul to turn towards mystical contemplation, that is, to turn towards the path into the spiritual, supersensory world.

The first sign would be an inability to contemplate and to use the imagination, a reluctance to contemplate. We must remember that these words were written in the time when the consciousness age had not yet dawned. Now the consciousness age is dawning upon humanity, now the human observations about nature arrive, as they are presented by modern natural science. You really have to take into account the historical development of humanity. You have to take into account that St John of the Cross did not have people around him who were permeated with and steeped in those conceptions that are trickling out from natural science everywhere today. St John of the Cross only had people around him who went to the Catholic church with faith, who received their worldview from the faith preached from the pulpits of the Catholic Church. You had to speak differently to them than to people of the twentieth century, who are steeped in scientific views.

What does that actually mean: steeped in scientific views? All people today are—whether they admit it or not, down to the last peasant in the very last hut, if they are not illiterate. And even illiterate people today are already steeped in scientific conceptions in their ways of thinking. But anyone who looks at the world today as it must be looked at in accordance with the meaning of today's world, must—because natural-scientific conceptions only tell them about what is dead—come to the realization, if they have a living need for knowledge, that these natural-scientific observations make them incapable of stopping there. Exactly what St John of the Cross describes in the first sign occurs. This sign is fulfilled by the natural-scientific conceptual mode itself. Back then, when he was writing, it was fulfilled in some, today it is fulfilled in all who even begin to think. This difference must be taken into account. If St John of the Cross were writing today, he would say, certainly, at that time, mystical contemplation had to be recommended to those people who felt incapable of looking at things externally and setting the imagination in motion. Today, all those who are only devoted to barren natural-scientific conceptions are at a certain point incapable of devoting themselves only to these barren natural-scientific conceptions,[26] namely then when they have a longing in their soul to find any way at all to the divine-spiritual. St John of the Cross spoke to just a few candidates; today the candidates are all thinking people. That is precisely the progress of humanity. So what St John of the Cross assumes to be fulfilled by the sign is fulfilled today, when a person living in the scientific age feels that very urge.

The second thing is the observation that a person no longer has any desire to occupy the imagination of the senses with particular external or internal impressions. At the moment when natural science cannot help but give the human being nothing but a view, a perception of how they have developed out of the animal world, there truly arises in the soul the awareness that they no longer have any desire merely to behold what the senses reveal in the outer world! They simply reveal that human beings are descended from the animal kingdom—then a person no longer has that desire. Then, because the time has come—at that time only for some, now for all thinking people—a person turns to that which is the developmental view, namely to the path into the spiritual world, precisely in the sense of John of the Cross.

The third is the experience of joy in feeling, in the innermost part of the soul, in being alone in the mindfulness of God. Well, this most intimate joy will certainly be felt by anyone who in this scientific age has only absorbed those concepts which natural science offers, as soon as they can find their way into the supersensory world.

Once again, we are confronted with the fact, the significant fact, that it is precisely modern spiritual science that so rightly fulfils what such a person as John of the Cross meant and demanded for his time. But the stream of development flows onwards, and today fulfilment is different from what it was at that time. Something else additionally comes into play. Anyone who looks into the development of humanity today with an honest sense of truth will say to themselves, the sense for supersensory knowledge must be kept alive in people because we have entered the scientific age. Such demands as those of John of the Cross are simply fulfilled when a person today embarks on the path that is mapped out, for example, in *Knowledge of the Higher*

Worlds. How is it Achieved?. But if they embark on this path today, then what is revealed to them is not what was revealed at the time when St John of the Cross was writing, but what is revealed to them today is what lies in the path of human development. And then we can no longer speak in the way that St John of the Cross spoke just in the sense of positivist Christianity. For there is the serious fact to which we referred yesterday and often before, that today human beings either unconsciously or consciously pass the Guardian of the Threshold in a certain regard. There they learn to recognize how they must speak not only of a unitary God, but of the divine hierarchies. There they learn how they must contrast the ahrimanic and luciferic with the divine hierarchies. But just as the Catholic Church wanted to prevent people from believing in Copernicanism until 1822,[27] so today it wants to prevent people from entering into the supersensory knowledge that is really demanded by the times. Why? Because it does not want people to become attentive to that which wants to flow into human development from spiritual heights.

Certainly, there may also be some, and there are some, who in a certain sense honestly say the following: the human being today truly is not prepared to confront directly with their soul that which enters from the spiritual world; that will only bring them harm. When they step before the Guardian of the Threshold, they cannot distinguish deception from reality. So let us make it as horrible as possible for them to embark on the path of the spiritual themselves, so that they will not be at risk. There may be such people; they do not take into account the necessities of the time, they calculate with a limited, narrow-minded conception, but they may be honest. But the majority of those who say such things today as that a person should not go down the path of supersensory knowledge—they don't mean things that way. A certain feeling of fear of the truth is holding back the influx of this truth from many different sides. This feeling of fear, this is what widespread church confessions have in their official representatives; but so do certain masonic and similar societies.

I have already drawn attention to this from another point of view.[28] There are also some people within these societies who are honest from their point of view; but the power with which they halt the progress of humanity is terribly strong. For the following is the case. There are people, especially in the Orders with high degrees,[29] who say that, as a rule, the human being is not quite ready for the spiritual world to be presented to them directly, therefore they should be held back from direct entry into the spiritual world, they should not be allowed to enter, they should only be allowed access to the practice of the ceremonies prescribed in certain old rituals. Refer them to all kinds of symbols that do not introduce them directly to the spiritual world, but only symbolically demonstrate the matter, but even there possibly to symbols that are really quite old. I have told you[30] that in this respect certain masonic Orders, let us say, are at variance with the favourite instincts of most ladies. After all, most ladies like to be young, most masonic societies like to be as old as possible!

In this respect, if possible, they point to an ancient ritual or ancient tradition. Not always, although very often, it is meant in a false way; but it is sometimes honestly meant when they say that the rituals, which are ancient, can no longer endanger people when they are performed before them today because these rituals are spent, they are ossified, they are only a shadow of what they used to be. And besides, human souls have lived for so long with these rituals, or with the symbols and with what they represent that they have become accustomed to them: they are no longer shocked by the impression of an immediately experienced truth. Acquaint people with what is quite old, what only exists as a shadow, then they are less at risk.

All these things may indeed be advocated, but they must fall away in the face of the necessity today at the turning point of time. The calamity that would come if the human being were to repel the incoming spiritual tidal wave would be greater than all the other calamities. The real duty towards all the spirits of the world who are connected with the development of humanity is to acquaint the human being with that which today is necessarily taking place in the subconscious, in the soul of every human being, simply through the present laws of the world. To call this up into consciousness in the age of the consciousness soul, that is a necessity. And also with reference to what today arises so powerfully as social demands makes it necessary today to get to know what is actually present in human souls. For outwardly existence is becoming ever more mask-like, ever more mere phenomenon.

It is quite possible that today we have the experience in our soul of passing by the Guardian of the Threshold, but through the materialism of the time we suppress the awareness of it. But that doesn't mean that what you repress, what you don't become aware of, isn't there; it is there nevertheless. A person passes through the Guardian of the Threshold—but because of the way the times are they repress it. What it then presents itself as can be something completely different. It might be the actions of Lenin, it might be the actions of some Spartacist.[31] We must be attentive to this in the present, that we have arrived in an age when, through the deceptive impulses of materialism, the passage through certain spiritual impulses can mask itself outwardly in a way that endangers humanity in the worst possible way.

The times are serious. But we really have regard for that seriousness if we simply have the honest will to engage with our common sense with the interpretation of those things which can be extracted from the spiritual world by a real spiritual science. We will speak more about that tomorrow.

Third Lecture

DORNACH, 5 JANUARY 1919

You will have seen from yesterday's reflections how easily the whole course of human development can be misunderstood, and how it is misunderstood in particular by many quarters at the present time, to the detriment both of present-day knowledge and of the present-day social striving of humanity. Let us today set before our souls some results of spiritual science which are of such a nature that they can, I would like to say, illuminate from the other side things which are mysterious if we restrict ourselves to the ideas which the present has of them. I have told you that the human being will only be able to deal with the present if they decide to really reorient themselves by approaching the spiritual path—both with regard to their relationship with external nature, since the old means of orientation are no longer sufficient, and with regard to the relationship of human being to human being, since there too the old means of orientation are no longer sufficient to see what impulses are necessary for the present social structure of humanity. If we want to come to terms with these things, we must seriously consider that because of the way the human being is placed in the world today between birth and death, they only see the outer manifestation of their actual being, just as they actually only enter into a relationship with the outer manifestation of their fellow human beings.

Life is organized differently for the different periods of human development, and we are endeavouring to really study these things specifically with reference to the present human being. For in the present period a great deal will be decided for the human being on earth. Up to the fifteenth century and, we might say, because things don't happen in one fell swoop, up to the present, the human being was actually still more or less under the legacy of old concepts, old impulses. This fifth post-Atlantean period is, in a certain respect, something extraordinary in relation to human development. For as you know, if you take the whole evolution of the earth, it is divided into seven successive great epochs, of which the fourth was the Atlantean, and the present fifth is the post-Atlantean; then the sixth, then the seventh will come.

The Atlantean period contains, in a sense, a kind of decision. For until then, the entire existence on earth was a repetition of the earlier existence on Saturn, the Sun and the Moon. The Atlantean period contains a kind of decision, but only the beginning of a decision. Things were only prepared there which are actually not to be developed until the following earth evolution. So that up to the Atlantean time the human being was really only that which they already were in other forms as a Saturn, Sun and Moon human being. In the Atlantean time, however, they were only a hint of what they were to become as an actual earth human being. Then it continues, and now we are in the fifth post-Atlantean period. In the post-Atlantean period, through the ancient Indian, ancient Persian development and so on, increasingly specific conditions already arose. But the Greco-Latin period, the fourth post-Atlantean period, again only provides a kind of repetition, albeit in a different form, of what was already present in Atlantis on another level of existence.

It is only now, in the fifth post-Atlantean period, in a time that has begun since the fifteenth century, that human beings are located, as it were, in such a way in their overall development that quite noticeable new impulses, noticeable in their being, appear. They were not so noticeable before; now they appear noticeably in their being, and still they are only hinted at. The terrible catastrophic events of our time, of which we can already say that they will shake humanity quite monumentally, are the expression of the fact that new conditions are entering into the development of humanity. And I have indicated to you how these new conditions are to be characterized from a certain point of view by pointing out how it is clearly evident that a spiritual wave is flooding in, originating, as it were, from a rise in the development of the spirits of personality.

Now, if we look at this particular condition of the soul in which the human being of the present time exists here on earth from a spiritual-scientific point of view, we notice quite strongly how human beings are actually only aware of the way the being of nature is revealed, as well as the being of their fellow human beings, when they perceive something or when they are active outwardly in the will and have no knowledge of the real beings into which they must grow in a certain way in the course of their development; and into which they will have grown when that development will have progressed. The human being, as you know, stands in the world in such a way that they perceive, if we characterize it roughly, the surrounding world in the mineral realm, in the plant realm, in the animal realm and in their own realm, in the human realm. These are the things that are visible around the human being. And in the visible human realm there also takes place that which emerges from volition and which is supposed to find a certain order in the social structure.

Well, people have often reflected on—but with insufficient thought—how the human being relates to their environment. The results of this reflection have been incorporated into various theories of knowledge. But not very much can be gained from these theories of knowledge. And that which is taught by the book today in these theories of knowledge to young people who are then supposed to speak philosophically to the world, that is really quite inadequate stuff. Because a true insight into what actually reveals itself in the human environment can only be gained by looking at the matter from a spiritual-scientific perspective. On the one hand, the human being can look at the mineral and plant realms, on the other hand at the animal realm and the human realm itself. Both, mineral realm and plant realm as well as human realm and animal realm, reveal themselves to them in such a way that, if they are now honest in the theoretical sense, they notice contradictions in this revelation. They cannot come to terms with the way the mineral realm and the plant realm reveal themselves on the one hand, and the animal realm and the human realm on the other. And if people think they are managing, it only stems from a certain obtuseness. They do not want to go into all the doubts which spring from the observation of the realms of nature because they are too lazy to do so.

However, if we advance a little in knowledge, if we train ourselves a little in the direction indicated in *Knowledge of the Higher Worlds. How is it Achieved?*, then in a certain respect both the view of the mineral and plant realms and the insight into the relationship with the animal and human realms are transformed. People today already have an unconscious feeling of this transformation which does not, however, come to consciousness. It remains unconscious, just as I have said, that today the human being steps with a lack of consciousness before the Guardian of the Threshold as part of natural development. It is actually always a certain fear of the truth that unconsciously prevents people from really advancing in such a way that they come to this transformation. I am talking in imaginations, in imaginations that are translated into words. There is no other way to really characterize things accurately. For if we bring to life in ourselves what can be brought to life by applying to ourselves what is described in *Knowledge of the Higher Worlds. How is it Achieved?*, we shall always feel something like fear when we look at the mineral and plant realms with this transformed power of cognition.

You see, you need not shiver, you need not get goose bumps when these conditions are characterized. People avoid them because they are afraid. From this you must understand that of course when you describe such conditions, it is also the case that you can get goose bumps to a certain extent; that's precisely why people are afraid. When we look at the mineral and plant realms with advanced cognition, there is always a sense of a smell of decay, a smell of decay that characterizes like a living feeling what lives in the mineral and plant realms. On the other hand, when we look at the animal and human realms in transformed cognition, we always have a feeling which we can characterize in such a way that we are inclined to say, actually— you will forgive me for putting this imagination into words—human beings, even the most advanced ones, always remain children as long as they remain in this physical body, real children in comparison with what is in them in reality. It is simply true that there is much more in the human being than they can develop, reveal out of their being between birth and death.

You see from this, because in such supersensory knowledge we gradually ascend more and more from appearances to true reality, that—by looking at this world outside as it is—we are actually only dealing with appearances. For the smell of decay, of which I spoke to you, and the childishness of human beings—forgive me—conceal themselves. The smell of decay finds, if I may say so, a nose that is too dull on our physical human being, the etheric nose is not sufficiently developed. And the childishness of human beings does not really allow us to admit that it is there, because we as human beings are too conceited for that.

But that's how things are. And by keeping apart what I have just characterized, we point out at the same time that there is much more in the human being than can be activated. We can then raise the question, well, in minerals, in plants, humans do not perceive realities; in animals, and not even in their own human nature, they do not perceive realities either. What, then, is the human being actually attuned to here on earth? For, strangely enough, they are attuned to beings that belong neither to the mineral and plant realms, nor to the animal and human realms, but lie in between. They are attuned to a kind of plant-animal or animal-plant. If there were beings here on earth who were neither plants nor animals, but who were merely plants in their inner organization, but who could walk, beings who did not have muscle and blood, but whose anatomy was like that of plants, who had only such cells and such tissues as plants, but who could move at will like animals; or if animals walked about on our earth who, when they died, left behind something like a plant corpse: then the human being in his whole condition of soul would really be attuned to such beings. They would, human beings would actually be able to grasp such beings here in their earthly existence. But the strange thing in turn is: these beings cannot be in earthly existence, these beings can only be found in other worlds. For their part, they are such that they could not thrive in earthly existence. So we can say, human beings actually lack that cognitive faculty—and this is particularly visible in the present day—which enables them to penetrate directly into the nature of minerals and plants and also of animals and human beings. And the beings whom they could perceive directly according to their whole constitution, these in turn cannot stay on earth. This is how strangely humans are positioned as regards their relationship with surrounding nature.

But human beings also have a strange relationship to themselves here on earth. On the one hand, the human being is a conceptualizing being. But when they exercise their conceptual faculty, then they lose their own nature in the conception. And this own nature, which cannot come to light in the conception, they actually only have through the fact that something, the will, works its way up from the unconscious. If the will did not work its way up, if we did not feel the will within us, the whole world would seem spectral to us if we could only picture it as a conception. We would have a spectral world in front of us, like the world of scientific concepts is approximately; that would then really be our world. Imagine if the world looked like the natural scientists or zoologists describe it, imagine if there were nothing other than what is written in books about botany and mineralogy—the real plants and rocks contain much more than what is written in books, but imagine if you were led into a world as described in books, where there was nothing more than what is described in books: it would only be a spectral world, a spectral ghost world. It is only because the will always has a say that this world is not a world of spectres.

If you could fly, not with a machine, but fly yourself, that is, if you didn't need the ground beneath your feet, if you could move freely without the ground, then you would come close to perceiving the world in such a spectral way. If you were only watching the world with your eyes in a waking state, it would indeed appear very spectral to you; not as much as the naturalist describes it, but it would nevertheless seem very spectral to you. You have a solid sense of the existence of the world only by having your feet on the ground. And this pressure with your feet on the ground, that gives you the feeling, which is related to the will, which is only weakened will, that you are not merely in a spectral world, but in a solid world. If you did not have this feeling but were only looking, then the world would seem very spectral to you. Because you don't tell yourself what is going on in your subconscious. In the subconscious there always takes place what the human being actually says to themselves, in the subconscious they say to themselves, actually, the world looks like a spectre! But if the world were as my eyes show it to me, I could not stand firm, I would have to sink down. And I'm not sinking down after all, so the world is not as my eyes show it to me. This conclusion is continually drawn in the unconscious. That's how complicated the very ordinary, most mundane relationship with the world is. It is always an unconscious conclusion, which in a certain sense comes from the will. So in pure conceptualizing we actually lack—if I want to express myself in a scholarly, that is, pedantic way—the subject, that drops away. That we have a subject, that we feel together with the world, comes from the will.

And again, when we have volition, when we develop will, we actually lack the object. The object, that doesn't enter our consciousness properly and solidly. If I simply want to move this little booklet from the left side to the right side and actually do it—well, the actual object of volition, that doesn't come to consciousness. You see the path that the little book takes, the conception, it appears in the will like an apparition, but the actual object of the will does not come to consciousness. So that the human being, both in conception and volition—this is again grotesquely expressed, because an imagination must be put into words—so that the human being is actually a cripple, forgive me, both in conception and volition. Their conception is spectral and their volition is incomplete.

What the human being really is, that is actually neither in the conception nor in the will, it is again in the middle between the conception and the will. But the thing is that this cannot come to our consciousness in ordinary life. Just as the plant-animal cannot enter into external nature, so the human being cannot become aware of what they actually are. That is why I have often expressed this fact to you from another point of view, by telling you that a person perceives the real I like a hole in the events of life. You see, you just have to be aware that you can also perceive holes. The human being knows nothing about sleep, they wake, sleep, wake, sleep, wake, sleep; but as they survey their lives, the consciousness that has been left blank, the hole in consciousness, appears to them in the course of their lives, and they see the holes in consciousness of sleep just as they would if they had a surface that was white and had black holes where they could not actually see anything. But that's how it is with our I also in our waking life. In truth, our I is not raised into consciousness, but in consciousness there is only a hole of this I, and the perception of this hole draws our attention to the fact that we indeed have the real I.

These things, which still seem like a fantasy to the present-day coarse human being, must gradually become the elementary consciousness of people. For life cannot in the future be founded on such beliefs as could be done in times past because the remnants and after-effects of atavistic clairvoyance were still present. In the future, life will have to be based on clearly transparent foundations. It will have to be part of everyday conceptions that we look at the mineral and plant realms as Goethe did,[32] who looked only at the phenomenon, who did not believe that anything other than, at most, the basic phenomena, the archetypal phenomena, revealed themselves in the phenomenon, but that the phenomena reveal laws of nature not expressible in thought. Goethe never searched for laws of nature, that would have seemed very fanciful to him. He wanted to follow the phenomena, for the outer world shows us nothing in the mineral and plant realms other than the observations, the phenomena. This is how a person must look at the outer world, so that they are aware, I actually only see something external in the mineral and plant realms; and when I face the animal and human realms, I actually only see something that is like an embryo of the whole being. And that is how it has to be.

You see, in the mineral and plant realms there are in reality beings who reveal themselves only to a certain extent when the human being looks at them because, let me put it like this, they cannot reveal themselves in any other way. For in the mineral and plant realms there lives something which can only be fully recognized if we—please understand me correctly—look back to the world out of which we emerged when we entered this physical existence through birth.

If you were able to retain that consciousness which goes backwards beyond birth in your memory after birth, if you would therefore be able to regard being born as such an event in your life as, say, the transition from the fifteenth to the sixteenth year, if the thread of consciousness would not break because your consciousness was quite different before birth or before conception, then you would quite easily obtain quite a different view of the mineral and plant realms from the one you obtain only by looking at them from the standpoint of life between birth and death.

For you would then say to yourself, I have emerged from the spiritual realm through birth. I have entered this physical realm here. Why did I do that? Why didn't I stay there in the spiritual realm? Why did it entice me down to earth in the first place? For we can speak of such an enticement. Then you could say, if you could remember, it enticed me down to earth for the reason that suddenly, in the course of my development between death and a new birth, I entered a sphere where it seemed as if certain beings had fled away, as if they were supposed to be in it, were absent and were not in it. If I may express myself roughly, in the final period before birth, we experience in the spiritual world at every turn that we are missing beings who actually belong there and who are not there. Everything shows that these beings are missing. And when we now pass through birth, these beings are there in the minerals and in the plants, but like exiles, as if these beings were exiled from the world in which we were, and as if they could not fully flourish, would half die and therefore produce the smell of decay, would half die in the world into which we have entered. Before birth we long to make the acquaintance of certain exiles. We just know, there are banished beings, but where are they? Then we enter the physical world and perceive them, but, I might say, embalmed, mummified. For in the world we have entered they cannot be other than embalmed, mummified, desiccated. It is the completely correct sentiment when we approach the mineral and vegetable world in such a way that we see in it the beings who are banished from the spiritual world, from the sphere in which we were a short while before we had to enter physical life.

And when we look at animals and human beings and see their childishness, then we come to the conclusion, if we can develop a view of their deeper nature, that these animals and human beings, once they are here in the world in which we live between birth and death, are never finished, never actually bring their whole life, which is conditional on their inner being, to a conclusion. Anyone who looks at animals properly, who can look at them with complete inner living cognitive power, knows that animals are not immortal, but they also know that animals go through the whole tragedy of this non-immortality in their group souls. The group souls do, after all, endure beyond the individual life of the animal; but that part of the animals that is here on earth is, as I said the other day, actually sick, it is so that it perishes because it belongs to another world and is banished into this world. And the human being in their outer physical form is also banished into this world; therefore they remain crippled, they remain a child. The human being remains a child.

The animal in general has dried up in its nature when we take its physical form, for those things which belong to the animal and the human being are found when we pass through death and enter directly into the spiritual world, which we then regard after death. Because actually we describe a circle in the life between death and a new birth. The things that remain hidden from us here in the animal and plant realms, which is why we perceive that animals and human beings are exiles from the spiritual world—human beings in their outer physical form—are at first perceived by entering the spiritual world through the portal of death. We go through a development, and reach a point at which it becomes increasingly clear to us, after the cosmic midnight I described in the Mystery Drama,[33] that something is missing, and what is missing has, so to speak, run away from the spiritual world. We follow this through birth and then find it in the mineral and plant realms on the physical earth.

We are not actually surprised about the mineral and plant realms when we enter into existence through birth, because we expected them. That we also find animals here on the physical earth, and human beings with an outer form that is reminiscent of the animal, only more perfect, is something that astonishes us to some extent after we have been born with our predisposition to consciousness. But we begin to understand things when we know that with this outer form of animals and human beings a beginning is given which only continues to grow in the world into which we enter through the portal of death.

We might say, with regard to the abstract and completely desiccated beliefs that still remain into our consciousness age and that formerly were much more alive and really gave a person something; with regard to these beliefs, the things that people perceive here in the physical world and the things that they are supposed to conceive of as lying at the basis of the world that the human being lives through between death and a new birth stand too abruptly [side by side]. What human beings go through between death and a new birth therefore remains so questionable for people today, and can be so easily denied by the grossly materialistic spirit, because, having entered the age of the consciousness soul, that is, the intellectual age, human beings live only in mirror images in their consciousness, as I have explained. They can therefore only live in mirror images if they go beyond the perceptions into which, as I have indicated to you, the will impinges in rising to their feet. But if no will plays a part—and no will plays a part in immortal life after death, after all—and human beings are solely dependent on placing before their souls in the mirror images of conception that which is the world between death and a new birth, then this world becomes questionable to them, not only spectral, but questionable.

Indeed we can even say the following: if people were to insist on accepting only the natural sciences, on seeing only the spectral world that natural science provides, then they would actually be right to deny life between death and a new birth, and life after passing through the portal of death as such. For what natural science gives is only images, it is spectral. And this ceases when the human being steps through the portal of death. Natural science cannot contain anything of what the human being experiences in the realm after death and before birth. For you see, in the mineralogy books and in the botany books and in everything that is connected with them, physiology, geology and so on, in all the ideas that you can acquire at all about plants and minerals, you can only acquire something about beings that are banished here into the physical world. And again, in the animals and in human bodies you can also only perceive something that is banished here—including in the zoology books and anthropology books—and that, basically, if you think of it in the broadest sense, comprises all knowledge: you can only perceive that which lives here in banishment.

But if you consider that before birth you are missing the very beings—that is, they are not there—which you experience here after birth, that in animals and human beings the thing is experienced which is not present there, then you will understand that nothing at all of immortal life can enter into the ordinary natural-scientific conceptual life, that natural science is quite right from its own perspective when it does not concern itself, so to speak, with immortal life, because it lives in images. And therefore it is the case that in the period since the fifteenth century, in which the ideas of natural science have dominated in all circles, human beings have on the one hand, we might say, robust, raw nature, which is actually the only reality for them, and on the other hand a realm which they only seek to reach with the diluted mirror images of the age of the consciousness soul; a realm in which it actually seems to them as if they were saying to themselves, well, if I come to the conclusion that these are only mirror images I'm thinking about—and subconsciously they come to this conclusion, because then they become doubters of immortality—then I would be just as stupid if I believed that these mirror images and also my own mirror image would still be there after my death as I would be if I believed that people come out to meet me from the mirror on the wall, that they are not just a reflection of themselves, but that they come out to meet me.

It is simply in the character of this age of the development of the consciousness soul that human beings, if they do not want to advance to a spiritual comprehension of the world, increasingly lose their connection with the world into which they enter when they pass through the portal of death. And it fades from their conception, it fades from their conscious life, but it does not fade from their longing. And even the worst deniers of immortality have deep down in the sphere of the will, from which longing comes, they have a longing to know something of the world into which human beings enter through the portal of death, from which they have emerged by passing through the portal of birth. They have a longing. The present is indeed sick with this longing. And the various illnesses of the present come to expression because this longing prevails in human beings and the human being cannot find any conscious conceptions for this longing.

When something lives in the sphere of our will that the human being cannot manage conceptually—again, we have to develop very radical concepts when we talk about these things—then they start to rage. That is the essence of rage, of frenzy, that something lives in the sphere of the will which a person cannot encompass with their conceptual capacity. And if people do not take the trouble to enter into the comprehension of the spiritual world, in order to grasp through the comprehension of the spiritual worlds that which is already taking shape in the sphere of the will, then the rage in the world will become greater and greater, the rage which today arises for people as the next stage after the absence of a peace agreement[34] which people have been hoping for. This is not something you can talk about like in a bowling club where, according to the usual philistine ideas, people think they can find a remedy here or there by coming to an arrangement—no, this is something that is connected with the deepest essence of human development. The human being cannot resist that which develops in a person and enters their sphere of the will. They have no power over that. All they can do is decide to consciously penetrate the sphere of the spirit in such a way that they learn to understand that which penetrates their sphere of the will. In this way, orderly human coexistence will be able to develop in the future instead of a frenzy.

As you can see, it is not a matter that concerns the human being just subjectively, that the human being should turn towards the spiritual world which wants to reveal itself through a special wave of events in our time, but it is an objective necessity that the human being should turn towards the spiritual world in the age of the consciousness soul. For changes have simply occurred in the development of humanity.

Up to the time when the Mystery of Golgotha took place in earthly life, everything that the human being needed in order to stand here in the world with some degree of security came out of sleep. People slept differently, even if today's physiologists do not admit it, before the Mystery of Golgotha than they sleep now. Prophetic figures to whom great things were revealed in dreams, such as to the Hebrew prophets, therefore no longer exist in this form; for the Lord no longer gives it to His own in sleep. He gave it to them. That is precisely the great transition in development. And the images of the future were not only given to the prophetic figures, but thoughts were given to people from out of their sleep as late as the Greek period. When you woke up, you brought those thoughts with you. The human organism was still constructed in such a way that people brought their thoughts with them. That lingered on for a while, although the thing was that people actually became headless—forgive me!—as early as the fifteenth century. In other words, the head was no longer quite needed; the head could no longer bring thoughts with it from sleep.

It is indeed a result of spiritual science to recognize that since the fifteenth century our head has quite become a much less useful tool, much more dried up than it was before. But this only becomes really noticeable in the present time, and it will become more and more noticeable if a substitute is not created, so that what is extinguished in the head is in turn replaced from the spiritual world. For until our time, until the nineteenth century, the other nature, the chest nature of the human being, was still accustomed to what the head received from sleep during the Greco-Latin period. The chest nature was used to it, and there people still had the lingering impulses in their headlessness. They were still used to it. Let me put it this way: people still had the gesture of the thought, the shadow of the thought. But even this shadow will pass, people will have no thoughts at all if all they want is to abandon themselves to their heads.

And that's how it is, and it shows itself in the fact that people don't want to think. Fewer and fewer want to think. On the one hand, they would like to let nature dictate their thoughts, preferably just experimenting and let the experiment tell them what to think.

People do not want to think for themselves. They don't really have the confidence to do so because they believe that what they think up is not reality after all. And if you take the bare thoughts, it is not reality. But we can become aware that it is the thinking, not the thoughts, that must become active. The thinking becoming active in this way comes from the involvement of the spiritual world. And today, when you really begin to think actively, you cannot help but let the spiritual world feed into you. Otherwise you don't think, otherwise you think as little as natural scientists think today who would prefer to let the experiment or research into nature dictate everything; or as little as social researchers think today who actually, because they don't want to be active, because they don't really grasp social impulses which can only be grasped in activity, work with what can be researched historically, what is hereditary.

Just think how people have succumbed to this because they no longer have the impulses themselves through which the social structure can be formed, how they have succumbed to looking back to the time when thoughts were still being formed. People are just looking at it from the wrong angle. It was Rousseau[35] who demonstrated the natural condition to people because he felt that nothing can be gained from the present if we do not become active in the sense of knowledge of higher worlds. And modern socialism prefers to study the primitive conditions of humanity—that is the thing in which socialists in particular immerse themselves—to study primitive conditions, to study the most savage peoples and the most primitive peoples, in order to understand how human beings should be in the social context. Anyone who is familiar with these things knows that. Everywhere there is a certain fear of that which so necessarily enters as the first dawn of the connection with the spiritual world, a certain fear of active thinking.

That is why it is so difficult to understand those things that demand active thinking, such as my *Philosophy of Freedom*.[36] Here the thoughts are different from the thoughts that are common today. And when reading this book, people sometimes stop reading very quickly for the simple reason that they want to read it like any other book. But, you know, the other books that people particularly like today, well, you read them, sit down on the chaise longue, recline a little, then you become as passive as possible and let the mental images pass by. After all, that's the only way some people still read. Don't deceive yourself by thinking that they often read the newspapers differently, these people—those present are always excluded, of course—it's just that sometimes emotions are mixed in, worries are mixed in; but the newspapers too, which are so sensationally received, they are also read in such a way that the pictures flit by in this way. Well, that's not the way to read something for which the attempt has been made to present it in the way of the *Philosophy of Freedom.* You have to keep giving yourself a jolt so that these thoughts don't put you to sleep. Because it is not intended that you merely sit on the chaise longue. You can sit, of course, you can even recline your back, but you must then try to set the inner spirtual and soul being in motion from out of the whole human being, precisely by bringing the outer body to rest, so that all of the thinking is set in motion.

There is no other way forward, otherwise you fall asleep. Many indeed fall asleep in the process, and these are not even the most dishonest. The most dishonest are those who read the *Philosophy of Freedom* like any other book and then believe that they have really followed the thoughts. They didn't follow them, they just translated them like empty words; they only read the words and do not take away what actually follows from the words, as when you strike the steel on the flint. This is certainly what must be demanded of those things that must intervene in the present and in the near future in the development of humanity, for through them humanity will gradually rise in a healthy way into the spiritual world. The inner relationship of the human being with the spiritual world will ignite in active thinking, and then the human being will advance further and further upwards. They can already go very far today by observing things like those described in *Knowledge of the Higher Worlds. How is it Achieved?.* But there, too, it is sufficiently indicated that it is nevertheless necessary that coherent, if I may use the expression, connected thinking, where the thread of thought never breaks off but everything is pursued along the thread of thought, should preferably be developed.

From ancient times, this still more or less unclear and unconscious longing to move up with conscious thinking into the sphere where the spirits are—which one can do—this longing is mixed with a weary desire to persist in incoherent thinking. I already drew attention to this the other day: it is inconvenient for people to always have to progress with conscious thinking from one step to the next step. They would rather go through a more subconscious region that cannot be followed with the thinking, and only then in turn take the next step, you see? It is not the case that you cannot understand spiritual science as it is meant here and which, as you know, reckons in a healthy way with the steady pursuit of a thought, if you make your thoughts really active that is; but people only wish to understand it differently from the way it must be understood. Instead of a steady pursuit of a thought, people always want the line of thought to break.

If you immerse yourself in what spiritual science gives you, then you can already today, if you only immerse yourself really thoroughly—be patient, in today's age this can only be present in allusions—follow this development up to the point where the human being stands in the world; you can do so by developing the power of thoughts in order to follow Saturn, the Sun and the Moon with your thoughts as they are described in my *Occult Science. An Outline*[37] and penetrate as far as into your own life, penetrate into your own life with the thought thus given greater intensity. Then you come to certain conceptions, even if they look different from what you wanted them to look like, but they are absolutely in the context, in the coherence of thinking, which enlighten you about your being, about the way you are, about your character. For you can progress as far as your own being by really bringing to life what has been said about Saturn, the Sun and the Moon, and then about the evolution of the earth, and applying this to yourself as an individual human being; only you must proceed with the thought as far as your self-perception, not let the thought break off, but let the thought remain coherent, let it be connected. The things that the human being legitimately begins in this way today enlightens them to the degree to which they are supposed to be enlightened about their own, personal being. But if the line of thought is broken, something else, something calculated is mixed in with this longing which is still more or less unconsciously present in the human being. Human beings want to gain enlightenment about their nature. What do they do? They take an old, antiquated science, which is not to be disparaged in respect of its venerability, of course, but which needs an explanation if it is to be brought into the new age, and calculate star constellations, letting the line of thought break off at every moment; later the thread of thought can break off, and purely externally, without thinking, this being of the human being is supposed to develop, as they stand on earth.

You see, the Roman Catholic Church, as I described yesterday, denies what is most necessary today; but especially if we take something like the description of inner contemplation of John of the Cross, this can be accomplished if we live today in the spirit of developments, in accordance with *Knowledge of the Higher Worlds. How is it Achieved?*. What is contained in this book is—especially for the present time—the observance of what a person like St John of the Cross wants, whereas the Catholic Church denies this and still wants the old ways of St John of the Cross to be applied to people today, as indeed some people do. They are too comfortable; they do not want that active life in the spirit which is already present at a very strongly active level when we absorb such ideas as are given in spiritual science. They want to continue in more customary thoughts right into the immediate present, preferring to remain with the old, so that out of their non-thoughts may leap that which is meant to enlighten them about the present human being.

Of course no derogatory judgement is passed on that which is thus venerable; but it must be pointed out from every side that we must not deny that which lies in the spiritual necessities of the present evolution of humanity as it enters the age of the consciousness soul. It is a question of really understanding what is wanted by human beings today in the evolution of the world. I believe, if I may use the expression—after all, it is only a *'façon de parler'*—that the better attitude towards spiritual science will result increasingly from the right sentiment regarding precisely those things which people today find uncomfortable and do not want; and only when this better attitude towards spiritual science results will it also fertilize social life. Then the human being will be able to enlighten themselves about human life, because only then will they have the strong thoughts to enlighten themselves about human life.

For in such enlightenment about human life the present human being suffers from a very unfortunate circumstance. Whether you are a Leninist or a Trotskyist, or whether you are a Marxist, or whether you think that you can shape the social structure of people in the right way in any other way: in all this there lives an unfortunate circumstance which is not understood, which is not understood in practice, unless you allow yourself to be fertilized by spiritual science. After all, the human being has entered the age of the consciousness soul. They must consciously develop that which arises as social structure. There is no other way. They must consciously stand in the world; it is simply necessary that the human being consciously stands in it. But they should also consciously understand the relationship between people, life in society, social life. An unfortunate circumstance actually prevents them from doing so. The fatal thing is that the human being can only ever conceptualize one person. Just as two people—physical people, I mean—just as two things—physical things I mean again—cannot be in one place at the same time, which constitutes the law of impenetrability, so two people cannot be in human consciousness at the same time, two people cannot truly be conceived of in real terms at the same time. It is very important to take that into account. But you cannot live with the other person without a conception of them, and neither can you develop knowledge about social coexistence without a conception of the other person.

But the situation today is that a person, because they can only ever have a conception of one person, usually prefers to only have a conception of themselves, to only have a conception of their person. And social thinking is also content with demanding a coexistence where only the person themselves is ever imagined by themselves. The human being cannot get away from the conception of themselves; they often tell themselves they can get away from it, but in reality they can't yet get away from it easily today. Only if they make an effort to fulfil the expectations placed upon them by spiritual science will they gradually gain the possibility of getting away from themselves to some extent. For spiritual science places such thoughts in the world that attain very broad perspectives. In this way, the human being gets into the habit of getting away from themselves. Just as the human being today, when they become a spiritualist, becomes even more egoistic than they were before, so they become more selfless when they want to penetrate the spiritual world on the other path, on the path of spiritual science. Therefore spiritual science is not merely the transmission of a science, but is in fact the thing that is absolutely necessary for the education of contemporary humanity for social life. Therefore nothing good will come about if we do not start from this point, if we do not really consider: we have to start with the conception. You can't undertake social reform if you don't start with the school system, if you don't start with the way people are taught. And if you fail to do that, you fail to give people the opportunity to embrace concepts that encompass their longings. And they will become more and more frenzied, people will, if I want to be radical in what I say.

So that is the inner connection. It would be good if this inner connection were understood. It would be good if, above all, this inner connection were felt by everyone who approaches spiritual science and wishes to live in it up to one point or the other. This is something that needs to be considered by everyone who wants to take spiritual science and the spiritual scientific movement seriously. It cannot well be overlooked, it cannot well be disregarded, that when we enter into a relationship with spiritual science, spiritual science in a certain sense demands of the human mind that we expand our interests beyond our narrow personal interests. It is really the case that when we speak of spiritual science, we are simply speaking of things which make it necessary, if we are to relate to them properly, for the human being to detach themselves from their narrowest interests. They should certainly not be afraid that they will become an impractical person as a result; they will become a much more practical one. What people have gradually got themselves into by becoming so unspiritual is only the belief, after all, that they are practical. In reality, practitioners today are terribly impractical people. And it is the practitioners who have actually brought about this catastrophe for humanity.

And therein lies something tremendously important that you must actually always anticipate if you want to understand spiritual science properly: you have to detach yourself from your closest interests. You have to get away somewhat from your immediate personality, because it does no good to bring narrow personal interests into the spiritual-scientific movement. This always causes some kind of trouble in the connection through which you enter into a relationship with spiritual science. This, of course, is also what makes the spiritual-scientific movement difficult today. Sometimes people have the theoretical and abstract goodwill to enter into spiritual science with their own thinking and feeling and their will, but they cannot quite muster the strength to really enter into the detachment that must be demanded in order to understand correctly what is being said from the standpoint of spiritual science. So a kind of spiritual state that is not immediately present in today's world, but of which the opposite is often present in today's world, is required if the spiritual-scientific movement is to be beneficial.

This is what distinguishes the honest presentation of spiritual-scientific knowledge from everything else that occurs in the present, that this honest presentation of spiritual-scientific knowledge is not a personal matter, not the presentation of a personal opinion. If I had to take the view that I was only presenting personal opinions, that I was not presenting what is being revealed today, what is necessary for humanity right now, I would prefer to remain silent. For to assert personal opinions and personal aspirations in a spiritual-scientific movement is actually something impermissible. This should not happen. Such a movement as is sought here is only justified if there is the will to put forward only that which can be observed from out of the spiritual world.

After all, if you describe what a city looks like, you can tell it in an interesting or boring way, but what the city looks like does not depend on you. You are telling something objective. To the same extent what you yourself want, what you yourself think, should not be expressed in spiritual science. What is spiritually observed must be at work in spiritual science as required today. Anyone who actually only wants what is personal can therefore only inadequately understand what is supposed to prevail in a spiritual-scientific movement. They will always confuse that which is to prevail in a spiritual-scientific movement, as it is intended here, with something else, which in turn is only taken out of the personality.

How many people approach spiritual science and want to have justified by spiritual science precisely those things that suit them as their opinion. People are not always equipped with the open mind that is necessary for the reception of spiritual science. Rather, people often approach spiritual science with something quite different from such an open mind. People would like it if this or that were true and then in some way—admitting that the spiritual-scientific researcher can know something about the truth—they persuade themselves that the researcher is saying what they think is true. Then that feels nice. But you have to take note of this subtle difference; it is a subtle difference, but it is a tremendously far-reaching difference, a far-reaching significant difference, whether you really want to receive the communications from the spiritual world, or whether you actually only want to have confirmed what you yourself like as an opinion. And you will only find the difference in the most careful self-examination, in conscientious self-examination.

Some people who approach spiritual science do not notice the difference; but this difference must be noticed. And if you notice this difference, then you will indeed become aware that something of a new stream of life, which was not there before, must pass through a spiritual-scientific movement. It really cannot be the case that a spiritual-scientific movement is nothing more than a gentle breeze that comes to meet those who bring the philistine nature of their previous existence to this spiritual science and now believe that the things they would so gladly recognize as true out of this philistine nature, they will see confirmed by this spiritual science.

If we proceed seriously and conscientiously in this matter, if we do not merely want to have confirmed what we actually mean ourselves, then we will also have to deal with various things which, I would like to say, must appear as new things in a spiritual-scientific movement, and which must become harmful if we do not pay attention to them.

In a movement such as the spiritual-scientific movement, which is in its infancy, many things can be detrimental which are not so detrimental in old, dried-up movements that are no longer of any use or are of little use. We should actually engage with such subtleties. It is then connected with the endeavour to see our own opinions, our own aspirations, merely confirmed by spiritual-scientific revelation, that we actually unfold a strange kind of glossing over with reference to that which occurs, quite naturally occurs, within a spiritual-scientific movement. We must be alert in the spiritual-scientific movement to the fact that people's appearance cannot be taken in the same way as in a bowling club or anywhere else where people can reveal themselves in all their scope, which they have acquired through the outer world, where they do not need to acquire anything new. We must be serious about the fact that we should not bear witness to the intentions of spiritual research through our own conceptions, but we must really make ourselves prepared to take things in.

We should consider that something wants to flow into the world that is to spread further and further, so that everything we take in should actually be taken in with the awareness that some connections that are not yet comprehensible will only become comprehensible later. Such goodwill to always take everything in as a preparation, so to speak, will certainly not be the case for those who bring personal aspirations into the spiritual-scientific enterprise, for they want to get to grips with things as quickly as possible and reshape things according to their usual opinions. They do not reshape their opinions according to spiritual science, but they reshape spiritual-scientific knowledge according to their opinions. And so something often turns out particularly to be the case which I would like to characterize in the following way.

You see, the spiritual scientist has to judge the world in a certain way, the world of nature and also the world of human beings. This is what spiritual-scientific education consists of, that we learn to judge ourselves and our environment and our relationship to the environment anew, that we learn to look a little deeper into the world. Now it happens very often when it is a question of, let us say, how the relationship of three people works, that it is said, well, spiritual scientist B judges person A in a certain way. And you see, as soon as you go just a little beyond the sphere that is the ordinary philistine sphere, which is common today, then two points of view can always assert themselves with regard to such a judgement from person to person. One standpoint is the standpoint of reasonableness, the second standpoint is the standpoint of compassion. So that B can judge A, and depending on there being an inner necessity, B can quickly do something in relation to A out of pure compassion. If it then suits C to reject the matter because they do not think about it further, because they do not suppose that there could be a need for pure compassion, then they will make a judgement out of pure rationality and say, how can you do such a thing! Or else this inner necessity says that compassion should not prevail on this occasion, but that rationality should prevail for certain given reasons. Well, if it suits the other person better, they will now let compassion speak, and now they will condemn and say, what a lack of compassion in person B! What kind of a loveless person is this, what kind of a dry rational person is this! He only judges it from the point of view of rationality! And so the strongest misconceptions can arise precisely regarding those who strive to seize the inner nerve of existence, where they sometimes have to do something out of reason, sometimes something especially out of compassion.

If it suits the other person, they judge what has happened out of reason from the point of view of compassion, what has happened out of compassion from the point of view of reason, and they can always condemn or praise, as they wish. You don't get to the right thing this way, you only get to the right thing if you first ask yourself: I have to look at the case; I have to look at the reason why compassion or reason prevailed here. This gives rise to the small misunderstandings of life which often grow into the most terrible disasters in human coexistence, and which spiritual-scientific education is intended to help us overcome. Because life is such that it expresses itself dualistically, and because it expresses itself dualistically, we can always judge any case according to what suits us. However, this is taken into account very little, and it is not taken into account, above all, in relation to the teachings of spiritual science itself. The latter may have to be placed in the world out of certain intentions. Depending on what suits a person, they can choose one or the other point of view in the individual case, if they do not go into what the spiritual researcher has to do for deeper reasons. The latter can often be misunderstood. And if you do not engage with that which they must do out of inner commitment to the facts, then everything can be misunderstood, for the world happens to express itself dualistically.

For example, you can fall prey to the following mistake: you can fall prey to the worst kind of belief in authority precisely when you are so eager to want, to have confirmed, what suits you. In the very field in which spiritual science also wants to be active, which wants nothing more than to make the human being a completely free being who relies on themselves, belief in authority can of course assert itself, and very often does so on the widest scale. But the other pole of the belief in authority is the hatred of authority. And basically, a person who does not feel impelled towards spiritual science by entering into the facts that are revealed from the spiritual world, but who wants to have these truths borne by authority and who wants to believe in authority because that is more comfortable than engaging with things, is such that they can jump terribly easily from believing in authority, which always has a certain kind of love of authority, to hating authority. And such phenomena as have just occurred in our movement, such a jump from blind adoration of authority, which is sometimes even admitted with a certain shamelessness at the moment when a person has then gone over to hatred, such crossing over from blind adoration of authority to hatred, that is already something that is inwardly present as a danger. It is very important to consider these connections, because it is these connections that make it enormously difficult to shape a spiritual-scientific movement in a thriving way today. It must be shaped in a thriving way for the sake of the welfare of humanity.

In my life I have found quite a number of people who were spiritual people, who honestly sought a way into spiritual science, into, well, spiritual science of one kind or another, who had also advanced in a certain way in their development. A certain type of these were disappointed people, those who had been disappointed in one of the current spiritual movements, and whom you then happened to meet somewhere. How many today are disappointed by the Blavatsky movement, the Besant movement, other movements! The characteristic phenomenon is not that such curious reversals take place, as they do here in the anthroposophical movement, but that you find people here who are spiritually advanced in a certain way; and after some time you find them again, but they say, you are totally wrong! It's not uncommon to meet people like that. Spirituality is not very common generally today, but there are people like that who say to you after a while: you are actually wrong, because, you see, that you publicly expound the things you expound in spiritual science to the people, that serves no purpose at all! People are not inclined to accept it, they are not mature enough to do so. It only makes sense to train this in yourself and remain alone with it. I have found a lot of people like that who say that! And it is virtually a characteristic of the spiritually genuinely advanced person that it no longer occurs to them to speak about it to their fellow people, but they keep the matter to themselves. There are not so few of these people in the world.

I have never been able to agree with these people according to what I understand of the spiritual world, for a certain inner reason. These people are useful in a spiritual context, but they become hermits, even if they sometimes remain completely in a social setting. You can become a hermit, can't you, even though you wear patent boots and spend your time in hotels? So then you see this twofold human life that a number of people lead; they may even be modern hotel people, have patent leather boots and, if you like, even top hats, but lead this outer life in order to mask themselves, in order to conceal themselves inwardly, have their inner spiritual life which they do not want to share with their fellow human beings.

This seems like an action that is not right, that is a sin against humanity. For it is true: such people do indeed have an effect in spiritual life, what they experience enters into the spiritual stream. The human being is not just a closed being, so what they experience has value and meaning in the spiritual world—but the question of time always plays a role. Such people, who at present live in the way some of those I have met do, in such a way, they do indeed have an effect in the spiritual world, but this only comes to maturity after a long time, in later epochs of humanity. Then, however, if there were only such people who developed their spiritual existence as hermits and did not want to teach what they knew from the spiritual world, what they had developed in themselves, then outer humanity would already have so declined by the time the fruits of these people ripened that it would no longer be able to absorb them. Earth evolution would be endangered, the connection would be missed.

We live in this day and age in such a way that these particular truths of which we speak absolutely must be communicated to humanity. It does not work with the attitude expressed, for example, by an acquaintance of mine who was in a sense a spiritually advanced person. He came to Berlin. I asked him if he wouldn't like to hear a lecture of mine, just to see what is happening in the movement—it's a long time ago now that he said, no, giving a lecture and speaking to the people, that's no use! Sitting down together for an hour or so and talking a bit, I would find that very agreeable, but leave spiritual things out of it as much as possible; everyone has to sort it out for themselves! Making a courtesy call on one another, talking about everyday things, that's best, especially with these kind of spiritually striving people. And this attitude is very common. It would be more comfortable to live according to such an attitude. And comfortable is precisely what it is not in the present to go before humanity and communicate that which you feel an obligation to communicate. But it should certainly be taken into account in a spiritual-scientific movement that work is done out of inner necessity, that it is not a choice, but the fulfilment of an obligation, what happens in this way.

I have placed these words at the end of today's reflections because I always want to take the opportunity to draw attention to what is necessary if we want to take matters seriously, as we should take matters seriously with a spiritual-scientific movement in the present day. For what such a spiritual-scientific movement can otherwise be turned into, when personal aspirations, personal ambition are brought into it, can lead to serious damage, must lead to serious damage. It also has the dark side that the person who only thinks they find personal confirmation through spiritual science cannot distinguish whether the other person is also doing it purely out of personal ambition. This then gives rise to the very worst calamities.

Well, I wanted to draw attention to such things. We'll speak again next Friday.

Fourth Lecture

DORNACH, 10 JANUARY 1919

W HEN we spoke of what prevents people of the present day from finding their way to the recognition of the spiritual world as it must be intended by anthroposophically oriented spiritual science, we pointed out two things in the human soul constitution which cause this impediment in the human soul. This is the lack of courage, the lack of strength in the face of the recognition of the spirit, and the lack of interest in the real shape of spiritual life. Now, today in particular, I would like to address these things from a point of view from which I have so far made less reference to them.

When such things are discussed, it must always be borne in mind that ordinary, common sense—I have often said it—is sufficient to understand all things of spiritual science, to take in all things of spiritual science without preconception. We have, if I may say so, in our present time—through this fact that correctly applied common sense is sufficient to understand the things of the spiritual world—everything that the investigating spiritual scientist themselves has of the spiritual world; we have it in a certain sense merely through such an understanding, through its unprejudiced reception. And we have, if we only have the courage and the interest to take these things in through common sense, then the possibility ourselves to ascend slowly and gradually, according to our own karma, into this spiritual world. This is already necessary today and will be increasingly necessary for all people, to learn to understand the spiritual world simply through common sense in the way that the spiritual world is spoken of in spiritual science. The extent to which a person can make themselves mature enough to look into the spiritual world for themselves is quite another question; it is a question which can only be settled in each individual soul's innermost being, and which each person will also settle properly in the inner being of their soul if they simply try to understand the things of the spiritual world by means of healthy human reason, which is not impaired by natural science or other things.

Now it is above all a question of why so many people today avoid letting this common sense prevail in such a way that it can understand, or is prepared to accept, that which comes from spiritual science? Well, you can learn something about this question when you hear how things and beings in the spiritual world actually look when the spiritual researcher enters this world. More ancient times had their initiates speak about many things differently in relation to the spiritual world than they must be spoken about today. But of course there is also much that could be said in more ancient times in a similar way as it can still be said today. Thus, in particular, it has always been expressed in a way that is still correct today what actually happens when a person in an immature state of soul wants to enter the spiritual world. Today, this can happen in such a way that people say to themselves, common sense, so what! But we must at least make an effort with it if we want to grasp the spiritual world! People do not like to make this effort; they prefer to acknowledge this or that on the basis of a belief in authority. People today really love common sense much less than they believe, and so they would like to bypass this use of common sense, so to speak, and would like to penetrate the spiritual world directly, which seems easier to them, even if the judgement is perhaps made unconsciously, through brooding of all kinds, which they then call meditation and the like. This in particular is very common, that people actually want to penetrate the spiritual world by bypassing common sense.

But older people who have been initiated into these things have already said the right thing and keep repeating it today. If someone immature in their whole state of soul wants to penetrate the spiritual world, then it happens all too easily that after some time they let their whole attempt fail; let it fail approximately in such a way that they are left with a feeling similar to that of touching a hot piece of coal and being in the in-between state of getting burnt or letting go. This feeling is one that occurs very often in mediums. They do not try to use their common sense to the same extent as their zeal in the so-called exercises, which are of course very justified in themselves. But it has always been emphasized, common sense must not be excluded, and it must be actively, assiduously applied. If you try to practise for a while in such a way that you exclude common sense, especially also a certain moral self-discipline which you have not yet acquired, then this peculiar thing occurs, that you feel the whole thing as if you touch red-hot coals with your fingers, or rather do not quite touch them, but recoil. In this way people recoil from the spiritual world. As I said, this has always been emphasized. It has been emphasized because it is an experience that countless teachers of spiritual science have had in earlier times when it was practised atavistically, an experience that can also be had very often in the present day. It is emphasized, but today we must look at the reason why this sensation of touching and recoiling as if from red-hot coals actually occurs.

Now, in seeking to understand this fact, we can recall a basic truth of our spiritual science with which we are completely familiar, namely, how we behave as human beings when we contemplate our full lives alternating between waking and sleeping. If we retain the old terms, we can say that while we are asleep we leave the physical body and the etheric body in bed and flow out with the I and the astral body into the world that otherwise surrounds us, if I may put it like that. We are not then in the casing of our body when we sleep, we are poured out in the world around. Our consciousness as a human being is then very limited when we are asleep. If the state of sleep is not interrupted by dreams, which means a certain increase in the intensity of consciousness, but if we consider dreamless sleep, then our consciousness is so limited that we do not become aware of the infinitely significant sum of experiences that we go through when we are in the state between falling asleep and waking up.

Now what we really have to consider is not the abstract words that in sleep we are in the I and in the astral body outside the physical body, but we have to consider that our life is an immensely rich one between falling asleep and waking up. We just don't know it because our consciousness is then weakened, because our sleep consciousness is not yet as strong as that consciousness which we can connect with the tools of the physical body. Indeed, a tremendously intense experience is had by the I and the astral body within the world which we are otherwise also in, an intense experience. It is just that the human being is guarded by their ordinary earthly state from directly perceiving this life, this life which we unfold as an I and an astral body by initially squeezing our way through the same things, if I may express myself in this way, in which we are also when we use our physical body and its tools in the waking state. Life in the sleeping state is a tremendously rich one. But this life does not stop when we wake up and submerge ourselves in our physical body and etheric body. We are then also connected through our I and through our astral body with our environment in a way of which the ordinary consciousness has no idea. We just don't notice it. We can now look more closely at this relationship. We can ask ourselves: What is the actual relationship between our soul and spirit and our physical body?

It would be a very bad thing for our present state of how we experience things if we had to perceive all the time—which we don't do at all, but if we did, we would have to do it all the time, we couldn't help it—what we experience asleep with the things outside in space and time. For our body has a certain peculiarity in relation to these experiences. It weakens, we might say, these experiences. Everything that we actually experience in truth in our environment is weakened by our body, and we only perceive what our body has weakened, not our real experiences. Our real experiences relate to what we perceive of our surroundings through our body—and this is a very, very apt image, because it is actually not merely an image, but corresponds to an occult reality—our body or the experiences of our body relate to our real experiences in the same way as the sunlight that shines on the stone and returns from the stone in such a way that we can see the stone relates to the real sunlight that looks towards us from the sun above. Look at the stone on which the sunlight falls: you can look at the stone, you can tolerate the reflected, the rebounded light with your eyes. If you turn from the stone to the sun and look fixedly into the sun, you will be blinded.

This is roughly how it is with the relationship of our real experiences in relation to our environment and what we experience through the tools of our body. That which we really experience with the environment has the strength of sunlight, and that which we experience through the tools of the body has only that diminution of this strength which the diminished light which some object reflects back to us has of the strength of sunlight. We are sun beings in our innermost human being; but we cannot yet endure being sun beings. Therefore, just as we must look with our outer physical eyes at the weakened sunlight, because the direct sunlight blinds us, we must perceive our surroundings through the weakened experience of our body and its tools, because we cannot directly face what we really experience of our surroundings. As human beings we are indeed as if we were blinded by the rays of the sun, and what we know of ourselves and of the world is not of our nature, is not as if it were directly experienced in the streaming rays of the sun, but is like the light which is reflected back to us by the objects and which no longer dazzles our eyes. But from this you can see that when you now awaken in the world that the ordinary consciousness cannot bear, you have the feeling as if you were inside the ray of the sun, as if you were really living with the ray of the sun. And as really experienced it is even the very concentrated ray of the sun.

There you have the fact concerning what is often said, that people throw away the spiritual-scientific experience like hot coals. You enter a region of experience in which the soul experience is the same as when you physically burn your finger: at first you flinch, you don't want to burn it. You must not, of course, invert what I am saying: no one can come to a spiritual experience by physically burning their finger. That's why I said—in spiritual science we must always use precise language—like the soul experience when you burn your finger.

It is indeed the case that entering the spiritual world is not at all something that brings about bliss in the human being, but this entry into the spiritual world is such that it has to be acquired—there are, of course, many other such experiences—with that inner, we might even say wretchedness which is experienced, for example, when you burn yourself with fire. Spiritually, we experience exactly the same with the things and beings and processes of the spiritual world as when we burn ourselves, for example. The real experiences of the spiritual world must be acquired through such painful experiences. The thing that makes these experiences of the spiritual world a source of bliss, that gives satisfaction to life, is the afterglow in the thinking. The person who receives these experiences through having them communicated and who understands them through common sense can have this just as much as the person who enters the spiritual world. Only, of course, certain individual people must enter the spiritual world, otherwise nothing would ever be able to be experienced from the spiritual world.

This fact, which I have indicated, must be taken into account. Basically, it is not that difficult to deduce from external facts what I have now set out. You will find everywhere where the spiritual world is spoken of seriously, not quackishly, that there is always talk of the passage not through joyful but through sorrowful experiences. And you know how often I have discussed that the person who has acquired a little real knowledge of the spiritual world in life does not look back harshly on the pains of their life, on the suffering of their life. For such a person says to themselves: I certainly accept the joys, the uplifting moments of life gratefully as a divine gift and rejoice over my destiny that such joyful, uplifting moments have been granted to me; but I get my insights from my pain, I get my insights from my suffering. This is what everyone who has acquired real knowledge of the spiritual world will say. Here on the physical earth, knowledge of the spiritual world cannot be acquired in any other way than in this way.

And now you can understand why people recoil from an understanding of the spiritual world, even though this understanding can be acquired with common sense. People usually don't recoil only from those things in their understanding that they don't recoil from in their outer life. Now, of course, you would be most unwise and foolish if you wanted to arbitrarily burn your fingers to know what it is like. And likewise, when you burn your fingers, you pay so little attention to the soul experience that you do not acquire an actual experience of what it is like to burn your fingers there either.

Indeed, there is a psychological fact that can only be correctly understood if it is seen in the light that flows from these insights. You will perhaps have already noticed—I am not saying this to any one of you in particular, because naturallyI do not expect this of any particular individual, but of course I only believe that they have heard of these things—but you will have heard it from others and noticed in others that when they burn their fingers, they scream. Well, why do some people scream when they burn their fingers? For the simple reason that screaming drowns out the soul experience. People scream and moan in pain in general to relieve it. And so they cannot experience the full content of the pain in full consciousness either when they cry out; it is really a drowning out of pain, the expression of pain. In short, the human being does not have much experience in ordinary life of those things that are experienced in the spiritual world.

Nevertheless, it is possible to understand things through common sense because they have analogies everywhere in the outer physical world in which we have our experiences. The things of the spiritual life are by no means incomprehensible, but we must decide to enhance certain qualities of the soul, for example courage. You just have to have the courage that you don't usually have when you do something that you recoil from because it hurts. You have to have this courage, because entering the spiritual world always hurts. So you have to enhance certain soul powers. This is necessary, but very many people at present do not want to enhance soul qualities in the systematic way that is indicated, for example, in my book *Knowledge of the Higher Worlds. How is it Achieved?*. If they were to enhance them, then there would also easily reign in their conceptual ability, in their healthy human reason that which is necessary in order to understand, through this healthy human reason, the experiences of the finger in the spiritual world, which in this sense, as I have described, is a painful one. We happen to live in an age in which such an enhancement of the constitution of the human soul is necessary, because otherwise humanity will not be able to reach its earthly goal, because otherwise catastrophe after catastrophe would have to occur and chaos would finally come.

Now, however, in discussing these things, I have strongly emphasized something else at this very time when it is particularly necessary. This is that with the weakening of the soul's constitution, which already exists in the present human being, you can be an excellent natural scientist in the present sense of the word, and with this understanding, which is not healthy common sense, but common sense elevated by scientific authority, you can understand very well what is the outer side of our physical environment; you cannot understand it inwardly spiritually, but you can understand the outer side just fine. But what you cannot do with the concepts that natural science gives you, what you cannot do with the very expenditure of thought to which present-day humanity is accustomed, is to bring order into the social structure of human coexistence, which is becoming increasingly chaotic. In other words, the social demands of the present and the near future can never be solved by what we might call thinking about nature and natural phenomena. It is precisely on this point that our contemporaries still have an enormous amount to learn. It is precisely on this point that our contemporaries do not go along with what spiritual science must say from the innermost understanding of the essence of our world. Spiritual science, in spite of all the objections which are increasingly being raised today, must say on this very point, however much tinkering and fiddling is done in the field of social questions, all this tinkering and fiddling will lead to nothing; on the contrary, it will lead to even greater social confusion than already exists in individual areas of earthly existence if there is a failure to recognize that insights into social questions can only come from the spiritual comprehension of world existence. The social questions must be solved by spiritual science.[38] Everything else is amateurism in these fields.

Here we have to turn to something else in order to talk about things from a certain point of view. What is holding people back so much at present from approaching spiritual science is their lack of interest in spiritual life. Almost all contemporary natural scientists have this lack of interest in spiritual life. They are indifferent to spiritual life. They deny it or put into laws what they observe with the physical senses, what can be observed through the microscope or telescope; but they have no interest in what every look, every real look at nature reveals: that there is spirituality behind natural phenomena and natural facts. But this indifference to the spirit is especially present today among those who want to tinker and fiddle with social issues. And there is another special reason.

You will be able to gather from many things I have discussed recently that we are in a very special inner life of the soul when, as a person, we are faced with another person. I have expressed in radical terms the state of our soul when we, as human beings, face another human being. I told you that, actually, facing each other as one person to another always has something of a lulling effect on us. We actually fall asleep with regard to the innermost characteristics of our being as a person through the presence of the other person. That we are deceived by our outward behaviour about falling asleep in this way is not to be wondered at. For certainly we see the other person with our eyes, we even reach out to them and touch them, but that does not prevent our deeper human being from being lulled to sleep by the other person. Just as we fall asleep in the evening with regard to outer nature, so something in us falls asleep through the presence of the other person. But if it falls asleep, it does not therefore cease to be effective. And so there are always effects from person to person in social life about which people cannot have a clear consciousness precisely because they are together with people. It is precisely the most important things in social life that escape people in relation to ordinary consciousness, because for these most important things in social life it is actually precisely the conceptual faculty that is lulled to sleep and people act instinctively.

No wonder that in social life today, where the intellect is most easily lulled to sleep in the visual imagination, the wildest instincts prevail and are even declared to be quite justified as the wildest instincts, because clear thinking about these things is simply lulled to sleep by people being together. But at the moment when the human being enters the spiritual world, that which has been lulled to sleep awakens, and it becomes clear what prevails between one person and another. Therefore the solutions to the so-called social questions and social demands can also be found there. So they can only be found, as I have said here before, beyond the threshold of sensory consciousness. And what humanity will want in the future by way of so-called solutions to social questions, if they are to be true solutions to social questions, can only be won by way of spiritual science, that is, the science of the supersensory, because all human coexistence in its more intimate substrata is of a supersensory nature.

But if we want to experience spiritually those things which relate to the human being and humanity, which relate to the human social structure, then we must introduce into our whole conceptual faculty, into all that we experience, something of which you will see in a moment that it is scarcely present in ordinary consciousness today. There is only one thing here in the physical world of sensations, of feelings, which is the same as the sensations and feelings that someone must have if they do not want to investigate the social laws, the social impulses, with lack of substance but want to do so with substance. This only exists to a limited extent here in the physical world; and that is when there is a completely healthy, a completely correct relationship between father, mother and child, in the upbringing of father, mother and child. In everything else that can be experienced in the surroundings of the world between one person and another, this does not at first exist for ordinary consciousness.

Now try to understand maternal love, that love which the mother develops when she has directly given birth to a child, that maternal love for the child which springs unsurprisingly from nature—you can be quite radical about it—and now ask whether this maternal love is present in all the scientific investigations which scholars usually carry out—even those scholars who carry out studies in the social sciences. We must have such maternal love for the thoughts we develop about the social structure if these thoughts are to be of substance and not insubstantial. There is nothing else in human life that could be conceived in a socially correct way other than that which is conceived socially with maternal love.

And now take the various social reformers and social thinkers. Try, for example, to let something like the writings of Karl Marx,[39] Schmöller[40] or Roscher,[41] or anyone you like, work on you, and ask yourself whether they, in working out their so-called socio-political laws, let the same thing prevail in doing so which otherwise lives in the mother's love for the child, when this maternal love develops in a healthy way. But this is something that must be pointed out: a healthy solution to the so-called social question is not possible other than when this solution comes from thinkers who—you will understand what I mean when I express myself in this way—can develop maternal love in solving their problems. It is a very human thing on which the solution to the social demands in the present depends. It is not a matter of acumen or ordinary cleverness or scholarly belief, but it is a matter of increasing the capacity for love to the degree that maternal love develops, or we can also say the immediate, intimate love in the way that father, mother and child live together.

Now you will rightly raise an objection. You will say, well, on earth things are already arranged in such a way that the social structure has as its smallest unit, so to speak, the family, and on earth this family as such is, of course, fully justified, and surely the whole of humanity cannot become a family! That is an objection that will of course be voiced immediately. But if social laws were to be devised with maternal love, it would actually have to follow that the whole of humanity would become one family. That cannot be, of course. The person alone who accounts to themselves as to what is a true thought and not a quackish abstract thought will have to admit to themselves that, of course, a person cannot behave directly towards every child as they do towards their own child, that not every child can behave towards every other woman, towards every other man as they behave towards their father, mother, and so on. So not all of humanity can become one family. That is quite right, but precisely because that is right, there is another necessity.

There is no way at all that we can create a family out of the whole of humanity in the way that we live as physical human beings here on the physical earth, and anyone who wanted to do that would of course want nonsense. But we can do it in another sense. And in another sense, it even has to happen. We cannot relate to the physical human being in the way that father, mother and child relate. But when the insight takes hold in humanity that a soul and spiritual being lives in every person, that a divine-spiritual being shines out through the eyes of every person, that the message of a divine-spiritual being resounds from their words; when, in other words, it is no longer recognized merely in the abstract that the human being has an immortal soul, but it is recognized in direct feeling in the encounter from person to person that when I look into a person's eyes, infinity shines out at me; that when I hear a person speak, it is not merely the physical sound that speaks, but the divine-spiritual essence of their soul that resounds—if that becomes an immediate sentiment, in the same way we perceive a surface to be blue or red, we will be able to feel that the human being, in expressing themselves, is of a divine-spiritual nature. We will not merely acknowledge by faith that the human being has an immortal soul, but we will perceive this immortal soul directly in the human being's expression. At that point the moment has come when we can behave as if the whole of humanity were one great family, not in relation to the physical human being, but in relation to that which the human being harbours intimately within themselves as a soul and spiritual human being. For we can enter into this relationship with the soul and spiritual part of every human being. That is the only thing that will make it possible to solve the so-called social question. For this reason the solution of the social question is simply given in the recognition of the divine-spiritual nature of the human being, in the recognition that the part of the human being that walks around here as a physical body on earth is only the outer expression of something that shines out of eternity in every human being. We can relate to what shines forth from eternity in the human being in the same way that we relate in the right way to our closest family. We can do that, we can do that in every direction. If we recognize this, we can then muster that love of humanity which is as great as the love of family.

The objection does not apply, of course—and it would also be very superficial to look at things like this—that, yes, there are also bad people! My dear friends, there are also bad children whom we have to punish; but we punish them with love! The moment we see the divine-spiritual shining into the human being, we will punish where it is necessary, but we will punish with love. Above all, we will learn one thing that we only practise, I would like to say, instinctively, when we face another person as family: when we face another person as family, we punish, but we do not hate the person. We do not hate the person who is our son, even if we punish him, but we hate the vice that he has. We love the person; we hate his misdeeds and his naughtiness, because we know how to distinguish between the person and something that has befallen him. Once people understand the great, enormous difference that exists between love of a person and hatred of the misdeeds that befall a person, then a right relationship between person and person will arise. We never have the possibility, if we follow our innermost human nature, to hate a person. We have, of course, many grounds for hating human crimes, misdeeds, human weakness of character, human lack of character. The great error we commit in social behaviour then consists, as a rule, in transferring to the person that which we are supposed to attribute to the misdeed and the crime. Today we do it instinctively, but we must be aware that the more recent development of humanity lies along the line of separating hatred for the misdeed from the love that we nevertheless feel for the person.

The recognition of such truths would do more for the solution of today's burning social demands than many other things that circulate in the world today as socialist bungling or socialist dogmatism. It is difficult to speak effectively of such things in the face of materialism, which everywhere needs crude matter, for the simple reason that people today are often materialistic in their instincts—which is more harmful than the materialistic theories. The crime, the lack of character, you cannot see them, they are not materially present; but because people want to hate material things, they cling to material people with their hatred. This gives rise to countless misunderstandings.

Another bad misunderstanding that arises from this is that sometimes, in the other direction, the person is confused with what they do out of some misunderstood feelings and emotions. We become lax in judging what people do by saying, oh, we don't want to hurt the person, love of humanity forces me to turn a blind eye in this instance or that. If a matter is judged only in such a way that the eye is directed to that which is done as a misdeed, and the human being in their innermost soul life is not confused with the misdeed, then the right judgement will undoubtedly result. On the one hand, it is convenient to act righteously against someone if you don't like them anyway, as is often said; but it is also convenient to excuse mistakes by which a person can have a harmful effect in the outer world because it happens to suit you. In the overall context of humanity, a great deal depends on our being able to separate what our antipathy may really focus on from what the human being as such is directly.

I have often emphasized that what is spoken from this place in such contexts is not meant to be a critique of culture and contemporary conditions, but a simple characterization. Therefore, you will also understand when I say that so-called Western civilized humanity, the humanity of Europe with its American appendage, had to go through this stage for a while, not only to take things materialistically in scientific terms, but also to take life materialistically, by confusing people with their deeds in the sense indicated. This was a matter of education: in order for the other qualities to develop properly, people had to pass through the stage of materialism in this area as well. But people who have remained behind on earlier cultural stages have preserved many things from earlier cultural stages in which there was still atavistic clairvoyance. And in the wake of atavistic clairvoyance there lie quite specific tendencies of sentiment and states of soul. We Europeans can only be equal to what is coming at us from certain sides if we consider what has been said today. For let us not forget, for example, the following: thinkers who are regarded as very enlightened, such as Immanuel Kant,[42] speak—and this is only out of certain underpinnings not of Christianity but of ecclesiasticism—of the radical evil in human nature. And how widespread is this error—this is indeed what we can call it—that human nature is actually evil at its core! In the civilized world of Europe and its American appendage it is said that if human nature is not tamed, it is evil. That is actually a European view, that is a view of European ecclesiasticism.

There is part of humanity that does not hold this view, that has preserved a different view from earlier times. This is, for example, Chinese humanity. In the Chinese worldview as such, the proposition, the principle prevails that the human being is good by nature! It is an enormous difference which plays a much greater role than one thinks in that conflict of humanity which will develop. Of course, when you talk about these things today, people don't believe you any more than they would if you had talked in 1900 about the war in which we are now engaged. But it is true, nevertheless, that a conflict is also preparing between Asian and European humanity. And here very different things will additionally be at play than have been, or are, and will continue to be, in the catastrophic conflict in which we find ourselves.

There is indeed a great difference in the whole way of feeling whether you are convinced like the Chinese that the human being is good by nature, or like the Europeans that the human being is afflicted with radical evil by nature—that is indeed a great difference whether a person thinks this way or that way, from the point of view of the worldview of a people. The fact that one person thinks this way and another thinks that way is expressed in the whole temperament of life, in the whole state of the life of the soul. People mostly get hung up on the externalities of life's conflicts; they don't usually pay much attention to what lies at the bottom of their innermost natures.

I just want to mention one thing. You see, the fact that the European person, even if they do not usually admit it to themselves, is basically always convinced that the human being is actually bad and that they must first become good through education and through being tamed, being tamed by the State or other means, this fact is historically and necessarily intimately connected with something else: it is connected—not the fact itself, but the qualities of feeling that underlie it—with the fact that European people have developed a certain life in the soul in the form that is called logic and science. Therefore you will understand that real experts in Chinese affairs, that is, not European experts, but Chinese themselves, experts in Chinese affairs who have also become acquainted with Europe, such as Ku Hung-Ming, who has often been mentioned to you here,[43] emphasize that there are no equivalent words for logic and science in the Chinese language. So what we call European science, what we call European logic, the Chinese have no word for it at all, because they don't have that thing, because what the Europeans believe to be Chinese science is something quite different from what we call science, and what we call logic, something quite different from what we Europeans believe to be logic in the soul of the Chinese. That's how different people are on earth! That's what you have to focus on. Without focusing on these issues, it is not possible to have a fruitful discussion about the social problem. But if you focus on such things, then your spiritual horizon expands. And it is this broadening of the spiritual horizon that is necessary for a healthy understanding of spiritual science.

And if we ask about the various things—we have already touched on two things today, we can touch on a third—if we ask why people today still habitually distance themselves so much from spiritual-scientific knowledge, one of the reasons is that the horizons, the spiritual horizons of present-day humanity are very narrow. However much people show off, boast about their spiritual horizon in the present, the spiritual horizon of present people is a very narrow one. It shows itself in its narrowness in particular by the fact that, as a rule, people find it extraordinarily difficult in the present to get out of themselves with regard to certain things. And that not only influences their understanding, it also influences their whole life of sympathy and antipathy.

I would like to mention to you once again a fact that is known to a whole number of you—that is to say, the effect of this fact is known to a whole number of you—which I have already mentioned once. You know that a certain relationship existed years ago between the so-called Theosophical Society and those people who now form the Anthroposophical Society.[44] Now I have experienced strange things from prominent members of the Theosophical Society in particular. As you know, I already published communications from the so-called Akasha Chronicle at the beginning of this century,[45] communications of which I may say, as of all the rest that I communicate from the spiritual world, that they are based on personal experience. When these communications were read by a prominent member of the Theosophical Society, they could not understand that such a thing existed. I was asked: How do these communications come about? And it was not possible to come to an understanding at all, because the method of spiritual-scientific research that is really appropriate for today was completely unknown in that circle. There research was undertaken in a more medial way. They basically wanted to have the name of the medium or the medium-like person through whom these Akasha Chronicle communications came about. It was considered impossible that they could really arise in direct observation through a certain human soul state reaching into the supersensory. Human narrow-mindedness is expressed in such things. Even in such an important field, people only consider possible what they are familiar with, what is obvious to them.

Well, I have given this example in particular because you cannot penetrate spiritual science at all if you are narrow-minded. But in ordinary life today, this narrow-mindedness is the usual thing: always to refer everything back to the personal, familiar point of view. This is what those who profess to be part of our spiritual-scientific movement should consider above all. I will now say something which, if we were to say things only inwardly systematically, would perhaps not need to be said in this way, but which it is nevertheless necessary to say in the outer context of life.

Those who concern themselves more closely with our movement know how much the sources of this movement are being attacked, are being treated with hostility, are hated by some who were initially good supporters. I already spoke about these things from different points of view last time. Well, it is not superfluous to be clear about the reasons for such opposition from certain quarters. I talked about the reasons for such oppositions in one place or another last time. But such opposition is very often particularly intense when it occurs among people who belong to one or another, let us say, occult society. The hatred of some members of one or another society which is developing towards what is represented here as spiritual science is sometimes a really strong one, and it sometimes takes on grotesque forms, and it is not unnecessary to consider these things, for we should consider everything that can lead us to belong to this movement with complete seriousness. It is true that there is nothing in the world involving more quackery than the representation of spiritual matters by all kinds of societies. That is why it is so easy to be suspicious of what appears as a spiritual-scientific movement, because there is really so much quackery going on in the world. Anyone who wants to can easily find approval when they say: Well, once upon a time a society appeared which claimed that it dispenses the wisdom of the whole world; it was subsequently revealed to be quackery. And then another one appeared over there: again it was revealed to be quackery!

It must be admitted, there is endless such quackery in the world. You have to have discernment to distinguish what is true from what is quackery.

But a different case may occur. A certain insecurity in the soul may arise, for example. Such insecurity can consist in the following: such a person may become acquainted with what is being done here. If they do not have an open mind, if they pursue personal matters, then they can get into the following ambivalent soul mood. They can point out all the dangers, they can say to themselves: Oh, what is going on here? I have heard so often about secret or other societies; I have not encountered any knowledge, real knowledge, there! People talk about all kinds of things; it's written in books, it's spouted in rituals, but there is no living knowledge flowing there. Now, is that which calls itself anthroposophy of the same kind, or is it something else? In that situation they can get into an ambivalent soul mood. If a person cannot respond to what is really living here, they can say to themselves, in superficial terms: is this the same hoax as the hoax that is actually more pleasant for me because it does not make such great demands?

The things I am saying are not so far from reality. And they are spoken above all for the reason that I want to point out that seriousness and dignity—which I have often said—and discernment are necessary, so that the unpleasant thing does not happen, which very often happens, that real spiritual life surrounds you, while you would actually rather have the talk about spiritual life, because that is more convenient. It is precisely the fact that it is what I have emphasized in my book *Theosophy*[46]—that there is only talk about spiritual experiences—which gives rise to so much opposition. The opposition from the Theosophical Society came about only at the moment when it was noticed that it was claimed that real spiritual experiences were being discussed. That was intolerable. They wanted to have people who would repeat what was said there, who would repeat it with a certain zeal; but independent spiritual research, that was basically the great sin against the holy spirit of the Theosophical Society. And such independent spiritual research, it doesn't yet have it so easy in the world today. This is also what I wanted to indicate at the end of my reflections the other day. And it will indeed be necessary for you to consider these things in particular with a healthy sense, but also in all seriousness. The times are serious, and what we seek to receive as the remedy for the times from the spiritual world must be serious.

We will talk about that tomorrow.

Fifth Lecture

DORNACH, 11 JANUARY 1919

IF we want to consider the significance for the present of the entry of spiritual science into the world, we must not forget that this entry, as we can already see from the various observations we have made, will bring with it a considerable elevation of the human understanding of the Mystery of Golgotha. And we can say that the person who unites themselves with the insights of spiritual-scientific research, not only with ordinary, rational thought but with their whole soul, with their whole mind, will, if they are somehow connected with modern culture, always have to keep raising the question: How does the human being, transformed in a certain sense through spiritual-scientific knowledge, relate to the Mystery of Golgotha? We have looked at this most important event for humanity from many different perspectives. Today we will try to look at this event in humanity in such a way that we will endeavour to follow the current that proceeds from this mystery right up to most recent times. This can in a certain sense prove the fruitfulness of spiritual-scientific knowledge, that it succeeds, or at least can succeed, in a similar sense to comprehend spiritually world events, human events, right up to the present, whereas otherwise human observation usually shrinks back from a spiritualization of most recent history.

When we look at the Mystery of Golgotha, we are reminded above all that this Mystery of Golgotha cannot be grasped or understood if we only take a material view of world events as our starting point. We only come to a real understanding of the Mystery of Golgotha when we attempt to understand a spiritual event spiritually. Certainly you can say, the Mystery of Golgotha is after all a physical event in the physical world, like other historical events. But I indicated to you only the other day: the science of the present, if it is honest, cannot say that. It cannot recognize the Gospels as historical documents in the same sense as other historical documents, and it cannot accept the few historical notes that exist apart from the Gospels about the Mystery of Golgotha, which are highly contestable, as historical documents in the same sense as, for example, the historical reports about Socrates or Alexander the Great or about Julius Caesar or about the Emperor Augustus and the like. It is precisely this—we have often emphasized it—which constitutes the special relationship of spiritual science to the Mystery of Golgotha, that this spiritual science will present the Mystery of Golgotha as a reality at the moment when all other methods of humanity and all other ways of humanity will fail to approach the Mystery of Golgotha as a reality. For the Mystery of Golgotha, as a spiritual event, must be understood spiritually. Only through the spiritual comprehension of the Mystery of Golgotha can we also approach the external reality of this Mystery of Golgotha.

What is the most important thing in the Mystery of Golgotha? Nothing has changed, notwithstanding all the so-called liberalising theology of Protestantism: the most important thing about the Mystery of Golgotha is the thought of resurrection. And still the Pauline saying remains true: 'And if Christ be not risen, then is our preaching vain, and your faith is also vain'.[47] That is to say, what is necessary for Christianity, for true, real Christianity, is the possibility of realizing that Christ Jesus went through death and conquered this death by reconnecting himself after a certain time with the development of the earth. But this, of course, in terms of its inner lawfulness, belongs only to spiritual worlds.

Now I have also pointed out to you something else which, if honestly considered from the point of view of mere reason, could virtually burst your heart, because it represents one of those contradictions which must always exist in life and which logic always wants to remove: Christ was killed. The most innocent being that has walked the earth was killed through human culpability! We can look at this human culpability and regard it in the way we regard human culpability, such great human culpability. That is one side of the matter. But then we must look at the other side of the matter and say to ourselves: and if Christ had not been put to death, if Christ had not passed through death, there could be no Christianity in the true sense. That is to say, the greatest culpability of human beings was necessary for the greatest blessing to enter into the development of the earth, for the development of the earth to have acquired its meaning. We might almost say paradoxically, if human beings at that time had not incurred that culpability, that greatest culpability, the purpose of the earth would not have been fulfilled. And in doing so, we refer to one of those great, radical contradictions that exist in life and that logic always wants to eliminate from the world. Because what does logic try to achieve? Logic tries to achieve that if it finds a contradiction somewhere, it eliminates it. But logic does not yet know today what it is thereby doing: logic itself kills life for human comprehension with the elimination of contradiction. And therefore human beings do not arrive at a living comprehension if they merely want to shape this comprehension with abstract logic. That is why human beings only come to a comprehension of that which is alive if they seek to ascend above logic to imagination, inspiration and intuition.

Externally, the Mystery of Golgotha presents itself in such a way that at a certain point in time, in a little-mentioned province of the Roman Empire, the man Jesus is born, lives for thirty years in the way we have often discussed, then the spirit of Christ enters him, he lives as Christ Jesus for three more years, passes through death in the third year and is resurrected. At first, this event remains disregarded in the greater Roman Empire. Throughout the centuries, this event has the effect of not only completely reshaping the culture of the civilized world, but completely renewing it. This, first of all, is the outer side. We enter the inner side when we try to understand how this Mystery of Golgotha arose out of Judaism and in the midst of the pagan world. Judaism has something in its understanding of religion that is radically different from all pagan understanding of religion. We might even say that Judaism and paganism are like the two poles of religious understanding in general.

Let us first therefore look at paganism. All paganism—no matter whether what I want to say is hidden to a greater or lesser extent in paganism—proceeds from the assumption of somehow extracting the divine-spiritual from nature for human perception. Pagan religion is essentially at the same time perception of nature. More or less unconsciously, this is always based on the fact that the pagan looks at nature, that they feel, the human being also ascends from the coming into being and weaving of natural phenomena; that they feel a kinship as a human being in their whole existence, in their whole growth, with what is there in nature and what grows in nature. And then the pagan tries, as the culmination we might say of what they can gain as a view of nature, to grasp with their soul that which lives as divine spirit in this nature. In ancient times we see this in the fact that the human being is able to grasp the divine-spiritual out of their own bodily nature in visions, in atavistic clairvoyance.

In the highly educated Greek culture we see how the human being tries to grasp the divine-spiritual in pure thinking. But everywhere we see how the human being, in being a pagan, tries to pave a straight path for themselves from the contemplation of nature upwards to the crown of the edifice of nature in the perception of the divine-spiritual within nature.

Such a view—and this is also evident when we examine the essence of all paganism in depth, today I can only sketch things out—cannot arrive at a complete comprehension of the moral impulses of the human race. For no matter how much an attempt is made to recognize the divine-spiritual impulse from out of nature, this divine-spiritual impulse remains without a moral ingredient. In the highly cultured pagan religion of the Greeks, we see how the gods don't actually harbour many moral impulses.

In the radically polar opposite way—of course, everything is expressed outwardly in a more or less masked way, in that the essence is clothed in one guise or another, but in essence it is possible to say, the matter is expressed in Judaism in the radically polar opposite way. Judaism could be described, if we wanted to speak simplistically, as the actual discovery of the moral impulse in human becoming. This is the characteristic of the old Jewish religion, that the Yahweh impulse essentially weaves and undulates through humanity in such a way that its weaving and essence also introduces morality to the development of humanity. But this created a difficulty for the Jewish understanding of religion that the pagan understanding of religion did not have. This difficulty lay in the fact that Judaism was not in a position to establish an insightful relationship with nature. The god Yahweh undulates and weaves through human life. But if the human being now looks at the god Yahweh who brings the human being to birth, who now also punishes sins and rewards good deeds in the course of life, and then looks away from the god Yahweh to the natural occurrences in which the human being is also enmeshed on this earth, then there is without doubt some impossibility to bring the natural occurrences into harmony with the work of the god Yahweh.

The whole tragedy of this inability to bring natural occurrences into harmony with the impulse of the god Yahweh is expressed in the great, powerful tragedy of the Book of Job, where we are especially shown how purely in the course of natural events the righteous can suffer, can come to misery, and how in contradiction to what nature brings, he has to believe in the righteousness of his Yahweh impulse. But the whole underlying tone, this profoundly tragic tone of the Book of Job—which, I would like to say, echoes into the human soul in an unworldly manner with regard to nature—shows us the difficulty that lies between a pure conception of what the Yahweh being actually is and an open view of what presents itself before the human gaze and before human life mainly as the course of natural events in which human beings are enmeshed. And yet, this god Yahweh, this Yahweh impulse, what else is he for those who really understand the Old Testament but the innermost being that weaves in the human soul itself ? To what is the ancient Hebrew view driven by the fact that it is opposed in such a polar fashion to the view of nature that is so prominent in paganism?

The ancient Hebrew understanding is thus necessarily driven towards perception of a being which, separate from the Yahweh impulse, had a share in human nature as this human nature is on earth: the serpent in Paradise, Lucifer, Satan, a being which is opposed to God, to the god Yahweh, must have a share in how the human being has become within earthly existence. The adherent of the Old Testament must regard the god Yahweh as the innermost impulse to which they direct their worship, to which they direct their devotion; nevertheless, they are not able to ascribe to this Yahweh impulse the sole share in the creation of the human being. They must attribute an important share in the human being to what is then called the devil in the Middle Ages. And it is only amateurishness—even if people believe that it is terribly learned—when this opposition between the god Yahweh and the devil, the old serpent, is presented as if it were the same opposition as, for example, between Ormuzd and Ahriman in the Persian religion. The Persian religion is, after all, pagan in its fundamental nature, and Ormuzd and Ahriman stand opposite each other in such a way that it is possible to ascend to their essence from your view of the world if you ascend from your view of nature. The whole process of the cosmic battle, which the Persian religion imagines to be the battle between Ormuzd and Ahriman, is also such a process as the other pagan religions have incorporated into their religious concepts.

But that which is thought of as an opposition in the Old Testament between the impulse of Yahweh and the impulse of Satan, as it appears in the Book of Job, is a moral opposition, and the whole description of this opposition is thoroughly interspersed with moral notes in the Book of Job. There is indeed reference to a spiritual realm in which there is good and evil, which is something different from the realm of nature. And we can say, at the time when the Mystery of Golgotha was approaching in the development of humanity, humanity had come to the point of not being able to come to terms with these two main currents, with the pagan path towards the divine and the Jewish path towards the divine. But both were highly developed. For we must not forget, we must always remember: such a refined spirituality, such loftiness of human conceptual life as developed in Greek paganism, is something that is unique in human development. It has not been reached again since then, nor was it there beforehand. And conversely, such an adherence to the moral impulse of Yahweh, undeterred by natural events, as is portrayed in the Book of Job, is also unique, it is also not to be found elsewhere. The Book of Job is indeed one of the marvels of human development, especially in this direction.

Humanity was, in a sense, at an impasse at the time when the Mystery of Golgotha was approaching. It could proceed no further. It had understood, or tried to understand, on the one hand nature in the old sense, on the other hand the moral world in the old sense. It could proceed no further. Both, outwardly shaped, had reached a supreme peak in human perception, but it was impossible to proceed any further. Now it is truly the case that the evolution of the world takes place in opposites. It does not simply advance as conveniently as modern evolutionary theory imagines, that there is an ascending straight-line development in this way. This modern evolutionary theory thinks, first simplicity, then in a straight ascending line what follows, and so on. This development is not like that, but this development is based on another, in that certain impulses of development reach a peak, but at the same time as these impulses reach a peak, others develop which reach a low point. There are always two currents running: one reaches the peak of outer unfolding, and just as one reaches the peak of outer unfolding, the other reaches the peak of inner unfolding. And in the same time in which, on the one hand, human beings came to reach a certain height in relation to heathen understanding, on the other hand, to reach a certain height in relation to Jewish understanding, the things which developed within humanity on earth could not be reached in any other way than through such an event which—when it took place externally, as it were, like a world symbol—itself happened historically.

Thus it could only be the death of the spirit that gives meaning to the earth. Highest life, as this life developed in the course of antiquity, brought to its peak, meant at the same time inwardly spiritually the necessity of death. Only from death could then new life come forth. This death on Golgotha is therefore the necessary greatest contrast to the abundant life that the worldview attained in Greek culture and Judaism at this time.

Certainly, it is possible to present the matter from the most diverse points of view. We have already done that too. But we can also say the following, for example. We can say that all the old worldviews, which were all more or less based on atavistic clairvoyance, which only advanced to pure thought in Greek times, all these old world-views were designed to ultimately find the human being here on earth. And this had already happened—particularly in Greek culture, in another way in Judaism—just at the time of the Mystery of Golgotha. If we go back to even earlier times, we find that the human being is, in a sense, closer to the divine in what they think about themselves. They have not yet reached themselves with their understanding. In the time when the Mystery of Golgotha happened, the human being had reached themselves with their own understanding. When something like this happens, one of those events occurs where an occurrence turns into its opposite, as it were, through its own power.

If you look at a pendulum that swings to the left and to the right, you will find the following—I have used this image several times: as this pendulum swings here [draws], it falls back again by gravity to here, and as it has sunk down here by gravity, at this moment, because the line goes in the direct opposite direction to gravity, gravity cannot act. But the pendulum does not stand still. Why? Because by falling, as people say in physics—it is not spiritually correct, but we can use the word—the pendulum has absorbed so much inertia that it swings to the other side through its own inertia. But this inertia is exhausted, it becomes zero, at the moment when the pendulum has swung as far to the left as it has swung to the right. The movement to the left is caused by the pendulum's own inertia, but it exhausts itself. That is a general law of events in the world, that something happens, and in the happening the impulse of the happening destroys itself. Thus, at the moment when pagan and Jewish culture had reached a climax, the strength by which they had brought themselves up to that point was exhausted, arrived at zero. And it needed a new impulse to come into the world in order to guide the development onward. And this impulse was Christ, for whom the envelope of Jesus was prepared in the way we know about.

Thus we can say, if a human being had been able to see through what was actually going on in humanity at the time when the year zero was set in our calendar, they would have had to say, at this time humanity has met with the tragic fate that the forces which were given to it at the beginning of its development on earth have in the time in which we have arrived indeed brought this humanity to the highest development with regard to its inner soul constitution, but at the same time they have exhausted themselves. They are afflicted by the death of human culture, which proceeded in the sense of those impulses which the ancients received like an inheritance from humanity at the starting point of earthly development. Then a person who felt the fate of humanity in this way could look up to Mount Golgotha and see the outer historical symbol, the dying body of Jesus, the dying representative of humanity, and could gain from the resurrection the hope that a new impulse will not abandon humanity on earth, but will lead it on; but an impulse that could not emerge from what the earth had been able to give people until then. That is to say, humanity had to look up to something that the earth could not give by looking at Golgotha and feeling at Golgotha the possibility of a further development of humanity from Golgotha.

Looking up to something that came into the development of the earth as a new influence—that was something that had to be done, or should have been done, by anyone who had an inner understanding of the development of humanity at that time. That was what had happened, and that was the meaning of what had happened. Whether this event was understood to a greater or lesser extent in this way or that way is a matter for external history. What is significant for Christianity is that it happened and that it took place as an objective fact. Christianity is not a doctrine; Christianity is the view of this objective event taking place in the development of the earth.

And now we see how this view of Christianity is spreading in a curious way. I recently developed the same fact from another point of view. Today we shall only consider how the view of the Christ impulse entering the development of the earth spread over the countries of Judaism, of Greek paganism, of Roman paganism. If we look at the historical development with an open mind, we cannot help but say, it is true that Christianity certainly did not take root in Judaism, but despite the fact that the Gospels were indeed written out of Greek culture, it did not take root in Greek culture either, and certainly not in the Roman culture of the Roman Empire. You have only to take Catholicism, which is the remnant of the Christianity that developed out of the Roman Empire, and you have only to take from this Roman Catholicism the sacrifice of the Mass, which is indeed great and mighty in its way, and you will see what peculiar significance underlies particularly the spread of the Christian understanding through the old Roman Empire.

What is the Mass, basically? The Mass and also other ceremonies of the Catholic Church are in their grandiosity, their incomparable greatness, nevertheless taken from the old pagan mysteries. And as soon as you look at the ritual of Catholicism and understand it correctly, you have in this ritual a reproduction of the path of initiation in the old pagan mysteries. The main parts of the Mass, proclamation, offertory, transubstantiation, communion, represent the journey of the initiate from the ancient pagan mysteries. The Christ impulse had to be clothed in the form of the old pagan mystery in order to spread through the regions of the Roman Empire. And the way in which what was lived through in the perception of Christ Jesus presented itself to those who were familiar with the results of initiation in the old heathen mysteries, you can read about that in my book *Christianity as a Mystical Fact*.[48] There is set out how on Golgotha, on the stage of world history, something was set forth which otherwise, in the mysterious depths of the initiation into the mysteries, always presented itself as a single human experience on a different plane.

And so we see that the mystery of Christianity is immersed in pagan ritual as it spreads across the cultured lands of the fourth post-Atlantean period, which we call the Greco-Latin period. That which is had as the idea of the Christ impulse lives on in the ritual, it lives on in the sacrifice of the Mass. Basically, it still lives on today in the sacrifice of the Mass in Catholicism. For a true Catholic is one who feels Christ Jesus in all his mystery when the host, the bread transformed into the body of Christ, is lifted up at the altar. In this ritual action the real Catholic, who feels the pagan form of Christianity, feels that which he should feel. There is not a direct relationship to Christ Jesus, there is a relationship that seeks to approach the human being through the form of pagan ritual.

In a quite different, intimately human way, Christianity first appears when it comes to the Nordic barbarians from the civilized countries of the South, which have immersed it in paganism or Judaism. These Nordic barbarians therefore also initially confront Christianity in such a way that they take up this Christianity in a much more primitive form. And for a long time these Nordic barbarians were Arians,[49] that is, they did not embrace the complicated ideas that were simply embodied in the pagan ritual, but they more or less imagined Christ Jesus as a kind of ideal man, as an elevated, idealized human being raised to the divine, as the first brother of humanity, but still as the brother of humanity. They were not particularly interested in the question of how Christ relates to some unknown God; but they were extremely interested in the question of how human nature relates to Christ's nature, what relationship the human heart, the human mind, can have directly to the ideal human being Christ Jesus. And this is combined with the views about the external, human, social structure. The Christ becomes a special king, a special leader of the people. In the same way as they imagined that they follow the leader in whom they have confidence, they wanted to follow the Christ Jesus as the especially illustrious leader. Something occurs here that we could call the search for a personal relationship with Christ Jesus, in contrast to the complicated relationship, expressible only in the realized imaginative image of the ritual, that we have gained in the South.

How does this happen? Well, these barbarian peoples, to whom Christianity is penetrating in the North, are the seed of that which is to appear later in human development as the fifth post-Atlantean period. It is just that they had not yet even become quite human beings in the time when the people of the fourth post-Atlantean period had already arrived relatively at a high point. They still absorb into a primitive human entity that which can enter a highly developed humanity only in the form of the realized imaginations of the ritual. The hearts and minds of the barbarians receive in an intimate, personal way that which, in the sweep of human nature into high spirituality, was received in the South only in a pagan form.

And so we see that in a very different way the seed of the Christ impulse falls into the southern hearts and into the hearts of the Nordic barbarians. These Nordic barbarian hearts are far less mature than the hearts of the peoples of the South, and into their immaturity the Christ impulse descends. The noteworthy fact is that throughout the South, throughout Christianized Judaism, throughout Christianized Greek culture, throughout Christianized Roman culture, Christianity established itself in such a way that the Christ impulse approaching humanity is preceded by the conception of Christ which is shaped in the way that it could be shaped in accordance with the old experiences of the soul. For these ancient people had a significant soul life, a soul life that was grandiose in a certain sense. The Nordic barbarians had a primitive, simple soul life that was only accustomed to the very nearest, to the very closest relationships of a personal nature between person and person. And into these close relationships flowed the Christ impulse. These people had no conception of scientific knowledge as it was developed by the Greeks, of a political view of a State structure as it was developed by the Romans. This did not exist with the northern barbarians. Their conceptual life in the soul was, we might say, free. They could not think much. They could hunt, they could wage war, they could farm a little, they could do other things—you only have to read about the ancient Nordic barbarians, but they did not have any developed science. The Christ impulse was not preceded by any conception; it could come to the people itself as the Christ impulse. Therefore we can say, Christ came to the southern people in such a way that he had to come to a halt in front of the conceptual life with which they approached him. These southern people erected a gateway: first you must come through it, they told Christ. This gateway was still the one that was constructed from the old, traditional ideas. The Nordic barbarians had no such gateway; the entrance was wide open, the Christ impulse entered there itself. There is only a slight difference between the people or peoples who lived out their lives as Nordic barbarians, to whom Christ came, and Jesus himself as an individual human being to whom Christ came. In Palestine, Christ came to the single person Jesus. Then the impulse spread across the southern countries. There the gateway of the conceptual life was everywhere; he could not enter into it as he could into the person of Jesus. When the Christ impulse came to the northern barbarians, it could not, however, enter the individual people everywhere—they were not Jesuses—but it could enter the folk souls who received him as Christ in a certain way. And a similar process took place between the folk souls and Christ as between Jesus and Christ.

This is the inner secret of this journey of Christianity through the southern countries to the northern barbarians. But they really weren't very advanced, these northern barbarians. And even though Christ was able to enter directly, it did not look very distinguished in the dwellings that he was able to enter. Primitive, the most primitive ideas were there. Let me put it this way: that which was already highly developed in the south, but on an earlier level, was still unfolding as if beneath the cover of cosmic development. What was highly developed in the south on the fourth post-Atlantean cultural stage, the Greco-Latin one, was still quite embryonic in the north and was waiting until later. So that we can say, we have the fourth post-Atlantean cultural stage and we have the fifth post-Atlantean cultural stage. As we know, the fourth post-Atlantean cultural stage, 747 years before the event of Golgotha, runs until the year 1413, and then things continue; we are now living in the fifth post-Atlantean cultural stage. If we take any point of the fourth post-Atlantean cultural stage, let us say a point in the fifth century before the event of Golgotha, development was advanced in the Greco-Latin countries, and very behind among the Nordic barbarians. It was waiting for things to unfold later, the same point came much later. That is to say, in the north people reached the point, albeit at a higher level, at which people in the south were previously at a much later time. It's important to consider something like that. For it is only by doing so that we come to understand how the inner development, the inner unfolding of human life is shaped over the earth.

Just consider how high this Greco-Latin culture was at the time when in this Greco-Latin culture that great man—we cannot just call him a philosopher—Plato[50] rose, Plato who raised the human mind to the ideas. These are not the abstract ideas that contemporary people blather about; these are spiritual beings themselves, to whom Plato looks up when he speaks of ideas. Anyone who really knows Plato realizes the height at which this ancient Greco-Latin culture of the fourth post-Atlantean cultural period stood. At the time when the great Plato stood out in Greek culture, Nordic barbarian culture had to go through a great deal before it in turn brought forth from its own flesh and blood, albeit now for the fifth post-Atlantean period, the same as had been brought forth from Greek culture when Plato was there.

And when did the Nordic barbarian nature work its way up from its own flesh and blood to such a height as Plato had already reached in an earlier epoch? That was at the time of Goethe. Goetheanism is to the fifth post-Atlantean period what Platonism is to Greek culture. How many years pass in a cultural period? As you know, if you take 1413 after the Mystery of Golgotha, and 747 before, that makes a cultural period; that is 2160, just over 2000 years. That is also roughly the time that passes between Plato and Goethe; a cultural period, only deferred, lies between the two.

And in looking at Plato, one thing emerges in Plato that shines out magnificently from the rest of ancient culture. In Plato we encounter what lies in the words in which Plato's philosophy rises to religious consecration, where he says: God is good[51]—where he gets an intimation that the view of nature in accordance with ideas must be connected with the moral order of the world: the divine is good. And with that, the expectation of Christianity enters Greek culture.

But this would indicate an expectation with Goethe in the Nordic world, an expectation of a renewal of Christianity. Who could look at Goethe inwardly in any other way than to see in him an expectation of a renewal of the understanding of the Mystery of Golgotha! The boy Goethe,[52] the seven-year-old, still stands before nature like a pagan, reprises Greek culture. He takes a music stand, places all types of stones and rocks on it as representatives of the processes of nature, lights an incense cone directly with sunlight, which he captures with a burning glass, in order to offer a sacrifice to the great god of nature. Pure pagan nature worship; nothing of a Christ Jesus lives in it. In it lives the god who can be looked at in nature. And Goethe is intensely honest down to his innermost being. He does not profess himself outwardly to any deity, to any divinity, with which he cannot honestly connect himself inwardly. Accepting the conception of God that a priest tells him, that he cannot do; learning outwardly something that does not well up from his innermost soul, that he cannot do. Thus as late as 1780 there wells up from within him his prose hymn to nature,[53] that wonderful prose hymn to nature, which begins: Nature, we are surrounded and embraced by her. Without warning and unbidden, she gathers us into the cycle of her dance and sweeps us along until we have grown tired and slip from her arms. ... Everything is nature. We are part of her; she sweeps us along. Even that which is most unnatural is nature. The greatest philistinism has something of her genius. She has placed me within, she will not hate her work. Everything is to her credit, everything is her fault.

This view itself wells up intimately from his innermost being, because Goethe seeks it as honestly as he must seek it as a representative of his stage of humanity, in which there is nothing Christian. Throughout the prose hymn 'Nature' you will find a wonderful inclination towards God, almost like the seven-year-old boy who builds his pagan altar from products of nature, but nothing Christian. For Goethe stands as an honest representative in the fifth post-Atlantean period, which for him is the period of expectation. That it cannot stop with the pagan, however, is expressed in Goethe on the one hand in that he also arrives scientifically at his grandiose view of nature, which is expressed in his morphology, in his theory of colours; on the other hand, it is also expressed in that he must go beyond this view of nature, beyond this paganism. And from this point of view, take the innermost impulse of *Faust*, take from this point of view, in particular, that which Goethe has secreted into the *Fairy Tale of the Green Snake and the Beautiful Lily*, the rebirth of the human being which expresses itself in this *Fairy Tale of the Green Snake and the Beautiful Lily*, and then try not to remain superficial, but to penetrate that which lived in Goethe's mind—then the thought will come to you: here there lives in a human soul a new Christ impulse, a new impulse of the transformation of humanity as happened through the Mystery of Golgotha, a striving for a new understanding of this Mystery of Golgotha. For the whole of the *Fairy Tale of the Green Snake and the Beautiful Lily* exudes a mood of expectation.

Where Plato stands in Greek culture, Goethe stands within the fifth post-Atlantean period. The question, where does Goethe stand, leads us to say, just as Plato with his definition of the divine as the good pointed to the mystery of Golgotha for the understanding of the fourth post-Atlantean period, so Goethe, with the words that resonate from the *Fairy Tale of the Green Serpent and the Beautiful Lily*, pointed to a renewed understanding of the Mystery of Golgotha, which must come. That is the answer to the question: Where does Goethe stand?

How can we imagine human events in a spiritualized way right up to the present day? Outer historical understanding, which only lists people and events in succession, actually says nothing at all that could really take hold of the human being inwardly. But if you look at the inner events, if you see how Goethe is standing at the same point in the fifth post-Atlantean period where Plato stood for the fourth, then the spiritual wave that has been flowing through the world up to the present day is revealed to you. In modern days, history usually becomes quite unspiritual in its approach for contemporary humanity. Goetheanism is at the same time a mood of expectation for a new understanding of the Mystery of Golgotha.

There is no other way to understand what happened at the turn of the eighteenth and nineteenth centuries than by trying to penetrate the inner workings of humanity in this way. A person can evoke many uplifting ideas in human hearts when they try today to renew certain feelings that were aroused in ancient paganism, let us say, when people looked up to the idea of the great Isis of the Egyptians. But certainly also at the time of Plato, the ideas about the Egyptian Isis as the impulse that reigns throughout all of nature resonated with people. If we hear about Isis today, if we hear about Isis without renewing with all our might what people felt at that time, it stays with the words. If we are honest, it stays with the words. If we don't get intoxicated with the sounds of the words, it stays with the words; it does not touch the heart.

What can the modern human being do if they want to awaken the same ideas in their inner being that were awoken in the human heart in ancient times when Isis was spoken of? The modern human being can let Goethe's prose hymn about nature act on them. Modern humanity is addressed in the same way as ancient humanity was addressed when Isis was spoken of. Here also there resounds directly from the mysterious depths of the cosmos what resounded when Isis was spoken of to ancient people.

And let us consider how we do an injustice, an injustice to the development of the cosmos and an injustice to our own hearts, if we do not want to hear in this way, if we prefer to place ourselves purely outwardly, because there is an ancient aura, into the way in which Isis was spoken of by the ancients. When Isis was spoken of by the ancients, an ancient sacred mystery sounded out of it all. And the language of our time may speak of the same mystery, as truly and really as deeply as it came from the lips of the Egyptian priests when Isis was sung about. We must not misjudge it when depth prevails in the new spiritual life. Then we will also feel ourselves properly as human beings again, if we do not become prosaic in our feeling, if the sacred sounds out to us in the way it desires to sound out from the newer impulse of historical development. And then, when we prepare ourselves, let me put it like this, in a pagan way by means of something like the prose hymn, with all the expansion of the soul that can come over us, with the ancient deepening of the soul that can be experienced in our inner being, with all the elevations of the soul that become tangible to us, and then immerse ourselves in something like some of the scenes in *Faust* or in the *Fairy Tale of the Green Snake and the Beautiful Lily*, we will find there the expectant mood of a new understanding of the Mystery of Golgotha expressed by the most modern of all human beings.

This is something I wanted to indicate to you about finding Goethe and Goetheanism; not only in the way it is often done, but finding the Goethean spirit in the whole course of human development in order to understand the immediate present, so as to give strength to those impulses which we need if we are to place ourselves properly in the present and in the immediate future. We must place ourselves into it not asleep, as I have often emphasized, but awake, if we are not to sin against the course of human development. More about that tomorrow.

Sixth Lecture[54]

DORNACH, 12 JANUARY 1919

WHAT I wanted to point out yesterday is that the actual content, the deeper content of the Christ impulse, which came into the world through the Mystery of Golgotha, has not communicated itself completely to humanity all at once, not even in the relatively long time that Christianity has existed, but that more and more of the content of the Christ impulse will communicate itself to humanity in the future; that, in other words, the words of Christ Jesus are profoundly true: 'I am with you always, even unto the end of the world.'[55] And Christ did not mean to be idle among human beings, but actively revealing himself, entering into their souls, encouraging souls, strengthening souls; so that when these souls know what is going on in them, they can find the way, they can find the connection with Christ, they can feel strong within their earthly struggles.

In addition to all this, however, it is necessary, especially for this our time of the consciousness age, as far as it can already be the case today—and as I have said, the content will flow forth ever more clearly and richly for humanity—to make clear today what actually belongs to the revelation of the Christ impulse. In order to understand this point correctly, we must first thoroughly understand that the human race has really developed and changed in the course of the earthly ages. This change can best be characterized by saying that if we look back to very, very ancient times on earth, far back before the Mystery of Golgotha, we find, when we look more closely, that the corporality of the human being was more spiritual than it is today. And it was this corporality of the human being that caused those visions to arise which in a certain way revealed the supersensory world to atavistic clairvoyance. But this ability, this power to familiarize oneself with the spiritual world in atavistic clairvoyance, was gradually lost to humanity. And just at the time when the Mystery of Golgotha dawned, there was a crisis. The crisis had come which showed that the corporality of the human being had declined most in its power in relation to the revelation of the spiritual.

Now, from that time on, from that crisis, a strengthening of the soul-spiritual, of the soul and spiritual power, corresponding to the weakening of the bodily power, had to occur. But here in the earthly body we have to consider the tools of our body. The human being would simply not have been able to acquire the strengthening of their soul and spirit, which became necessary with the decline of the body's strength, if help had not come to them from a region which is not a region of the earth, but which is extraterrestrial, if something had not come to the earth from outside the earth: namely the Christ impulse. Human beings would have been too weak to advance by themselves.

But this becomes particularly clear when we look at the ancient mysteries. What were these mysteries actually for? On the whole, we can say that the great and broad mass of our ancestors—that is, of ourselves, for in our previous lives we ourselves were the very people we call our ancestors—were in very, very ancient times possessed of a much duller consciousness than today. They were more instinctive beings. And those people in this instinctive existence would not have been able to find their way into the kind of cognition which, however, is necessary for the salvation of the human being, for their preservation, for the growing consciousness of their power. Then certain personalities, called to it by their karma, who had just been initiated into the mysteries, were able to reveal to others, who led more of an instinctive life, the truths which may be called the truths of salvation. But such revelation was only possible in ancient times out of a certain constitution of the human organism, of the being of a person, which is no longer present today.

The mystery ceremonies, the mystery practices through the different degrees consisted of the human being really becoming someone else in the mysteries. This can no longer be easily imagined today, because it is no longer possible to such an extent through such external practices today—I recently described them for the Egyptian mysteries. Human nature was really transformed by the generation of certain emotions, of certain inner soul experiences, in such a way that the spiritual detached itself in full consciousness. But first the pupil of the mysteries was prepared in such a way that this spiritual part did not detach itself in such a chaotic state as it does today in sleep, but that the human being could really perceive in the spiritual. This was the great experience that the mystery pupils went through, that after their initiation they knew of the spiritual world in the same way as the human being knows of the physical and sensory world through their eyes and ears. Then they could reveal what they knew of this spiritual world.

But the time was approaching when human nature could no longer be so easily transformed by those practices which were those of the ancient mysteries. Human beings change in the course of history. Something else had to come, and the other thing that came was precisely that what the human being experienced on a certain level in the mystery, the inner resurrection, actually took place as a historical fact on Golgotha. So now this had become a historical event. A person, Jesus—because as a person walking around outwardly, he was just the person Jesus—had gone through the Mystery of Golgotha. But those who were his intimate disciples knew that after a certain time he appeared among them alive—in what way we will not examine today—that therefore the resurrection is a truth.

So we can say that once upon a time, in the course of this evolution of humanity, it happened that in one place on earth, through an extraterrestrial force, the Christ impulse, a human being had overcome death, so that the overcoming of death could be among the experiences of earth existence itself. With this, however, something had happened in the historical development of humanity which is incomprehensible to the reason in particular which was now specifically to develop, which lay in the advancement of human beings. For human reason cannot comprehend that a human being dies, is buried and is resurrected. For the salvation of the earth's evolution something was therefore necessary, something had to happen in the physical course of this earth evolution, which is incomprehensible to reason, a reason which can be well applied in relation to the natural existence. And actually it is honest to admit that the further human beings advance in the development of their reason—and development in the consciousness age is predominantly the development of the intellectual—the more incomprehensible the event of Golgotha must become for the mind which is at first directed towards outer nature. So that we can say, the person who is only aware of the way ordinary reason is used, as it is directed towards natural existence, must honestly confess to themselves little by little that they do not grasp the Mystery of Golgotha. But they have to give themselves a push, because they nevertheless have to grasp it. That is the essential thing, to be able to give ourselves a push, to simply think beyond common sense. That is the essential thing, that is something that must occur as a necessity, to give ourselves this push in order nevertheless to learn to understand something that is seemingly incomprehensible to the highest human power.

The more intellectual development progresses, on which the flowering of science depends, the more the understanding of the Mystery of Golgotha had to take a back seat to this intellectual development. It was for this reason that it was not the educated Hebrews, not the educated Greeks, not the educated Romans, who were first chosen, as it were historically, for the understanding of the Mystery of Golgotha in the way I have explained the Mystery of Golgotha to you; they transposed it into other conceptions, as I explained yesterday, but it was the primitively educated barbarians of the north who took into their primitively educated souls Christ who came to them, just as he came to Jesus of Nazareth. It would indeed be possible to say, in the sense I explained yesterday, that Christ first came to the human being Jesus of Nazareth in the event of Golgotha. Here humanity was first of all made aware—the humanity that was the Hebrews, the humanity that was the Greeks, the humanity that was the Romans—of the most important thing that was happening in the earth's existence. But then Christ came again, united with the people who populated the north, the east of Europe, who had no such education as the Hebrews, as the Greeks, as the Romans. There he did not unite with a single person, there he united with the folk souls of these tribes. But we also had to emphasize yesterday that these tribes gradually developed. They had in a certain sense to catch up at a fifth stage with what the Hebrew, Greek and Latin peoples had gone through at a fourth stage. And we stressed yesterday that it was only in the age of Goethe that the age of Plato was reached in relation to a later stage. With Goetheanism itself, the Platonism of Greek culture that was there for the fourth post-Atlantean period had returned for the fifth post-Atlantean period. But Goetheanism was not yet so far advanced that it was faced with the whole new conception of the Mystery of Golgotha, but, as I said yesterday, in anticipation of it.

This mood of modern humanity towards the Mystery of Golgotha—it can be studied correctly in particular if we really understand the personality, but now the spiritual and soul personality of Goethe correctly. The question is a thoroughly spiritual scientific one: Where do Goethe and those who were associated with him, various minds who were in contact with him, where does Goetheanism stand at the turn of the eighteenth to the nineteenth century in relation to the development of humanity, in relation to the conception of the Christ impulse? We could begin by looking at this: where does it actually stand externally within European development, this Goetheanism?

Here it is good to recall something about which I have often spoken to you during the years of our catastrophic time.[56] Here it is good to recall the answer to the question: Where actually do the European peripheral cultures with their American offspring come from? We must not forget that anyone who looks impartially at these European peripheral cultures knows that the culture of England, France, Italy, the Balkans, as far as it has advanced, but behind it even the culture of the European East, has radiated from Europe's centre; all of them radiated out. It would, of course, be a terrible misconception to believe that what is Italian culture today is anything other than what has radiated from the centre of Europe to Italy, only overlaid with the Latin nature that has remained in the language and in the outward form. It would be a terrible misconception to believe that English culture is anything other than that which has radiated from the centre of Europe and is actually only enclosed, again by language and the like, in a different nature, in fact much less than Italian or French nature. But everything that is France, England, Italy, and in many respects the European East, has radiated from the centre of Europe. And in this centre there has remained what has now resulted after the cultures have radiated out, what has remained as the womb out of which Goetheanism has developed.

Today we are faced with the fact, which must be accepted without emotion, that what has radiated into the periphery is working with all its might to destroy, also to destroy in spirit and soul, that from which it has radiated, situated in the centre of Europe. One day the world will look at this most monstrous phenomenon of human history in a completely different way than in our present time, when this world is preparing to worship fourteen cadaverous thoughts of the West[57] as idols. One day humanity will understand that what happened was what can be called the absolute desire to destroy that which radiated out to all sides. The tragedy of this will, of course, be fulfilled.

For it lies in the thrust of this fact that in a further developmental step there appears for Europe the thing—with the exception of the last decades, where it can be said that other forces have been at work—which has been initiated and developed through the centuries by the fact that from Europe's centre the personal traits of those who shaped the cultures in the most diverse ways also radiated everywhere. Oh, on this point humanity today is so little inclined to form an unbiased judgement! I may say that I myself was intimately connected with the work of my old friend Karl Julius Schröer[58] when, in order to give the matter a completely secure academic basis, he studied the last traces which were to be found of the various dialects, the various languages, the various characteristics of the sections of the peoples which should be regarded as the German sections of the peoples of northern Hungary, Transylvania and otherwise of the various regions of Austria. Anyone who considers all that followed on from the modest dictionaries[59] and grammars of the Zipser Germans and the Transylvanian Saxons in Schröer's studies, which I had the privilege of discussing with him personally as a researcher of the spread of Central European culture, as he was at that time, may say that Schröer is still connected with a knowledge which unfortunately is no longer taken into account in the turmoil, in the hurricane of events today. But look at this Hungary, where a purely Magyar culture was to be established in the course of the last decades, since 1867,[60] look not with political falsehood and political delusion, political hatred, look in accordance with the truth: then you will discover that in the areas that were later to be Magyarized as the lands of Magyardom, people moved in from the Rhine as the Transylvanian Saxons, people from further west as the Zipser Germans, people from what is now Swabia as the Banat Germans. All this is the ferment that forms the basis for Magyar culture, over which something is only cast which then basically formed very late as Magyar culture. But at the basis of this Magyar culture—even if not in what can be expressed through language, but in the feelings, in the emotions, in the whole people—there has always flowed into it those things that have come over the centuries from the middle of Europe.

As astonishing as this may be, you could study the same for all the peripheral regions of Europe if you only take the history of Europe as a whole. In the east, the Slavic wave came towards what radiated from the centre, overlaid what radiated from the centre with the Slavic wave; from the west came the Romanesque wave. And through a tragic concatenation, which, however, has an inner historical necessity, the periphery then turned against that which remained in the centre in the womb; turned in such a way that from this turn one fact is quite clear—this may or may not be believed, it may or may not be easily ridiculed or scoffed at: the things which have remained behind in the centre of Europe, the things which have grown out of Goetheanism, grasped in soul and spirit in their reality and in their truth, these things today find no understanding in the average knowledge of the periphery at its best. And we could say that everywhere, even as far as the American regions, people speak of the actual substance of the central European being as if they had no idea of it. It is impossible to have any idea of it. But world history will bring that to light. That is what can give you strength in a certain sense, being able to hold on to that.

Certainly, on New Year's Eve[61] I presented to you here a picture, calculated by a person who can calculate well, of the future conditions of central Europe. They will not differ from this if everything comes to pass, if even just a part comes to pass of what the peripheral countries want. But this central Europe, whose destruction has been decided as far as its external existence is concerned, whose destruction will probably also come to pass for the next few years and decades—for that is how it has been decided in the council of the peripheral powers—had in its womb the final form of what we characterized yesterday; that had in its womb the final form of that which is nevertheless important as a ferment for the development of humanity. It must enter, this development must simply continue that I characterized with regard to Magyardom. This radiating out will continue all the same.

The only thing that will have to be understood, especially in central Europe, is something which has, however, been little understood in central Europe in recent decades: something will have to be understood of the nature of what lies in the intentions regarding the threefolding of the social system, as I have described them to you. Central Europe in particular will be called upon to understand this threefolding. And perhaps when this central Europe has no external state, when this central Europe is tragically forced to live in chaos, only then will people begin to understand that old views, for which the periphery of Europe is now fighting, must be overcome, because these old views cannot be maintained by the periphery of Europe either.

The old concept of the State will fade away; it will make way for threefold division. And that which is Goetheanism will also have to enter into the outer life. Whether you call it that or not, it doesn't matter. The key thing is that in Goethe's worldview lies a preview of what simply must also become clear in relation to the external social organization of humanity. But we can only see through all of this if we make an effort to understand this representative, this most complete representative of German nature, Goethe, who is such a complete representative of German nature because he is so devoid of all national chauvinism or anything that is merely reminiscent of national chauvinism or nationalism as they are understood today.

We must try to comprehend this representative of modern times, this most modern of people, and at the same time this person who in his being has the most productive influence on intellectual culture. It cannot be said that humanity has actually advanced very far in comprehending Goethe. Goethe felt himself a loner within his milieu. And even if Goethe was one of those personalities who was able to develop the social manners, even develop the, if I may say so, social dexterity and social grace to establish any possible relationship with this milieu: the actual Goethe who lived inside this person living in Weimar, who later appeared outwardly as a fat privy councillor with a double chin, the inner person who lived inside this fat privy councillor with a double chin, he felt lonely. And lonely in a certain respect he still is today. He is lonely for a very specific reason, and lonely is what he was bound to feel. Such a feeling of loneliness in his culture, of not being understood, was perhaps at the root of the strange words he uttered in later years: The Germans will perhaps be different in a century from what they are now; they will perhaps then have turned from scholars into human beings.[62]

This statement must really touch us in the depths of our soul. For, you see, when the Goethe and Schiller Archive and the Goethe Society were founded in Weimar after the death of the last Goethe grandson, the former was founded by an assembly of people—truly, I want to say it in the best sense of the word—by an assembly of scholars. The Goethe service was set up at that time by people, by personalities who had truly not yet turned from scholars into human beings. Indeed, we can go even further. You know how much I admire Herman Grimm,[63] the art historian, the fine essayist, and I have never made a secret of this admiration, and have spoken to you in various ways of the veneration I have for Herman Grimm. I have also absolutely admitted to you that I consider the book on Goethe by Herman Grimm to be the best that has been written about Goethe by way of a biography and monograph. But now take this book by Herman Grimm: it is written out of a certain human love and vision; but try to form a picture of the Goethe figure that stands before you when you have let this book work on you! What is this Goethe figure like? It is a spectre nonetheless, a spectre, not the living Goethe! You can't get rid of the feeling if you take these things seriously and with due worth. If Herman Grimm had met Goethe today, or if he had met Goethe during his lifetime, he would have been ready at any time to say, because he had absorbed the deepest reverence for Goethe in the tradition that was built on Goethe: Goethe is predestined to become the intellectual king not only of central Europe, but of all humanity. Indeed, if it had been up to him, Herman Grimm would have done everything to serve as a herald, if it had been a question of making Goethe the king of cultured literacy on earth.

But you can't get rid of the other feeling, that if Herman Grimm had started talking to Goethe or Goethe to Herman Grimm, Herman Grimm would hardly have found any understanding for the innermost part of Goethe's being. For what he describes in his book is certainly the best of what he knew about Goethe, but nothing other than the shadow that Goethe cast on his entire surroundings, the impression he made on his time. There is nothing, not even the slightest hint of what lived in Goethe's soul; a spectre from the eighteenth and nineteenth centuries, not what lived profoundly in Goethe.

This is a striking phenomenon that we must place before our souls with all seriousness and dignity. And if we now look back from this—not Goetheanism, but from these Goethe followers, who even a hundred years after Goethe are truly much more scholarly than human—if we look back from this to Goethe himself, then among the many great things, among the many grandiose things that confront us in Goethe, we see one thing above all. Take *The Mysteries*,[64] which were recently recited here by Mrs Steiner, take the *Pandora* fragment, the *Prometheus* fragment,[65] take other things, take the circumstance that *The Natural Daughter*[66] contains only the first part of a trilogy that has not been completed, take the circumstance that in this fragment a greatness that lived in Goethe expressed itself: then you have the remarkable, the quite remarkable fact that when Goethe made an attempt to express something great, he did not reach the end, because he was honest enough not to round things off outwardly, as poets and artists do, but to stop when the inner well-spring dried up. That is why so much is unfinished.

But there's more to it than that. The matter goes so far that we can say, *Faust* is indeed complete in an outward respect, but how much in *Faust* is inwardly decayed, how much in *Faust* is like the figure of Mephistopheles himself! Read what I have said about Faust, about the figure of Mephistopheles, in the little booklet about Goethe[67] which has recently been published, where I speak of how Goethe has presented in Mephistopheles a character who does not actually exist, in that the two figures, Lucifer and Ahriman, have been mixed up and whirl about chaotically. And in the course of this week you will find presented here the last scenes before the appearance of Helena, before the beginning of the third act in the second part of *Faust*: something that Goethe completed in his old age, something that on the one hand is grandiose, deep, powerful, but on the other hand, despite being finished outwardly, is completely unfinished inwardly, contains everywhere the seeds of that which lay in Goethe's longings but did not want to enter his soul. If we look at *Faust* in terms of its human scale, we have a gigantic work before us; if we look at it in terms of the greatness that would live in it if Goethe had been able to bring out in his time everything that lay in his soul itself, we have a decayed, fragile work before us that is everywhere unfinished in itself.

This is perhaps the most powerful testament that Goethe has left to his descendants, that they should not only acknowledge him like a scholar today, or even like a person who is highly educated in a certain way. That's easy, but Goethe didn't make our attitude towards him that easy. Goethe must live among us as in a living way and continue to be felt and thought about. The most important thing in Goetheanism is not found in Goethe, because Goethe was not able in his time to bring it into his soul from the spiritual sphere, because only the seeds of it are everywhere. Goethe demands that we work with him, think with him, feel with him, that we continue his task as if he were standing behind us everywhere, tapping us on the shoulder and giving us advice. In this sense, the entire nineteenth century and right up to the present day has, one could say, abandoned

Goethe. And the task of our time is to find our way back to Goethe. Basically, nothing is more alien to real Goetheanism than the entire external culture on earth from the late nineteenth century or indeed from the twentieth century, with the exception of some of the spiritual things that have been pursued. The path must be found back to Goethe through anthroposophically orientated spiritual science.

This can only be understood by those who are able to respond properly to the question: Where did Goethe actually stand in reality? You have the most honest confession of humanity from Goethe—I characterized it yesterday, that he actually started out from paganism, which also corresponded to the Platonism of his age. The boy erects a pagan altar to nature. The man Goethe then receives the strongest influences not from traditional Christian ecclesiasticism, which always remained fundamentally alien to him, because his worldview is the worldview of expectation towards the new understanding of the Mystery of Golgotha. Those who complacently embraced the Christian faith in the old traditional sense, or even wanted to undertake all kinds of merely external reforms within this Christian faith, they were truly not inwardly related to him in spirit and soul. He actually always felt as he did at the time he was travelling with two apparently good Christians, with Lavater[68] and Basedow[69], with two people who stood for an advanced, but still old ecclesiastical Christianity, when he said: 'Prophet on the right, prophet on the left, the child of the world in the middle.'[70] That's how he actually felt when he was between two people in his age. After all, as he indeed said, he was always the decidedly non-Christian in relation to the Christians around him, precisely because he was supposed to prepare humanity for the expectant atmosphere towards Christ.

And so we see that three people have the greatest influence on his intellectual culture in a remarkable way. These three people are actually people who are, in a certain way, children of the world. Ordinary Christian preachers would not have been conducive for Goethe. The three personalities who have had the greatest influence on him are, after all, firstly Shakespeare.[71] Why did Shakespeare have such a decisive influence on Goethe? Simply for the reasons that Goethe set out to build a bridge from the human to the transcendental, not out of an abstract orderliness, not out of a porous intellectuality, but out of the human sphere itself. Goethe needed to hold on to the human sphere in order to find the transition from the human to the transcendental within the human. Thus we see Goethe struggling to shape, to mould the human, as Shakespeare did do to a certain extent, to work out of the human. Take a look at how Goethe handles *The Story of Gottfried von Berlichingen with the Iron Hand*, the autobiography; how he dramatizes this story, changing it as little as possible, creates the first figure of his *Götz von Berlichingen*; how he then develops a second figure out of it, transforms it to a greater extent, more contoured, then a third figure. In a way, Goethe seeks his own honest path by taking up Shakespeare's humanity, but wants to shape something transcendental out of this humanity.

He can only do this when on his journey to Italy—read his letters[72]—he believes he can recognize from something kindred to himself, from the Greek works of art, how the Greeks proceeded according to the same intentions, divine intentions, according to which nature itself proceeds. He needed his true path, his individual, personally experienced true path. He was not able to believe in what those around him were telling him; he had to find his own way.

The second intellect who had a tremendous influence on him was certainly a decided non-Christian, namely Spinoza.[73] In Spinoza he had the possibility of finding the divine in the same way as a person finds this divine when they want to pave the way from the human to the transcendental. Spinoza's thoughts are basically the last manifestation, for the intellectual age, of the ancient Hebraic drawing near to God. Spinoza's thoughts as such are very distant from the Christ impulse. But Spinoza's thoughts are such that the human soul finds in them, as it were, the threads to hold on to when it seeks that path: there, within the human being, there is my being; from this human being I seek to penetrate further to the transcendental. This path, which he could follow, which he did not merely have to have preached to him, which he could follow by following Spinoza—this path Goethe regarded in a certain sense as his own at a certain age.

And the third intellect who had the greatest influence on him was Linné,[74] the botanist. Why Linné? Linné for the reason that Goethe did not want to have any other botanical science, any other science of living entities than one that simply places living entities side by side in a series, as Linné did. All abstract thinking that discovers all kinds of thoughts about plant classes, plant genera and so on, was not something Goethe could relate to. His interest was to allow a person in the form of Linné to have an effect on him who placed things side by side. For Goethe wanted in his own way, from a higher standpoint than those who look at plants in an abstract way, to pursue what Linné conscientiously placed side by side as plant forms, to see the way the spirit works through this placement side by side.

It was particularly these three minds who were basically able to give Goethe what was not in the innermost centre of his life, but what he had to receive from outside; it was particularly these minds who had the strongest influence on him. Goethe himself had nothing Shakespearean about him, for when he reached the height of his art, he created his 'Natural Daughter', which truly has nothing of Shakespeare's art, but strives towards a completely different side; but he could only develop his innermost nature by modelling himself on Shakespeare. Goethe's worldview has nothing of an abstract Spinozism, but what Goethe had in his innermost being as his path to God, he could only gain from Spinoza. Goethe's morphology has nothing of the side-by-side arrangement of organic entities as in Linné, but Goethe needed to be able to take from Linné what he himself did not have. And the things he had to add were new.

And so Goethe grew up, grew into his forties, schooled by Shakespeare, Linné and Spinoza, and steeped in the views of art that presented themselves to him in Italy, where he said in respect of the works of art: 'There is necessity, there is God.'[75] And as it was appropriate for his time, in a strongly unconscious way, but also to a certain extent consciously, what we might call his passage past the Guardian of the Threshold took place within him. And now, when you consider his passage past the Guardian in the early nineties of the eighteenth century, compare the words that sound like the words of worship to Isis in ancient Egypt in this prose hymn 'Nature' just recited to you by Mrs Steiner, where Goethe still feels quite pagan, with that which confronts you in a powerful imagination in the *Fairy Tale of the Green Snake and the Beautiful Lily*: then you have Goethe's path out of paganism into Christianity. Here we see in images what Goethe was after his passage through the threshold location, after his passage past the Guardian of the Threshold; that is there in images which he himself could not intellectually dissect for people, but which are nevertheless powerful images. What are we compelled to do if we want to understand the Goethe who wrote the *Fairy Tale of the Green Snake and the Beautiful Lily*? Compare what is written in the Goethe booklet already mentioned[76] about the *Fairy Tale of the Green Snake and the Beautiful Lily*: such are the facts with which we are confronted when we consider that Goethe created this *Fairy Tale of the Green Snake and the Beautiful Lily* as a mighty imagination after his passage past the Guardian of the Threshold.

This *Fairy Tale of the Green Snake and the Beautiful Lily*, it arose from the transformed soul, after this soul has overcome the pagan feeling as it is still expressed in the prose hymn: Nature, we are surrounded and embraced by her. Unbidden and without warning, she gathers us into the cycle of her dance and sweeps us along until we have grown tired and fall from her arms. ... Even that which is unnatural is nature. ... Everything is her life, and death only her artifice to have much life—and so on. This pagan Isis mood, it transforms itself into the deep truths which cannot now be grasped with reason, which lie in the mighty imaginations of the *Fairy Tale of the Green Snake and the Beautiful Lily*, where Goethe to all intents and purposes sets forth how all that which the human being can find through external empirical science can only lead to the aimless flitting about of the will-o'-the-wisps; but how that which the human being must develop in their innermost being leads them to train their soul forces in such a way that the snake sacrificing itself can be a model for them, sacrificing its own being for the development of humanity, so that the bridge can be built between the two realms of the sensory and the supersensory, between which rises the temple, the new temple, through which we can have a sense of the supersensory realm.

Certainly, this *Fairy Tale of the Green Snake and the Beautiful Lily* does not speak of Christ. But just as Christ did not demand of a good follower that they should always say, Lord, Lord!, neither is only someone a good Christian who always says, Christ, Christ! The way in which the images are framed, the way in which the human soul is conceived in its transformation in the *Fairy Tale of the Green Snake and the Beautiful Lily*, the sequence of the thoughts, the power of the thoughts, that is Christian, that is the new path to Christ. Because why?

There were already many interpretations of this fairy tale in Goethe's time; many more have been added since then. We tried to shed light on this fairy tale from the point of view of spiritual science. I may speak here—in this circle it may be said, after all—about this fairy tale. It was at the end of the eighties of the nineteenth century that it first—if I may express myself trivially—dawned on me about this fairy tale. Never again did I then leave the path that is meant to lead further and further to an understanding of Goethe on the basis of these powerful imaginations, which are set out in the *Fairy Tale of the Green Snake and the Beautiful Lily*. We can say that the reason which guides us quite well in finding scientific truths, the reason which guides us quite well in gaining the external view of nature particularly as it blossoms in accordance with the present time and its conditions, this reason fails completely if we want to understand this fairy tale. Here it is necessary to allow our reason to be fertilized by the conceptions of spiritual science. Here you have translated into our time and its circumstances what is necessary for all humanity to understand the Mystery of Golgotha.

To understand the Mystery of Golgotha, the reason must first be trained. It needs to give itself a jolt. It does not need this jolt to understand external nature. It has become increasingly impossible for both Latin and Germanic culture—Latin culture, because it is too strongly in decadence, Germanic culture, because it has not yet risen to this level of development—to train the soul out of mere intellectuality to such an extent that it can find the new path to understanding the Mystery of Golgotha. But if you develop within yourself the possibility of transforming the forces of your soul in such a way that you begin to find as a natural inner language the transition to the imagery to which Goethe aspired, then you will train your soul forces in such a way that you will find the way to a new understanding of the Mystery of Golgotha. That is what matters.

Goethe is not only important because of what he has produced, Goethe is important above all because of what he turns our souls into when we immerse ourselves with complete dedication in his innermost being. Then, little by little, humanity can also consciously find its way past the Guardian of the Threshold, a path that Goethe fortunately still travelled unconsciously, which is why he was unable to complete precisely those works in which he wanted to express himself most deeply. A flickering and shimmering of the conscious and the unconscious, of the attainable and the unattainable lived in Goethe's soul in particular. When we allow something like the *Mysteries* to affect us, when we allow something like *Pandora* to affect us, like all those things that Goethe did not complete, then we have the feeling that there is something in this incompletion that must be released in the soul of Goethe's descendants and that must be completed as a great spiritual creation.

Goethe was lonely. In terms of what Goethe really was, Goethe was lonely, lonely in his development. Goetheanism has much that is concealed. But even if the nineteenth century has not yet accomplished that scholars have become human beings, whereas Goethe worked his way from his scholarship to a human conception of the world, it is precisely with the help of Goethe's impulse that development must progress. I said yesterday and repeat it today: the force that is connected with the Mystery of Golgotha was once connected with the single man Jesus of Nazareth in a little-known province of the Roman Empire, and then with the folk souls of central Europe. But then it went inwards. And from what was weaving inwardly in central Europe emerged such achievements as Goethe's and the whole of Goetheanism. But the nineteenth century in particular did much to let Goetheanism rest in its grave. In all areas, the nineteenth century did everything it could to let Goetheanism rest in its grave.

Those scholars who founded the Goethe Society in Weimar at the end of the eighties were much more suited to be the gravediggers of Goetheanism than to awaken anything of this Goetheanism.

The time has certainly not arrived in external life in which Goetheanism can yet live. This is related to what we have now discussed many times: the spiritual-scientific renewal of human souls. Whatever may befall this Europe, which now in a certain sense wants to commit suicide: the grave that is being dug first and foremost by the thoughtlessness of modern culture, this grave will also be a grave from which something will rise. I have already pointed out that the Christ spirit has united with the folk souls of central Europe; Goetheanism arose in the womb of these folk souls. There will be a resurrection, a resurrection that should not be imagined politically, a resurrection that will look completely different, but it will be a resurrection. Goetheanism is not alive, Goetheanism still rests in the grave as far as external culture is concerned. But Goetheanism must rise again.

Let the building that we have tried to erect here on this hill also be a sign that we honestly resolve, resolve as courageously as is necessary in the present, to bring Goetheanism to resurrection. To do this, however, we must have the courage to understand and see through the un-Goethean nature of the Goetheanism that has so far called itself such, and to step up to the being of Goethe itself. We must likewise learn to affirm Goethe's spirit, just as the end of the nineteenth and the beginning of the twentieth century denied it, denied it in all possible areas. Then the path of spiritual-scientific knowledge, which is to be attained in the absolute sense, will be connected with the historical path of the revival of Goetheanism, but also with the impulse that can come from this revival of Goetheanism for the new understanding of the Mystery of Golgotha, for the correct understanding of Christ, as is required for our time.

Our time will perhaps find the signpost to the Christianity of the future that humanity needs in the decidedly non-Christian Goethe, who, like Christ himself, demanded that people should not always say, Lord, Lord—but that they should carry his spirit in their hearts and minds; who, in the form of Goetheanism, does not always say, Christ, Christ, but who preserves in his heart all the more of that which has flowed out as reality into humanity from the Mystery of Golgotha, so that this heart may gradually transform the abstract and intellectualistic knowledge, the knowledge about nature of the present, into knowledge through which we look into the supersensory worlds, in order to give human beings strength for a deeper cognition of the world and for the organization of the social structure to be fit for human beings. We will talk more about this next time.

Seventh Lecture

DORNACH, 24 JANUARY 1919

With reference to everything that is connected in a deeper sense with the understanding of social life in the present day, a reflection seems useful which can follow on from our last remarks about Goethe, which we made in connection with the presentation of our *Faust* scene.[77] Such a discussion seems to me to be useful because it is precisely with regard to the social life of the present day that the nineteenth century forms an extraordinarily significant turning point in the development of humanity. People's way of thinking changed much, much more than is usually thought, especially in the middle of the nineteenth century. Now, we could certainly, if we wanted to refer to this turning point, also take as a starting point minds other than specifically German ones; we could perhaps take Shaftesbury or Hemsterhuis. However, if we were to take the English or the Dutch mind as a starting point, Shaftesbury[78] or Hemsterhuis,[79] we could hardly—and this may be said quite objectively—delve as deeply into everything that leads to an understanding of the relevant subject as we can by drawing on Goetheanism. And in our present day, when so many things are preparing to destroy that which was born of this central European spirit, to a greater extent and more thoroughly than we think today, it may not be without merit to draw on these things, which will probably have to live on in humanity in a completely different way than most Germans, even today's Germans, imagine.

After all, if you look honestly and impartially at the present, you must feel something depressing today at a statement like that from Herman Grimm,[80] that is to say, of an outstanding mind, from not very far back—you really do not need to be German in this respect— if you have any feeling for central European culture. Herman Grimm once said that there were four minds, four personalities, to whom the German looks up when they want, as it were, to receive the direction of their life, and he names as these four minds as Luther,[81] Frederick the Great,[82] Goethe, and Bismarck.[83] Grimm says, if the German can no longer look up to the guiding power of these four minds, then he feels, as it were, without a firm foothold and abandoned in the context of the nations of the world. Today, it is somewhat depressing to hear this statement, which many people—not including me—did not doubt was true in the 1890s. Yet we have to admit the following to ourselves, especially in the face of such a statement: Luther does not actually live in essence in the traditions of German nature. Goethe never really came to life, as we have had to emphasize time and again, and Frederick the Great and Bismarck belong to works that are now a thing of the past. So that the time would have come when the central European German, the German in general, would have had to feel abandoned and without a foothold among the nations of the world. Today, we don't feel deeply enough to really fully exhaust something like this in our souls. We are too superficial. However, such a fact should at least give people food for thought: the fact that not quite three decades ago something was a matter of course for an enlightened mind that today is an impossibility. If contemporary humanity were not so superficial, many things would indeed be felt much more deeply than is the case today, where the lack of feeling for what pulses through the world sometimes makes one's heart want to break.

If we look backwards at the development of humanity from the nineteenth century to the eighteenth century, we see a great moment. It was that moment which was at work in Schiller[84] when he wrote his *Letters on the Aesthetic Education of Man*, that moment when Goethe was inspired by what had been discussed between Schiller and Goethe at the time when Schiller was writing the *Letters on the Aesthetic Education of Man*. This prompted Goethe, for his part, to realize the impulse that lives in Schiller's *Aesthetic Letters* in his *Fairy Tale of the Green Snake and the Beautiful Lily* in his own way. You can read about the connection between Schiller's *Aesthetic Letters* and Goethe's *Fairy Tale of the Green Snake and the Beautiful Lily* in one of the essays in my last little Goethe booklet. Today I will only mention as much of it as is necessary for our reflections.

With his *Letters on the Aesthetic Education of Man*, Schiller not only wanted to write a literary essay, but he basically wanted to do a political deed. The beginning of the *Letters on Aesthetic Education* immediately reveals this. There is a link to the French Revolution, and Schiller endeavoured, so to speak, in his way, from his educational perspective and point of view, to say what can go through people's minds as a result of the volition arising from the French Revolution, from the revolution at the end of the eighteenth century in general. Schiller did not initially expect anything special from a major political upheaval, from which the French revolutionaries had promised themselves everything. On the contrary, he expected much more from the people thoroughly educating themselves. And in his *Letters on the Aesthetic Education of Man,* he wanted to talk about this self-education of the human being required by the time.

Let us place the basic idea of these *Letters on the Aesthetic Education of Man* before our souls once more. After all, we've done it several times before. Schiller wants to answer the question in his own way: How does a person achieve true freedom in social coexistence with other people? Schiller would never have expected anything from merely the fact that the social institutions in which people live should somehow be organized in order to lead people to freedom. Rather, Schiller demanded that the human being themselves should achieve this state of freedom within the social order through inner work on themselves, through self-education. In a sense, Schiller believed that a person must first become inwardly free before they could realize freedom on the outside. And so Schiller said to himself, the human being is actually caught between two drives. On the one hand, they stand facing the drive that comes from physical nature—Schiller calls it the drive in the needs of everything that a person's sensory nature itself produces in terms of desires and so on. Schiller counts this as a sensory drive, as something that the human being is compelled to do by a certain purely physical necessity. And he said to himself, if the human being follows this drive, they can never be free, because they only follow this sensory drive out of physical necessity.

The sensory drive is contrasted with another; this is the drive of the necessity of reason, of logical necessity, of the necessity of thinking. To a certain extent, the human being can now also surrender to this drive of the necessity of reason as the other pole of their being. But that does not make them a truly free human being either. Because if they logically follow the necessity of reason, they are still following a necessity. And even if this necessity of reason is consolidated and established in an external state or similar law, the human being, if they obey this law, also obeys a necessity. So by following their reason, they are by no means a free being. The human being is therefore caught between reason and the senses. If they follow the senses, they follow necessity, not freedom. If they follow reason, they also follow necessity, albeit an intellectual necessity, but a necessity nonetheless. They are not a free human being. The human being can only be free in Schiller's sense if they neither unilaterally follow the sensory drive nor unilaterally the drive of reason, but if they can manage to bring their drive of reason closer to their humanity, if they bring it to the point where they not only submit to logical or juridical necessity like a slave, but if they make the content of the law, the content of the necessity of reason, their own being.

In this respect, Schiller is indeed a much freer spirit than Kant, for example, whom he otherwise followed in many respects—to Schiller's detriment, we may say. For Kant regarded following the necessity of reason, surrendering to the necessity of reason, as precisely the highest thing that the human being can strive for; absolute subjection to what Kant calls duty,[85] that is, to the necessity of reason, is regarded by Kant as the highest thing in the human being. Schiller says, 'Gladly do I serve my friend, but unfortunately I do it because I am so inclined, and so I fear that I am not virtuous,'[86] because Kant would demand that it is a duty to serve one's friend, Schiller thinks. 'Duty, thou sublime and mighty name,' says Kant, the only time he becomes poetic, so to speak, 'that dost embrace nothing charming or insinuating. ...' Schiller says: 'Gladly do I serve my friends, but unfortunately I do it because I am so inclined. And so it often bothers me that I am not virtuous.' He says this satirically with regard to Kant. So we must get so far with our humanity that we do out of inclination, out of love, as something inwardly self-evident what the unfree person does in terms of content as the result of duty, of the categorical imperative. That is one thing.

Schiller thus wants to pull the necessity of reason down to the human level so that the human being does not have to submit to it, but can develop this necessity of reason as a law of their own being. He wants to move the necessity of reason down to the human being. He wants to elevate sensory necessity, the sensory drive; he wants to spiritualize it so that the human being no longer merely follows what sensory nature urges, but that they embellish and ennoble this sensory nature, that they may follow it because they have elevated it to its summit. By meeting in a middle state, Schiller believes, sensory nature and reason meet, the human being becomes a free being.

It seems as if today's humanity can no longer really feel what Schiller felt when he presented this middle state as something that is actually worth striving for in human beings. He then presented, as it were, the ideal state in which this interpenetration of the necessity of reason and sensory necessity is always fulfilled, and found the ideal state in artistic creation and artistic enjoyment.

This is quite characteristic of the Schiller-Goethe period, that something was sought in art that should govern the rest of human activity. This is the antithesis of Goetheanism to all philistinism, that in true, genuine art something is sought which is an ideal state to be striven for. Because the artist creates in sensory material. Even when they create in words, they create in sensory material. And they would produce fine stuff, at most symbolic, abstract stuff, if they were to abandon themselves to the necessity of reason in their work. They must eavesdrop on the material and its shaping in order to create what they want. They must spiritualize sensory nature by shaping the material. But by shaping the material, they must give the material a form that makes the material no longer act as material, but that it acts as the spiritual acts. So the artist blends the spiritual and the sensory in their creation. When all human activity in the outside world becomes such that the human being does everything that is obligatory and lawful out of their own inclination, just as a person creates artistically, and when everything that is sensory nature is performed in such a way that spirit lives within, then freedom in Schiller's sense is achieved for the individual person, but also for the State and social structure.

In other words, Schiller asks: How must the various forces of the soul interact in the human being—the state of reason, the state of the senses, the aesthetic state—if the human being is to stand as a free being within the social structure? Schiller sought that which should be striven for in a certain interaction of the soul's forces. And he believed that if such people, in whom the necessity of reason permeates the necessity of the senses, and the necessity of the senses is spiritualized by the necessity of reason, if such people form a social order, then a good condition of this social order will be the necessary consequence.

Goethe spoke a lot with Schiller and corresponded a lot with him at the time when Schiller was writing his *Aesthetic Letters*. Goethe was a very different person to Schiller. Schiller had a tremendous inner passion for poetry, but was at the same time a sharp thinker. Goethe was not a sharp, abstract thinker in the same sense as Schiller, was even less passionate about poetry, but he was precisely equipped with what Schiller lacked, what Schiller did not have: with thoroughgoing, fully human, harmonious instincts, spiritualized instincts. Schiller was the reflecting human being, the rationalist human being: Goethe was the instinctive human being, but the spiritualized instinctive human being. The way they faced each other, Schiller and Goethe, became a problem for Schiller himself. If you read the beautiful essay that Schiller wrote on 'Naive and sentimental poetry', you will always have the feeling that Schiller could just as well have written, if he had wanted to make it personal, about Goethe and me—About Goethe and Schiller. For the naïve poet is Goethe, the sentimental poet is Schiller. In this essay on naive and sentimental poetry, he really only describes himself and Goethe.

Goethe, who was an instinctive person, did not find the matter so simple. He had, as I just said, many discussions with Schiller while he was writing the *Aesthetic Letters*, about this problem. Any abstractly philosophical discourse, even that on the necessity of reason, sensory necessity and the aesthetic state—which, after all, are also abstractions if we contrast these things—any such 'philosophising' was actually repugnant to Goethe in his innermost being. He allowed himself to do this because he was receptive to everything human and because he said to himself: all these people are philosophizing, so you have to engage with something like this. He was never completely dismissive. This is best demonstrated when he is put in the position of having to talk about Kant. Goethe was in a very special situation. Kant was regarded by Schiller and many other people as the greatest man of his century. Goethe just couldn't understand this, that Kant should be considered the greatest man of his century. But he wasn't intolerant at all; he wasn't a person who only stubbornly believed in his own judgement. Goethe said to himself: if so many people find so much in Kant, then you just have to let them proceed, indeed, you even have to make an effort to explore what you don't find very significant, perhaps because there might be a secret meaning after all. I had the copy of the *Critique of Judgement* · that Goethe read in my hands; he had marked important passages. You can see how Goethe endeavoured to get into reading Kant's *Critique of Judgement*. But then, well before the middle, the markings become less frequent, and finally they dry up completely. It is clear, he did not get to the end.

And when the conversation turned to Kant, he didn't really get involved in the real content of such a conversation. He was uncomfortable talking about the world and its mysteries in philosophical abstractions. And so it was also clear to him that you cannot make it quite so simple if you want to understand the human being in their development from necessity to freedom, as Schiller did. You see, there is something extraordinarily great in these *Aesthetic Letters*. Goethe recognized this greatness. But it was too simple for him. It was altogether too simple for him to reduce this complicated human being, especially the complicated human being of the soul, to three categories: necessity of reason, aesthetic state, necessity of the senses. There was much, much more for him in this human soul, and things could not be juxtaposed like that for him either.

He was therefore moved to write the *Fairy Tale of the Green Snake and the Beautiful Lily*, where there are not three but about twenty soul forces, which are not expressed in concepts but in multifaceted, metaphorical figures, which then culminate in the golden king who represents—not symbolizes, but represents—wisdom, the silver king who represents appearance, the bronze king who represents might, and the love that crowns them. But everything else is also soul forces; you can read that up in my essay.

Goethe was thus moved to place this path of the human being from necessity to freedom before his soul. For him, the problem just became tremendously more complicated. He was the spiritualized instinctive human being. Schiller was the—let me use the expression, you won't misunderstand it—a sensualized intellectual; not an ordinary intellectual, but the sensualized intellectual.

Now, if we honestly consider the way the times have developed, we can say that such a way of looking at things, as each did in his own way, Schiller on the one hand in an abstractly philosophical way, Goethe in an imaginative artistic way, such a way of looking at things, quite apart from the form, is also not very suitable for people today in terms of its content. A very close older friend of mine, Karl Julius Schröer,[87] who was also once an examining commissioner for candidates for the secondary school teaching profession, wanted to test these people on Schiller's *Aesthetic Letters*, who were then to teach children from ten to eighteen years of age. Well, they couldn't have made more of a fuss! People who would have taken it for granted that they would have been asked about Plato, that they should have interpreted the Platonic dialogues, such people were not remotely concerned with knowing anything about Schiller's *Letters on Aesthetic Education*, which represent a high point of modern intellectual education.

Well, the fact is that the middle of the nineteenth century represents a tremendously profound turning point in human intellectual history, much more so than we can imagine today. On the far side, to the front, lies that which is still represented in Schiller and Goethe, and after the middle of the nineteenth century, right up to us, it is indeed the case that there lies something quite different, which can understand what preceded it only to a very limited extent. It would be much better if people today would simply admit to themselves that we have crossed a kind of abyss that can only make us understand the near past before the middle of the nineteenth century if we use very specific means of understanding. And it is fair to say that what we now call the social question—understood not in the narrow sense, but in the broadest sense, as it is not yet actually understood by humankind, but as it should be understood and must gradually be understood—this was not even known before the middle of the nineteenth century. This was only born in the second half of the nineteenth century, as it entered the consciousness of humankind.

And we can only gain an understanding of this fact if we ask ourselves: why is there nothing in such representative, significant reflections as Schiller endeavoured to do in his *Aesthetic Letters*, as Goethe pictorially placed before the soul in his *Fairy Tale of the Green Snake and the Beautiful Lily*, why is there, despite Goethe's clear reference to political structurings in his fairy tale, nothing at all of the distinctive way in which we must think about the social structure of people today? And why do we today need to really think about this social structure in the sense that I have often discussed here? We simply can no longer be quite the same as Schiller and Goethe were. We practise Goetheanism least of all when we don't want to continue to develop Goethe, but only want to ape him.

If we engage with Schiller's *Aesthetic Letters* and Goethe's *Fairy Tale of the Green Snake and the Beautiful Lily* with inner understanding, we realize that there is something of a tremendous spirituality in them that has since left humanity, that is no longer there. There is something at work here that very few people today have any real feeling for. Anyone who reads Schiller's *Aesthetic Letters* should have the impression that there is a different soul and spiritual element in the style of writing itself from that which prevails today even in the most outstanding minds, and to believe that someone today could write something as immediate as Goethe's *Fairy Tale of the Green Snake and the Beautiful Lily* is utter folly. Because this spirituality has not been around since the middle of the nineteenth century. This does not speak directly to people today; it can only actually speak through the medium of spiritual science, which expands the field of vision and can also really engage with the past. And it would actually be best if people would admit it to themselves that without spiritual science they would not understand Schiller and Goethe at all. Any *Faust* scene can prove this to you.

And if we investigate what is at work there, not so much in the assertions, but in the way these assertions are made, then we find that there is still the very last remnant, the last echo of the old spirituality in human beings at that time. People are still talking out of the old spirituality there. The old spirituality ultimately only dissipated and fizzled out around the middle of the nineteenth century, and around the middle of the nineteenth century people all over the world began to think in such a way that thinking was no longer governed by the spirit as such, but only by the human element when left to itself. Of course, this is only true in general. Schiller and Goethe, as well as their contemporaries, still harboured echoes of the old, we might say atavistic, spirituality. This is only lost slowly and gradually.

When people repeatedly claim that the time when Christianity arose marked the end of the old spirituality, this only signifies one stage; the last offshoot lies in what lived at the turn of the eighteenth to the nineteenth century in such manifestations as the two mentioned today. It lived in people in such a way that those who thought abstractly, like Schiller, had spirituality in their abstract thinking, and those who had spiritualized instincts, like Goethe, had it in their spiritualized instincts. But it was alive in some way. Now it must be sought by way of spiritual science, now the human being has to wrestle their way to spirituality out of freedom. That is what matters. And without an understanding of this watershed in the middle of the nineteenth century, it is impossible to truly grasp what is of particular importance today. Just take this fact, for example. Schiller looks at the social structure. He then wrote his *Aesthetic Letters* with the French Revolution in mind. But he looks at the human being by wanting to answer the question: How should the social conditions be organized? This is not the social question in today's sense. This is a purely humanistic conception that Schiller uses for humanity in general, a purely humanistic conception.

Since the middle of the nineteenth century, the focus is no longer so much on the human being, but on what is outside the human being. And today, when talking about the social question, it is after all common practice to actually exclude the individual person with their inner struggles, with what they make of themselves through their own self-education, and to look at the conditions, at what lies in the social structure. People today expect what Schiller expected from self-education, from the reorganization of external conditions. Schiller said: if people become what they can become in the middle state, then they will create a proper social structure of their own accord. Today, people say, if we set up a real, proper social structure, then people will become as they should be within it.

So in the course of a short time the whole sentiment, the form of sentiment, has really turned round. It is very important to bear this in mind. A Schiller, a Goethe, they would not have been able to believe that the self-educated human being leads to a proper social structure in coexistence if they had not still felt the universally human in coexistence in the human being themselves. In a way, they had a sense of human society in the individual person. But it was no longer effective. At the time of Schiller and Goethe, people could to a certain extent make intellectual, beautiful observations about the best self-education—it was simply the echo of the old atavistic life; it was to a certain extent an image of the old atavistic life, but there was no longer any real impulsivity in it.

Nor is there anything with social impulsivity in what people think up today about the best social conditions in which people should live. For Schiller, human society was still present in the individual for observation, but no longer effective. Today, the human being is present but not effective in the hypothesis, in the imagined social structure. The human being must first be found once again in the observation of the outside world, in the view of the outside world. And indeed the human being must be found in a sweeping sense. Schiller still believed that human society could be found in the individual. We have to look at human society as a whole, at the world, and be able to find ourselves, the human being, outside.

Only real spiritual science does this in a sweeping sense. Take my *Occult Science. An Outline,* take that which still causes the most offence today, the theory of evolution, the evolution of Saturn, the Sun, the

Moon, the Earth: the human being is in it everywhere. Think how the other way of looking at things, the cosmological way of looking at things, has lost the human being. Think of the grotesque—as Herman Grimm rightly says[88]—insane Kant Laplace theory! Consider, there is a general cosmic nebula in slow motion, then that which is in rotating motion continues to develop, and finally the human being appears as if shot out of a pistol. Take evolution as it must be taught by spiritual science, take the first state that can be described, the Saturn state. You have the first predispositions of the human being in it; nowhere do you have the mere abstract world, the mere abstract cosmos, everywhere you somehow have the human being inside the thing. The human being is not isolated from the world.

This is the beginning of what the time wants instinctively out of very dark, very sinister impulses. The time before the middle of the nineteenth century looked at the human being and believed that the world could be found in the human being. The time after the middle of the nineteenth century only any longer wants to look at the world. But that is fruitless. This ultimately leads to theories that are virtually devoid of human beings, if the human being is not already found in everything worldly. That is why this spiritual science really serves the otherwise darkest but justified instincts. It is, if I may use the nauseating journalistic expression, what is truly contemporary, because it serves the impulses that the time produces from within itself. What people want without knowing what they want is fulfilled by spiritual science: to look at the outside world and find the human being in the outside world. But that is what matters. And that is what is still frowned upon, even abhorred, today, but which will have to be fostered if any salvation on this point is really to materialize in the future.

People today should absorb such writings as Schiller's *Aesthetic Letters*, I would say, in order to free their minds, which are otherwise firmly immersed in material, physical existence. You become freer in the mind when you let these things work on you. But then you have to advance towards a new understanding of the world. You can't stop at these things. Today we may understand Schiller, we may understand Goethe in the sense of Goetheanism, but not in such a way that we stop at Schiller and Goethe, but that we recognize what is fruitful in them precisely with the help of what spiritual science offers today.

And so there must also be an expansion of the teaching about the human being if we want to find the human being in external circumstances, in the outside world. The important thing will be to really understand the external social organism in which people live. But you will only understand it when you look at the human being inside the social organism. Humans are threefold beings. They are also active in all ages in a threefold way, with the exception of our age, in which the human being, because they are supposed to focus on themselves, on the single point of their own self in the consciousness soul age, to a certain extent concentrates everything on a single force within them; otherwise they are also active in the development of humanity in a threefold way. Because today, everyone actually has the feeling that as a human being, everything flows from a single source. They think, well, if I am presented with a question, if life presents me with a task, then as a human being I make this judgement out of myself. However, this is not actually the whole being of a person from which judgements are made, but the being of a person firstly has the person in the middle, then something above and something below. That which is in the middle is the respective judgement, acting from judgements. That which is above it is afflatus, that which is seen through religion or other spiritual afflatus as something higher, supersensory. And that which is below the respective judgement is experience, is the sum of experiences: afflatus—respective judgement—experience.

People today pay little attention to either. Afflatus: old superstition, must be overcome! People today also pay little attention to experience, otherwise they would take more account of the difference between youthful ignorance and older knowledge through experience. However, not only do they not take it into account in their consciousness, but neither do they do so in practice. Thus they will not experience anything, people today, because they do not believe in experience. Most people today, when they have grey hair and wrinkles, are not much smarter than when they are twenty years old, because people don't believe in experience. You really do get ever smarter in life, but you always remain stupid; but you gain experience, and experience is the other pole of afflatus. Afflatus can come at any age; experience can only come by living through the time between birth and death. In between there is then the respective judgement.

I've often said it: today you can read judgements, critical judgements from the youngest of people who haven't looked around in the world at all. It even happens that old people produce something, write thick books, and the youngest of spring chickens judge them critically. This is not the way to really progress as a human being. The method by which we progress as human beings is that we draw ourselves up on our age, that we strive for it, that we consider it more capable of judgement through experience.

So the human being is also a threefold being in practical activity, and they are a threefold being in every respect. If you read my book *Von Seelenrätseln*,[89] you will find the head human being, the sensory and nervous human being, corresponding to afflatus, the chest human being corresponding to the respective judgement, and the extremities human being correspond to experience. I could also say, the human being of sensory and nervous life, the human being of rhythmical life and the human being of the metabolism. This threefold nature of the human being is not taken into account today. That is why we also do not arrive at the corresponding cosmic corollary. It is not possible to arrive at the corresponding cosmic corollary because there is no desire to ascend from the sensory to the supersensory. People eat today, that is, they combine external food with their organism, and they think, well, there's the organism inside, it cooks things up, it takes out what it needs; the other things, it lets go unused, and so the story continues. That on the one hand.

On the other hand, I look out into the world with my senses. I take in sensory things and process them with my reason, and now I feed them into the soul, just like food into the body. What is out there, what the eyes see, what the ears hear, I then carry within me as a conception; I then carry what is out there as wheat, fish, meat, whatever, inside me by digesting it, cooking it and so on.

But this does not take into account the fact that everything that is food also has an interior side. What we see with our external senses and what we experience with our external senses in food has no connection to our deeper nature. You can take care of your daily metabolism with what your tongue tastes, what your stomach digests, digests in such a way that it can be verified with the usual science of today, but you can never take care of the other metabolism, which, for example, leads to you shedding your first teeth and getting new ones at about the age of seven. What constitutes this metabolism does not lie in what is grasped by the ordinary senses from the food, but lies in the deeper forces of the food, which today no chemistry can somehow bring to the surface. What a person takes in as food contains a deeply spiritual side, that spiritual side which is also very active in the human being, but only when they are asleep. For the spirits of the highest hierarchies, seraphim, cherubim, thrones, live in what your food is. Your food has an external side when you taste it, when you dissolve it in pepsin or ptyalin;[90] but there is something that shapes the world in this food, that shapes the world in such a way that the forces that live in a—I would be better to say—sub-sensory way in the food are the impulses for the change of teeth, for sexual maturity, for the subsequent metamorphosis of human nature. That lives within there. Only the day-to-day metabolism is taken care of by what people know through external science. This metabolism, which goes through life, is taken care of by the highest hierarchies, which are contained in food as substrates. And behind what the senses see, the beings of the third hierarchy spread out in reality: angeloi, archangeloi, archai. So that you can say, sensory perception: third hierarchy, nutrition: first hierarchy, and in between is the second hierarchy, which lives in breathing, indeed in all the rhythmical activity of the human being.

The Bible still described this quite correctly. Those spirits who are the Elohim, with Yahweh, are introduced into human beings through the breath. Ancient science still knew these things atavistically quite correctly. If you enter into a real understanding of human nature here, you will also be led out into a real cosmology.

This approach is in turn inaugurated once again by spiritual science. It once again seeks out the human being in the outside world, turning the whole world into a human being. But we cannot do this if we do not consider the threefold human being, if we do not know that the human being is really a trinity. Today, afflatus and experience are suppressed. Humans do not do justice to afflatus and experience. Nor do they do justice to what goes into the senses, nor do they do justice to what goes into food, for in the course of life food is merely what the outer senses present to them. However, this is only an ahrimanic distortion of food, it is not a focus on what lives deeper in all creatures, for example in food. Spiritual science does not lead to contempt for matter, but to the spiritualization of matter. And if anyone were to look at food with contempt, they would find that spiritual science then even grotesquely tells them that the highest hierarchies, seraphim, cherubim and thrones, live in the food itself.

Thus our age conflates the threefold human being in an unclear, chaotic way, makes them a *monon*.[91] In practical terms, for the social structure, the antithesis [of the threefold human being] exists in that everything is made a *monon* of State legislation. That is the exact antithesis. Everything should be integrated into the law of the State. So we see a trinity that is made up of three components: firstly, of the natural basis of life, of all the economic aspects of life, the economy. Secondly, of legal regulation, which also corresponds to the middle of the human being, the rhythm. And thirdly, the intellectual life. And we see how this trio wants to unify itself. The economy, the economic part, is to be gradually foisted on the State; the State is to become the sole entrepreneur. After all, intellectual life was already foisted on the State a long time ago. The same thing that is represented on the one hand by the human being, who no longer understands themselves, is to be represented on the other hand by the State, which is no longer understood because the human being is no longer to be found within the social structure. These three parts of the social structure—economy, legal regulation and intellectual life—are as radically different from each other as the head, chest and abdomen. If you want to foist the economy on the State, it means the same as if you wanted to eat with your lungs and heart instead of your stomach.

Human beings only thrive when their three systems are outside each other, and in being outside each other interact with one another. In the same way, the social organism can only thrive if the three components really work alongside each other as independent components and are not crammed into a *monon*. Because all legal regulation, which in humans corresponds to the rhythm, the respiratory system, which also only regulates between the stomach and the head, corresponds to an absolutely impersonal element before which all people are equal. This is also expressed in the saying: all people are equal before the law; there is nothing of the human in it. That is why all people have to take care of it, that is why there is general representation in this area, that is why there is also a certain desire to stand still in these matters; but therefore also something that has remained sterile on both sides. We have to breathe. But if food is not added to the process of breathing on the one hand and sensory perception on the other, then we are not human. We must have a State that regulates legally in impersonal laws. But if the semi-personal aspect of the economy, where the human being participates, and the completely personal aspect, namely the completely personal intellectual life with regard to the external life of the State, do not work into this State, then the State organism is just as impossible as if the human being wanted to live only as a breathing human being. As little as the stomach can do in the present human being what the heart and lungs do, and the head can carry out its activity if it also becomes heart and lungs, just as little is it possible, if a healthy social structure is to come about, for you to foist the two other systems on the State: the economic system, in which the human being must be present, the endeavours of which cannot be completely detached from the human being, and the intellectual life, which must come to the State as well as to the human being in the same way that what they eat comes into the human being from outside from nature. This must become a new doctrine that must be considered fundamental: that the social structure is threefold. You can't place yourself in the world as a human being and not eat anything; you have to get the food in from outside. You cannot place the State in the world and not give it its nourishment—it is the other way round here, which is why I wrote the other way round—from the intellectual production of people.

The intellectual production of people is the same for the State as external physical nourishment is for the individual. And you cannot set up a State without on the other hand giving it a certain natural basis in the economy. For the economy is exactly the same for the State as is the element in the individual human being which is supplied to the respiratory process from the other side, which is supplied to the human being through sensory perception.

Sensory perception:	Third hierarchy }	Second hierarchy:
Nutritional substance:	First hierarchy ∫	breathing
Afflatus	Head human being —	Sensory and nervous life: 1. Natural basis, business, economy. Semi-personal, fraternity
Respective judgement	Chest human being —	Rhythm: 2. Legal regulation, impersonal, equality
Experience	Extremities —	Metabolic human being: 3. Spiritual life, personality, freedom.

You can see from this that real knowledge of human nature and real knowledge of the social structure are mutually dependent, that you cannot arrive at one without the other. Just as the human being is a head human being, chest human being, metabolic human being, that is, sensory and nervous human being, rhythmical human being and metabolic human being, so the State is not a single organism, but the social structure is: State and economy and intellectual life.

Nothing short of this must become the ABC for social insight in the future. And the sin that is committed in relation to the human being by eliminating afflatus and experience is committed today by socialist thinking in that it ignores the semi-personal, on the one hand, in the kind of social thinking in which fraternity must prevail as such; and in that it ignores, on the other hand, the intellectual life, in which freedom must prevail, while equality must prevail in the impersonal element of the law.

You cannot introduce fraternity into the State; but you cannot bring about an economic organization without fraternity. That is the great error of contemporary socialism, that it believes it can somehow create a healthy social structure through State regulation, above all through the socialization of the means of production. All forces of the social organism must be called upon if a healthy social structure is to be created. In addition to equality, which is the only thing that is being striven for today and which is quite rightly sought for, everything that is a matter of law, fraternity and freedom must prevail. But they cannot prevail if there is no threefolding. If someone says, liberty, equality and fraternity must prevail in the State, and the State is omnipotent, then that is the same as saying, you do not need a head and you do not need a stomach, but you should only have a heart and lungs, because the heart must think, and the lungs must eat or drink. Just as it is nonsensical to demand that the heart and lungs think and eat, it is just as nonsensical to demand that an omnipotent body politic run the economy and provide for intellectual life. The intellectual life must be self-sufficient and only work together in the same way that the stomach works together with the head and the heart. Things in life do work together, but they only have the right effect when they are given their individual form, not when they are packaged together abstractly. This is what needs to be recognized first and foremost, and without this insight we will certainly not make any progress. And the facts of the present in particular prove that this realization must be achieved. It is quite remarkable how people today do not see this connection between materialism on the one hand and abstract thinking on the other, especially with regard to the social question.

A strong reason for the emergence of materialism is that the State has gradually seized all free corporative, school-like institutions. If you go back to the times when things were still based on an atavistic feeling that arose from clairvoyance, you will see how the necessity of the working together of the three components was still felt. It is only since the sixteenth century that this has gradually merged, with the rise of materialism. Look at the universities in earlier times: they were free corporations, and they placed themselves completely independently in the human social structure. In the past, if a person wanted to become an eminent lawyer, they went to an important university of law, let's say Padua; if they wanted to become an eminent physician, to Montpellier or Naples; if they wanted to become an important theologian, to the university in Paris. This did not belong to any State, it belonged to humanity, because it was an independent component of the social organism.

Today, it doesn't help a person living in Switzerland at all if they become an important physician in some other country, because in that case they are nothing at all in Switzerland in the field of medicine, because today the part that should only do regulation has absorbed economic productivity and also intellectual productivity. And this has introduced an unhealthy element. You see, people can forget that they have a head and that they have a stomach. They have forgotten it in more modern science, because they deal with themselves as if they were only a respiratory human being. But in the field of reality, this leads not only to wrong theories, but also to wrong institutions and wrong establishments. Any school that is directly under the sole control of the State is an impossible establishment. You don't need to see through this if you're short-sighted, but it's still an impossible establishment that gradually leads to disaster. Any undertaking that goes beyond the merely regulatory, that wants to be productive, is, if it is run by the State, a disaster. That is what is important. You cannot pour anything into the lungs, not even water when you are thirsty. If it happens at some point, you can see what harm it does.

But today all kinds of economic undertakings and even also the undertakings of intellectual life are poured into that which is only supposed to take over the legal regulation of what exists. Today, you are even regarded as quite deluded if you clarify the only elementary, fundamentally correct thing in this area. Well, the radical parties, they still go so far as to consider the separation of Church and State. They want to separate this part of intellectual and spiritual life, the Church, from the State under certain circumstances, because they hope that people will then only be interested in the State. Then the Church will die off completely in this way, in a clever roundabout way.

But if you were to expect the same people to do what is necessary, that primarily schools were left to their own devices so that intellectual life could be restored to its productivity, then they would object very firmly. Every mechanism that intervenes in intellectual life from a regulatory perspective must necessarily lead to infertility, to sterility. And equally it must be wrong for an initiative that is necessary for economic life if pure regulatory life intervenes. Police, security service, everything that is societal law—not private law and not criminal law, that belongs to the third component, to intellectual life—belongs to the regulatory system. Everything that is the economic system is a system of its own; it must have a corporative organization, semi-personal. And everything that is intellectual life must be based on the human individuality and can never flourish if it is not based on the human individuality. The human individuality in its intellectual production is for the State exactly the same as food is for the lungs and heart, which must pass through the stomach and not directly into the lungs and heart.

So you see the other pole. Schiller arrives at ultimate humanness— the middle condition—and even links to the next condition, to art. In a sense we are compelled to start with the most robust, the roughest, the coarsest and look for the human being inside; but we must take this path, otherwise there is no salvation for the development of humanity in the present and the near future. Schiller boldly stated in his *Aesthetic Letters*: Human beings are only fully human where they play, and human beings only play where they are human in the fullest sense of the word. Schiller regards play as the actual ideal condition, if we of course conceive of play as Schiller does: that the necessity of reason has been guided down to inclination and inclination has been guided upwards, that it has been given intellectual content in the same way as the necessity of reason. He then calls the seriousness of life a game, because we act like a child at play, who does not obey any duty either, but abandons themselves to their drives, yet in a certain respect freely abandons themselves to their drives, because the necessities of life do not yet reach into childhood life.

Schiller's *Aesthetic Letters* thus capture something like a pinnacle of the human being: human beings are only fully human where they play, and human beings only play where they are human in the fullest sense of the word. And so, on the other hand, it is necessary that now, when we have to start with the most robust part of the cosmos in order to find the human being within it, with the most coarse part of the whole cosmos in order to find the human being in the whole cosmos, that we have to say to ourselves: humans will only truly advance humanity by understanding how to elevate even the smallest things in everyday life, even the most mundane games, to the great seriousness of cosmic existence. That is why we have to say that a turning point has come for humanity in the present, where seriousness is knocking terribly on our door. That simply has to be acknowledged. More about that tomorrow.

Eighth Lecture

DORNACH, 25 JANUARY 1919

W HAT I was particularly concerned to do yesterday was to show, using the example of Schiller's *Letters on Aesthetic Education* on the one hand and Goethe's *Fairy Tale of the Green Snake and the Beautiful Lily* on the other, how before the middle of the nineteenth century the whole way of conceiving of and feeling about the world was different, especially among outstanding minds, than it was after the middle of the nineteenth century. It is examples such as these in particular that really show what a considerable and significant turning point there was in the middle of the nineteenth century. We have spoken about this turning point in the whole development of humanity from various points of view, we have pointed out that in the middle of the nineteenth century there is to a certain extent a crisis of materialism, a crisis insofar as the materialistic way of feeling is gaining the upper hand in the whole of human conception and feeling, worldview, view of life and so on.

Now anyone who wants to take a close look at these things, who has the courage and the interest to take a close look at them, will notice in all sorts of things what a shift has actually taken place. Take the scene with the Cabiri[92] on the basis of today's conception, try reading everything in this *Faust* scene that refers to the Cabiri, try really to follow every single line with deeper interest, and you will see how Goethe, through his spiritualized instincts, was still thoroughly immersed in anticipatory cognition. Through such conceptions and performance in the mysteries as the Greeks had, for example, based on the Cabiri, something supreme was expressed for the human being in relation to the striving for knowledge and the like. Goethe rightly associated these Cabiri with the path that should lead from homunculus to homo. He rightly associated these Cabiri with the mystery of human becoming.

Three Cabiri are introduced. We are talking about three human constitutional elements to begin with. Before we go into the truly inner aspects of the human being, we will talk about three human constitutional elements: the physical body, the etheric body and the astral body. By talking about these human constitutional elements, it immediately arouses the criticism of those people who think they are particularly clever today, who think they are particularly scientific today. For example, such people argue: why divide, subdivide the unified human being? After all, the human being is a unit; it was schematic to peel the human being apart into such constitutional elements. Yes, but that is not how things are, it is not that simple.

Certainly, if things were merely based on a schematic division of the human being, there would be no need to attach particular importance to these constitutional elements. But these individual constitutional elements, which are apparently abstracted thus from the whole human being, are all after all connected with completely different spheres of the cosmos. Because the human being has a physical body as they have it today, the way this physical body has developed from its Saturn constitution to the present day, means that the human being is part of space, the sphere of space. And through their etheric body, the human being belongs to the sphere of time. So by belonging to the two totally different spheres, by being, we might say, crystallized out of the world of time and space, the human being consists of a physical body and an etheric body. There is nothing arbitrary or schematic about the division or structuring of the human being. It is actually based on the whole connection between the human being and the cosmos. And through their astral body, the human being already belongs to the extra-spatial and extra-temporal.

This trinity, the trinity of the human envelopes to a certain extent, is presented in the three Cabiri. The fourth 'didn't want to come'. And this is the one who thinks for them all! If we ascend from the three envelopes to the human I, we first have in this human I that which rises above space and time, even above the timeless, spaceless astral part. But this I of the human being only came to consciousness in the period that followed the Samothracian worship of the Cabiri. The Greeks, however, derived their belief in the immortal from the ancient sacred Samothracian teachings; but it was not until the Greco-Latin period that the consciousness of the I was to be born. That is why the fourth, which represents the relationship between the I and the cosmos, did not want to come. Far removed indeed from the mystery of the Cabiri, which in the first instance points to what was there in human becoming. The three highest, the fifth, sixth and seventh, are still 'to be sought in Olympus': spirit-self, life-spirit, spirit-human being. As we know, they come in the sixth and seventh periods. And nobody has even considered the eighth![93]

We actually see the mystery of humanity expressed in the old form, as it was concealed in Samothrace in those mysteries from which the Greeks took the best for their knowledge of the soul, for their wisdom of the soul, indeed also the best for their poetry, insofar as this related to the human being. That is the important thing to realize: as soon as we turn our gaze back to these old times, which Goethe tried to revive again, we look into a knowledge of the connection between the human being and the cosmos. Human beings felt related to all the mysteries of existence. Human beings knew that they were not merely enclosed within the boundaries of their own skin, but belonged to the whole, vast cosmos. And that which is enclosed in their skin is only the image of their particular being.

We can say that a reflection, a last echo of this view of the human being's connection with the cosmos can still be found in such writings as Schiller's *Letters on Aesthetic Education*, and can be found as, let me say, the pervading spiritual atmosphere of vitality in such writings as Goethe's *Fairy Tale of the Green Snake and the Beautiful Lily*. Goethe really did try in his own way to depict metaphorically what places a person in the community of human beings. There are then twenty soul forces that Goethe allows to appear in the form of the fairy-tale characters. But by allowing these twenty soul forces to appear, Goethe shows how these soul forces lead from one person to another in social life. In this fairy tale, Goethe has created imaginations of the course of social development through humanity. These imaginations, the way Goethe created them, the way he juxtaposed the king of wisdom, the king of appearance, the king of might, and the way he allows the king who chaotically combines all three—wisdom, appearance and might—to disintegrate into himself, the way in which he depicts this shows in his way what must be consciously grasped today in a very intensive way and from other viewpoints.

But we cannot stop at Goethe's fairy tale today. Anyone who wants to stop at Goethe's fairy tale and its depiction today is actually just playing. As you know, the same theme, the same impulses that Goethe portrayed in the fairy tale are depicted in my first Mystery Drama *The Portal of Initiation*.[94] But they are depicted in the awareness that something happened in the middle of the nineteenth century that makes it necessary for such things to be depicted today out of completely different, more emphatic impulses. Yesterday I drew attention to how the transition must be from looking at the previous age to the age at the beginning of which we stand. But that which we must attain again, that which was present in ancient times like the last echo of atavistic clairvoyance about these things, that is the consciousness of the connection of the human being with the whole cosmos, the consciousness of that mystery which you find expressed in the beginning of my second Mystery Drama,[95] where it is shown by Capesius how all the work of the gods ultimately amounts to representing the human being. Why is an awareness of this cosmic significance of the human being, of the human being's place in the entire cosmos, so particularly important for our time? Precisely because we are faced with having to spiritually grasp the most mundane thing: immediate external life. And this external social life cannot be grasped if it is not based on a real view of the nature of the human being. The moment you start to place the human being themselves in the social structure in their entirety, as some economists do today and as it even lives in the popular consciousness of most people, the moment you start to do that, you must fail with regard to the social question, because the human being projects with their being out of what the social question actually represents.

I told you yesterday that we must distinguish three constitutional elements in human nature. How you name them is another matter. Today we will call them the nervous and sensory human being, the human being of rhythm, the human being of the metabolism. We have to differentiate between three things in relation to a truly organically organized social structure: the intellectual part, the purely regulatory state, and business and the economy. The human being is in contact with such social life, the human being is within it. But to a certain extent they are already positioned in reverse in their threefold structure from the threefold structure of the social organism. Please note that it is always necessary to point out that we are not building constructs, not looking for analogies, not interpreting such things in abstract terms, but conducting real spiritual research.

So someone who compares the winter of the earth with night or sleep, and summer with waking, is on a hiding to nothing, while for the earth summer precisely represents sleeping and winter waking. Nothing is achieved by those who think of the development of humanity in analogy with the development of the individual. While the individual progresses from childhood to old age, humanity regresses from old age to childhood. Real research shows something completely different from what people fantasize about. Avoid concocting any analogies, but look at things as they are! If we consider the threefold human being, we first have the spiritual aspect of the human being in the sensory and nervous sphere. Then we have the middle in the rhythmical sphere, the lower in the metabolism. You can read more about this in my book *Von Seelenrätseln*. But I have drawn attention to this: the metabolism is actually the imprint of the highest, the spiritual. When we see the spiritual, the metabolism therefore corresponds to intuition, the rhythmical corresponds to inspiration, and the nervous and sensory life corresponds to imagination. Humans are threefold beings. But the proper social organism, too, towards which present-day humanity is striving in the fifth post-Atlantean period, is threefold. However, in observing this threefold structure, we must not ignore the following.

Where does the thing lie in the human being that is sought in the human organism—not in the whole human being, but in the human organism? Well, the world has a very confused view of this, and the real view, the true view—this seems confused to people. Today's honest-to-goodness physiologist thinks, as I said yesterday, that people eat, and in this way stuff food into themselves; then the organism selects what it needs from these foods and discards the rest. It transforms that into itself, and so it goes on, doesn't it, day after day. Now, I told you yesterday that this metabolic process only means the day-to-day metabolism, and that the other metabolism that takes a person from the first teeth to the permanent teeth, then on to sexual maturity and so on, is not directly dependent on this metabolism. The other metabolism, which extends over the long periods between birth and death, is not simultaneously connected with stuffing in and transforming food and so on, but is based on other laws and other substance processing. I already pointed this out yesterday. But what does this daily food that we take in actually mean? Here we come to a chapter in which we must again come into the most fierce conflict with the ordinary science of today.

Please, I don't want to now cause you not to eat; I ask you please not to draw any false, nonsensical conclusions from the things that are said for the sake of knowledge, for the sake of cognition, no one should draw any foolish conclusions from them! But why do we actually eat? Do we eat so that we have what is outside us inside us? No, we eat so that the various substances that enter us express certain forces, and our organism defends itself against these expressions of force, and we must have the stimulus for this defence through food. You can visualize this: as you ingest the food, it causes small explosions inside you; you need these explosions because you have to destroy them again, paralyse them again, annihilate them, and it is in this destruction that your inner strength actually develops. Human beings need stimulus, stimulation, and essentially what we eat is stimulation. Because what we are as human beings, we indeed actually get in a mysterious way from somewhere completely else.

As you remember, I have often said, the head is actually hollow. This enables it to absorb from the cosmos that which is productive in the human being. And this production is, in a sense, only lured out of the head. This is how the head in turn comes into its own. After all, the head is actually the least important part in many respects; it is the last remnant of the previous incarnation. It is that which, for example, could not think without the rhythmical activity. People always believe that the head thinks. It does not in reality think, but only reflects thoughts. But this is how it regains its glory, that it is what is actually productive. And in order to develop this production, human beings are dependent on the fact that, in addition to the rhythm, the metabolism also reigns in them, which is the constant stimulus. The metabolism is therefore the constant stimulus through which the human being enters into a relationship with the outside world.

So how is it with the social organism? Actually, here it's the other way round. What is internal in the human being, what the human being carries within themselves, through which they have their hollow head, what needs stimulation from outside through the metabolism, that is the basis for the social organism, just as food is for us. What is to us what we eat, is to the social organism what people produce from their nervous and sensory life. Thus the State, or rather the social organism, is an organic entity which, if I may use the expression, eats what people think up, what people invent, what comes from human intellectuality.

If you remove the actual basic force, the actual basic characteristic from human intellectuality, namely freedom, individual freedom, it is exactly the same as if you wanted to let a person grow up without giving them food. Free, individual people who place themselves in a coercive social structure and make their free intellectuality sterile, cause the social structure to die off, just as a person must die off if they are not given food. What human heads bring into the world is the food for the social organism.

So that we can say, what is productive from the nervous and sensory sphere is the nourishment for the social organism. That which is the rhythmical system in the human being corresponds in the social organism to everything that should actually be assigned to the State; as I said yesterday, everything that relates to regulation, to external legislation, that is, the laws of the State. So what, then, is the productive aspect of the State? That which comes out of the natural basis in the broader sense, the economic life. This is in a sense the head of the State. The economic life, the basis in nature, everything that is produced, that in a sense is the head. It is the other way round from the individual person. So we can just as well say, just as the human being is productive through their nerves and senses, so the social organism is productive through its natural basis. And just as the human being receives their metabolic activity from nature, the social organism receives its nourishment from out of the human head.

You can only really understand the social organism in relation to the human being if you turn the human being on their head. Here in the human head is actually the ground and soil of the human being. People grow from the top down, the State organism grows from the bottom up. If you want to compare it to a human being, it has its head at the bottom and stands on its head with its legs at the top. It gets its nourishment from the single individual person. This is how what the social organism is must be inwardly understood. Playing with analogies is irrelevant; but it is looking at the true reality, the real reality, that is what matters.

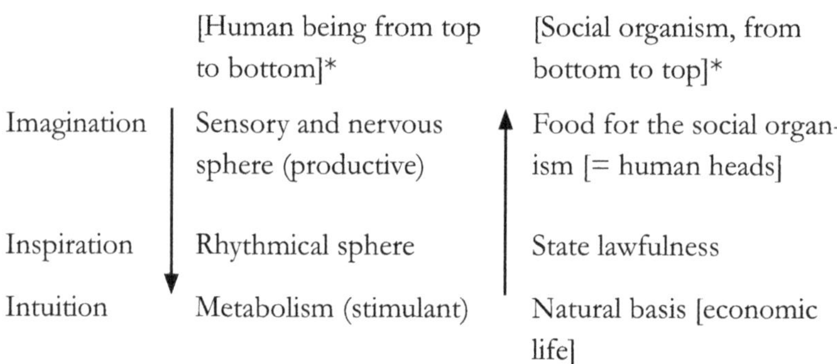

You see, it was in the course of the nineteenth century, just as this important watershed was making itself felt in the middle of the nineteenth century, that we witnessed the actual shift towards materialism, the turning away from the spiritual. It was the high tide of materialism. What actually happened there with regard to people's view of the world? Well, with regard to the human conception of the world, what happened was that people lost the spirit of the supersensory. They lost what was supposed to be produced by their hollow

---

* In square brackets: Added by the editors for the sake of clarity.

heads; what should enter into the hollow head is what people lost. They only wanted to rely on the randomness of experimentation with regard to all inventions and discoveries. As proud, as arrogant as people are about the achievements of the second half of the nineteenth century, study the history of ideas and you will see how even the greatest of these achievements are not based on the direct initiative of the mind, but on constellations that arose in the course of experimentation. People lost God, they lost the spirit, by no longer striving with their heads towards the spirit.

What would be the equivalent in the social organism? You would lose the natural basis, you would be squabbling away without taking the natural basis into consideration. This is indeed the character of social debates in the second half of the nineteenth century and to this day, most fiercely today. Because today people talk about social institutions, about the socialization of the human economy and the like: in this debate they leave out the actual basis of nature, the way in which production should take place, just as the materialists leave out what the head should do in the human being. If the materialistic age loses the spirit from its worldview, the corresponding social organism loses actual matter from the economy, from the social context. And in social development there lies the great danger that corresponds to the loss of the spirit in the materialistic worldview: the loss of production that satisfies humanity as much as possible, the loss of the greatest possible insight into what is productive.

Well, you cannot arrive at an understanding of the social structure if you do not train yourself in the threefold structure of the human being and thereby learn how the relationship between the science of the human being and social science must be organized. Otherwise, everything will be judged incorrectly. Our learned national economists, through whom so much misery has come into the world because others think the same way, because they only allow experiments to be valid, our learned national economists in fact know nothing at all about this relationship between the human being and the social structure. Because this can only be obtained through spiritual science. Our scholars of national economics, our teachers of political economy, are arguing in all seriousness about whether a piglet or a human being is of greater economic value. It is true that a lot can be said for either from the point of view of the arguments that people happen to have right now. Some claim that a piglet is more valuable in the economy than a human being, because the piglet represents something that can be eaten, that is, something that is suitable for consumption, something that has an economic value. You can't eat a person, indeed they even eat things themselves, they don't represent any economic value for some people. However, some people think differently, saying, well, yes, but people produce economic values, and these will then be there! So they indirectly help so and so many piglets to exist and so on. Well, as I said, people argue about such things! It is indeed a question that is debated among economists as to whether a piglet or a human being represents the greater economic value.

Well, that's just one bizarre example. But for those with deeper insight, what lives in our catastrophic present really does depend on such bizarre things. Because we can well say that the knowledge that is sufficient to make grandiose progress in the natural sciences, the knowledge that delivers magnificent scientific results, that marvellously enables us to compare the embryo of the piglet with the embryo of the dog, with the embryo of the human being, with the embryo of the bat and so on, and from this schematically to form the kind of thinking that is sufficient to produce all kinds of physiological, biological, mineralogical, geological things in the sense of the present day, this kind of thinking, this way of combining thoughts, is not sufficient to distinguish economically what is more important, a pig or a human being. And until people recognize that you can be a great natural scientist without being able to distinguish economically between a pig and a human being, there will be no remedy in terms of understanding the social question. This must be ruthlessly acknowledged by people, that what today constitutes the greatness of thinking in the field of natural science does not enable the economic value of a piglet to be distinguished from the so-called economic value of a human being. We will speak more about that tomorrow.

I HAVE often taken the opportunity in these reflections to draw attention to the fact that it is precisely with regard to the most important questions of life that people today can learn from the incisive, profound, even cataclysmic events of our time; how, however, learning from events in this way is actually already fostered as a method by very few people today. People usually think that they learn from events by judging the events and then considering the judgement they have made about the events as experience. This can be very satisfying for people. But for what is so necessary in the present, for social knowledge, it is not only completely inadequate, but also completely unsuitable. It is about not casting judgement on events, but really learning from events, letting events judge themselves. And you will experience this as the methods of spiritual science in the most diverse observations that are made here, when this spiritual science is applied to external physical events, for example to social events. And here I believe that we can learn in particular from an extraordinarily significant phenomenon of recent times with regard to social life. I have already alluded to the matter, but I would like to place the corresponding aperçu once more at the top of our considerations today.

If you try to discuss the social question today with a member of the working population, which is what matters in all things in today's affairs, and which on the other hand has primarily received the inner impulse for its views from Marxism, then you always learn that such a person initially thinks very little of social work and social thinking, of so-called goodwill or of ethical principles. You will find over and again that such a person behaves in the following way. Let's suppose you said that you saw the basis of a solution to the social question in the fact that, above all, the people who have certain leadership positions, namely the people of the so-called entrepreneurial class, should develop a social sensibility, that they should develop a sense of how a dignified existence must be created for all people. Let us assume that you were talking to such a person in the broad mass of the working-class population about raising the level of moral sensibility of the bourgeois classes.

As things stand today, this member of the broad mass of the working-class population will initially smile when you express such a view. They will say you are naïve to believe that emotions or emotional activity can solve the social question in any way today. All that flows from the feelings of the leading entrepreneurial class, such a member of the broad mass of the working-class population will say, is irrelevant. For this class of entrepreneurial people may imagine what they want with regard to their ethical and moral feelings, but the way the world is organized today, in that it is divided into an entrepreneurial class and a working class, the entrepreneur, however good a person they may be, must be exploitative. And the people of the working class do not want to know anything about raising social awareness, because they say, none of this will help, everything depends on the working class becoming aware of its class relations, on this working population itself bringing about such a transformation of the social situation from its own circumstances that the general impoverishment ceases or is alleviated. It is not a question of raising moral sensibilities, but of the class of people who are above all oppressed by the present capitalist economic order, of this oppressed, miserable class of people bringing about through struggle a different, non-capitalist economic order, a change in conditions, a change in the economic order.

This means, in other words, having no confidence at all in the power of thought, having no confidence at all that one can improve anything in the social situation of life through a correct understanding, through a correct conception of life. It was recently taken as a truth when a picture of a person with a rather long body and tiny legs appeared in a satirical magazine; he was depicted as the only one who was not yet in government in Germany, because all the others were already governing in some council or other, but he, with his short legs, always lagged behind, and so he was the only person in Germany who did not yet belong to a council and did not govern. That can indeed be taken as a kind of truth. We could well imagine that today, for example, the following could happen in one of the many councils that are being formed in the central countries. We can imagine that if we were to speak in such a circle today about what we must consider to be the right thing to do based on our understanding of human development and human needs, the people listening would say to us if they belonged to the working population: What are you talking about? You're a member of the bourgeoisie! Because you belong to the bourgeoisie, you think from the outset in such a way that your thinking is in line with the current economic order. It is much more useful for the improvement of the social situation if we render you harmless in some way and you have nothing more to say, rather than that we should hear anything from you that would be useful for the further development of the social situation.

Things have already been taken to extremes. And because things have been taken to extremes, it is necessary to acquire the ability to see clearly. Well, of course, most people today don't want to see clearly, least of all those who usually meet in congress councils, because they want to make judgements based on completely different things than clarity. But what every proletarian today, every member of the broad mass of the working-class population, if they are caught at the right moment—and this is what matters, because what really matters today is that they are caught at the right moment—should realize, is that they deny any possibility of bringing about a social improvement in the development of humanity through thoughts. Now we can ask them how they arrived at this view, how they came to the conclusion that an improvement in the social situation could only be brought about by changing conditions. There is only one answer that can be deduced from the facts. The whole tremendous impact—and it is a tremendous impact—of the modern social labour movement rests on the thought of Karl Marx and his followers. It is, however, a far-reaching thought. The thought that thoughts are worth nothing, that is, after all, Marxist theory. But it is a thought that actually gave rise to the current socialist sentiment. This socialist sentiment, which does not want to know anything about the impulsiveness of thoughts, rests on the impulsiveness of thoughts.

I once said in a lecture given to proletarians that anyone who looks around in world history and searches for the real forces at work in the development of humanity will find that never before, except in a single case, has a truly scientific impulse become a world-historical impulse. Investigate everywhere and look for the real impulses: they were never scientific impulses, except in one single case where the proletarian movement was renewed through Marxism. Lassalle[96] perceived this correctly when he delivered his great, emphatic speech on science and the workers. Because the only truly scientific movement as a political, social movement is the modern labour movement. It is therefore subject to all the flaws, all the hopelessness of modern science in particular, because it arose from modern science. But it emerges entirely from thoughts.

Think of this colossal contradiction that has been introduced into modern life: the thought that the thought is worth nothing has had the greatest impact as a thought in the last sixty to seventy years. That can be learned from the course of the last sixty to seventy years. And that is a powerful lesson, powerful because you can see that the effect of thoughts depends on something quite different from the content of the thought. You see, one thought, the thought of Karl Marx[97] was particularly effective. But if we examine its content, it is that the content of the thought is of no significance, only the economic conditions. It is something incredible, if a person has the talent to immerse themselves in this contradiction of thought, in this living contradiction of thought of recent times, for the understanding of the present.

And yet it is precisely what is so necessary in the present—to understand that the content of theories, the content of programmes actually has no meaning at all, that the effectiveness of the thought is based on something essentially different, on the relationship of the thought in question to the constitution of the people who get this thought. If Karl Marx had not realized his thought, as he expressed it from 1848 onwards in the *Communist Manifesto* and then developed it in his system of political economy and in his great work *Capital*, from 1848 until the 1870s, but perhaps, let us say, in 1800 or 1796, this idea would have remained completely ineffective; no one would have been interested in this thought. Here you have a key to an important matter. Imagine the works of Karl Marx brought into the world, say, only fifty years earlier, they would have become printer's waste! Starting in the year 1848, when the general state of life of the proletariat had become a specific one, these works did not become printer's waste, but became an international impulse, so that they now live on in Russian Bolshevism, live on in the whole central European chaos, which already exists and will become even greater, which will seize the whole earth.

This will make you aware that much more depends on whether things are said fifty years earlier or later than on the content. A content only has a meaning as a content in a certain time. That is also why it is not just some amusement on my part when I say, for example, of anthroposophical spiritual science, now it must be told, now it must enter people's hearts, because now is the time when people should receive it. This is something different. With Marxism, it was something that ignited on its own; in the case of spiritual science, it is something that must be embraced by people in freedom. If, on the one hand, you understand that people's understanding is really also something that is subject to development, then you will also comprehend many other things more easily, which, it may be said, is of the greatest possible necessity, to comprehend what people do not really want to accept. We encounter something monstrous in one respect today when we come across people's thoughts as they are now in so-called intellectual life, which is not, however, real intellectual life. Anyone who wants to check this can take random samples everywhere. Open, for example, an issue of a journal[98] published here in Switzerland, where a writer who often appears in this journal is once again holding forth on a certain question of the time. In this essay, in which he holds forth like this, he talks about what he actually understands by the nation. He talks about the guilt of the various persons involved in the War; he talks about how leading figures within the central European population should be charged, which on the one hand has a lot of merit—I have already explained here that the concept of guilt cannot be applied—but then he finds it necessary to say what he thinks the nation actually is. Now we see how this gentleman defines the nation in a sense: he includes in the nation nine tenths of the people of an area that comprises, for example, Germany, Austria, England, France and so on. And he says of such a nation that it is the totality of uneducated, unfree persons who are dependent on leaders in the broadest sense, that is, people in need of leaders.

This man thus defines the nation as the uneducated, reliant, dependent people who are in need of a leader in the broadest sense. Now, if we were to put most of today's figures who belong to the middle class or an even higher class of people through their paces, as they say, they would probably answer roughly the same thing if they were asked to say what they understand by the nation: it is the broad, uneducated, reliant, dependent humanity in need of a leader, nine tenths of humanity as a whole. Only one tenth, we would therefore have to say, is educated, self-reliant, independent and does not need a leader. This usually includes those who are confident enough to make a judgement about what the nation actually is.

With regard to such concepts, which are important in the most eminent sense if we want to form a social judgement, it is above all necessary to ask ourselves in a valid way whether this is a concept that accords with reality in the broadest sense of the word: to regard nine tenths of the population as an uneducated, reliant, dependent multitude in need of a leader. This is a question that everyone who wants to acquire an independent social judgement must ask themselves. However, if you want to arrive at an understanding about such questions, then you have to allow the intensity of thought to develop a little through what you can gain for such intensity of thought from spiritual science. Because everything else that gives intensity to thinking today is not enough, as can be seen from all the thoughtlessness that dominates the multitude today.

I don't know if you can call it a coincidence—in reality there is no such thing as a coincidence—but in the last few months I have found a saying quoted again and again when circumstances are discussed in this way in public, sometimes by one person, sometimes by another. This saying was: 'Only the most stupid calves choose their own butcher.' People find it quite natural to use this saying. Everyone takes it for granted that this saying makes sense. I don't find the slightest sense in this, because I believe that these would not be the stupidest, but rather the cleverest calves, because then they would choose as their butcher—since they have to die anyway, and these calves are not considered for anything else—the one who brings about this death most painlessly, while those who choose nothing will probably come off worst. The opposite would be true: only the smartest calves choose their own butcher. But just as these things are thoughtlessly accepted, so too are important judgements accepted that need to be changed; for people actually want to spare themselves the labour of thought, the activity of thought, when taking an overview of life; they do not want to use this power of thought.

Sharper thinking is what we need today in order to arrive at concepts that correspond to reality. No matter how tempting the thought may be for the so-called advanced person, as they are called in the sense of today's conventional wisdom, today's enlightenment, today's democratic consciousness, that the uneducated, the reliant, the dependent, those in need of a leader make up nine tenths of the entire population—this has no value in reality, for the following reason.

Let's start from historical fact, which can teach us a lot in this respect. The truth is that Christianity originated in an unknown province of the Roman Empire through the Mystery of Golgotha. Within the Roman Empire of the time, which had already absorbed Greek culture, lived a population that truly harboured a deep and meaningful wisdom. The Church had to make dreadful efforts to obliterate the traces of the old Gnosticism, as I once explained here.[99] But this Gnosticism was there. The highest knowledge was there. Indeed, the highest wisdom was already present at the heart of the Roman Empire at the time of the emergence of Christianity. This cannot be denied in any way whatsoever. But it was impossible for this supreme wisdom to have absorbed the historically strong impulse of Christianity. The strong impulse of Christianity—I spoke of it only recently[100]—was taken up by the northern barbarians, who did not have this wisdom of the southern populace. Only when the northern barbarians came to meet the wave of Christianity did Christianity unfold in the way it did for the rest of the fourth post-Atlantean period and also still for the beginning of the fifth post-Atlantean period. Not until today has another relationship come.

What must be taken into account here is that it is not the most highly developed, abstract spirituality for a particular age that is able to absorb the historical impulse in its greatest strength, but that it is precisely the seemingly backward being of people, which is more related to instinctive human nature, that can absorb the impulse in the strongest way. The judgement I just mentioned earlier about the nine tenths of uneducated, dependent humanity in need of a leader says little more than that this humanity differs in terms of its spirituality from those who consider themselves to be its leaders. But these so-called leading people, they already have a degenerate mind, a decadent intelligence.

In the nine tenths of so-called uneducated, dependent humanity in need of a leader there is, as we might say, an intelligence still latently concealed which is immensely more receptive to the strong spiritual impulse that is to be received today, which is immensely stronger than that to be found in the so-called intelligentsia with the decadent intelligence. That which today separates the bearer of spiritual impulses from the receptive broad masses is not the broad masses themselves, it is not the souls of the broad masses of humanity, but it is the leaders, it is the leadership. And this leadership of even the most socialist proletarians, this leadership, is itself completely saturated with the decadent reason of the bourgeoisie. This is what is necessary above all, a neat, clean acknowledgement that for the real impulses of spiritual development the path to the so-called uneducated, dependent people in need of a leader can truly be found if only we have insight into the peculiar effect of this intelligence.

No class of people has ever been more fanciful than the bourgeoisie, who frown upon imagination so much today. Because the most fanciful thing is today's practice. All things that want to be practical in life today are actually only practical because they have, so to speak, legally created the opportunity to force their way through, to push their way through, while the other, who has not created the opportunity to push their way through, no matter how skilful, no matter how practical they may be, they do not push their way through. It is necessary to have a feeling for the fact that in the broad masses today, which are not led but seduced by their leaders, something has really followed on from that time which is usually, albeit somewhat incorrectly, referred to in history as the time of the migration of peoples. At that time, barbarian peoples emerged, in a sense, who took in precisely that which the developed peoples could no longer take in.

Today a migration of peoples is striving upwards, not from some place, but from the proletarian underground of humanity. That is the important thing. But this migration of peoples must be accommodated. Make a hypothesis. Consider this, that all that is usually described in the history books as the migration of peoples, all these migrations of the Goths, the Huns, the Vandals, the Suevi and so on, later the Mongols, which are usually described as the migration of peoples, took place, but that as these migrations of peoples took place in the direction from east to south-west, they were not met by the wave of Christianity. Let's assume that this wave of Christianity had stayed away; imagine how different the world would have become! We can only conceive of the whole subsequent period in general, in that these barbarian tribes moved from the east to the south-west and were met by the Christian wave.

Today, the situation is such that the proletarian element is coming up from the depths. And today this proletarian element must be met from above by something spiritual, a spiritual-scientific grasp of social conditions, of the worldview in general. And anyone who does not want to believe that it is necessary for a new spiritual revelation to meet this migration of peoples which today is taking place, just not in a horizontal but simply in a vertical direction, anyone who wants to remain with the old spiritual revelation suitable for the horizontal direction, in short, who wants to remain with the Roman form of the spread of Christianity; anyone who does not want to find their way through the language of spiritual science to grasp the new revelation of Christ gone through the Mystery of Golgotha, is neglecting the most important thing that is necessary for the present. They are neglecting as much as would have been neglected at the beginning of the Middle Ages if the barbarian wave that rolled from the east to the south-west had not been met by the wave of the spread of Christianity.

At that time too, there stood between the wave of Christianity and the wave of barbarians all those people who were precisely the educated people of the Greek and Roman empires. Today, all those who want to hold on to the old concepts under the leadership of the so-called intelligentsia and, in particular, of a science which is completely unproductive in this field, are standing between the wave that is supposed to advance downwards as a spiritual wave and the proletarian wave that is going upwards. But what must be achieved is, above all, a lack of prejudice towards concepts such as those we developed here yesterday and the day before yesterday, which give us the opportunity to form a social judgement. You can't make a social judgement if you don't understand the social organism. Do you know what the result is when a really average professor of political economy, who is then followed by the others, or a real political leader talks about national and social contexts and so on, do you know what the result is in relation to the social organism? The social homunculus![101] This is what should finally be realized, that all those people who have tried to grasp the social organism in their thinking without the knowledge of threefolding have, with reference to the social organism, merely raised a homunculus, just as Goethe believed that through ordinary sensory and intellectual apprehension we also only arrive at the homunculus, not the homo.

You see, most people today are still unable to think in terms of the social organism because they lack the guiding principles for this kind of thinking. I have mentioned it before, that people in these fields proceed from the strange, grotesque idea that a single State or a single national territory is an organism in itself. They virtually want to build national organisms. That is nonsense in itself. I explained it once, if you want to compare something in relation to the coexistence of people across the earth, you can only look at the whole earth as one organism; a single State or national territory can only be one component of the organism. If you want to use the term 'organism', it must be a self-contained organism.

The person who wants to establish national economics, political economics, socialism in the territory of a single country is like a person who wants to establish the anatomy of the whole human being from, say, the hand only or the leg or the stomach. This matters to a much greater extent than people realize today. Because this three-fold structure that I have outlined to you does not provide the kind of abstract combinations that people are used to today, but rather provides a living introduction into the economic workings, into the social workings. Anyone who has only learnt the anatomy of the stomach will not understand the anatomy of the head and neck. But anyone who knows human anatomy will, when it comes down to it, be able to assess the stomach correctly, assess the head correctly and assess the neck correctly. This is how it is, that everyone who is famil-iar with the social organism in its inner living conditions—and this is something that must proceed from this threefold structure—knows how to place themselves in the right relations, be it that they have to assess the social conditions in Russia or England or in Germany or anywhere else.

Today you make the strangely sad discovery that people talk about countries as if these countries were there by themselves. They think they can bring about some kind of socialization or the like with regard to individual separated areas. This constitutes one of the fun-damental errors of our time and can in practice really lead to the greatest disaster. Today, it is simply harmful to believe that anything can be done on a certain limited territory without taking into account the fact that, since the middle of the nineteenth century, the earth has been a whole organism in a social respect. You simply have to take reality into account, otherwise you won't get anywhere.

You can see from this that it is above all a question of acquir-ing a lack of prejudice, of becoming truly equal through a lack of prejudice to the judgement that one can leave to things themselves. Because only by being unprejudiced can you learn from things. One statement that you will come up against again and again when social conditions are discussed in the way they are here is that it is hard to imagine how economic value is to be separated from human labour. The least able to imagine this today are the scholarly economists. If people learnt a little from history, they would say to themselves: Plato and Aristotle were not yet able to imagine that slaves did not belong to economic values; Plato and Aristotle still regarded the existence of a fairly large slave population as economically necessary. Well, today no reasonable person considers the existence of a slave population in the sense of the ancient Greek and Roman empires as an economic necessity. But people today still regard it as a necessity that human labour should be a commodity in the same sense as any other goods.

Now, let us endeavour to work[102] towards the gradual realization of the threefolding mentioned here. It can only be realized slowly. We are not working towards sudden overthrow here, but towards setting a direction, towards taking individual measures in line with this direction. And everything can be set up today in every detail that needs to be set up so that these guidelines are really adhered to, if you are not a mindlessly programmatic person, but if you are a person of living reality who wants to enter into the facts themselves, into the living movement of the facts; and that is what people should do today, that is what matters. If we work in the spirit of the direction that gradually introduces threefolding, by separating the three parts that have fused together in recent developments and have thus produced a sick social organism that has manifested itself in the last pathological catastrophe, if we try to drive apart that which has fused together into the three parts, as I always characterize them here, then we arrive at a healthy, realistic development. And then the gradual separation of the economic concept of value from the human concept of labour is achieved by itself. Just as the slave has ceased to be a commodity, human labour will cease to be a commodity. Not by making laws forbidding human labour to be regarded as a commodity, but rather by pursuing the real separation of intellectual, economic and State activities. In this way goods, which alone represent economic value as commodities, are detached from what is today crystallized in the commodity of human labour expended.

With regard to this, it is downright terrible to see the confusion of concepts among people who today often talk and want to have a say in the necessary reorganization of conditions. Let me give you an example of this. Here we have the broad mass of so-called Marxists who are clear about this: when I acquire goods today, acquire a commodity, this commodity contains the human labour through which this commodity was produced. In paying for the commodity, I also have to pay for the human labour that goes into it. And of course it is under today's circumstances; but that is precisely the point, that in the real process, not just in the concept, the labour should be separated from the actual commodity. To do this, it is of course necessary to acquire really clear concepts about these things.

Now it is easy to disprove[103] that stored-up labour is contained in the commodity as an economic value. Someone who is not a Marxist, who looks at the matter from a different point of view, says that it is wrong that the economy is driven to gluing together the labour and the commodity; it was precisely the other way round. Goods, finished goods that you have, are actually there today in the capitalist economic system to save labour. And indeed, goods with, in a sense, purchasing power are already available to save on labour. Imagine you are a painter; you paint a picture that is worth ten thousand francs and can be sold for ten thousand francs in today's economic conditions. You can then have so and so many people working for you for these ten thousand francs under today's conditions. The fact that you have the valuable object of this picture means that you can have so and so many people working for you. Just think, if you didn't sell the painting and you had to do everything yourself that you let others do for you, by selling the painting for ten thousand francs, what a lot of work you would have to do! You would have to make your own shoes and not only your own clothes, but you would even have to weave the fabric for the clothes yourself and the like; you would first have to get hold of the raw materials and all that—the economic process is incredibly complicated. But according to some economic thinker, it has nothing to do with the fact that labour is crystallized in the commodity, but with the fact that you save labour precisely because you have saleable goods. In other words, the economic value of goods is based on how much labour they save; not how much labour has been spent on this good, but how much labour is saved.

So today there are two parties, one of which claims that the economic value consists of how much labour has been put into these goods. Well, you really can't compare the labour that has been interwoven into a picture with the labour that has been saved by selling the picture according to the value it has in economic circulation. Under certain circumstances, a talented painter can produce such a picture, say, ready for sale in a month. Then his labour is what is crystallized into it in a month. But that is much less important than the work it saves. He then becomes a capitalist by saving labour; this is precisely what creates the capitalist economic order, that he can employ so and so many people through the labour he saves through his goods.

You have two opposing definitions here. One definition: the economic value of goods or commodities is the amount of labour used to produce them. The other definition: the economic value of goods consists of how much labour is saved by having these goods or commodities. Two completely opposite definitions, opposite in terms of their meaning in reality. For it would be quite different if any goods were really valued according to the labour of production or according to the labour saved. Because in the economic circulation process, neither one nor the other takes place. You only need to imagine one thing, if I am to continue the example: imagine that this painting I'm talking about, which is bought from the painter for ten thousand francs according to the ideas of a certain age, let's say in the present, imagine that this painting is still with the painter. So it's worth ten thousand francs. But let us assume that it has now been bought, that it is now in the drawing room of Mr Mendelssohn, who is not a painter; it hangs there, where only a few people look at it. If we now define the economic value of this picture, it is the sum of the labour expended. You see, you can't apply that, neither to Lenbach nor to Mr Mendelssohn, because for both of them there is no economic value in it.

So for Lenbach or any contemporary painter, the immediate value of course lies in the labour he saves; but no longer for Mr Mendelssohn, because he saves nothing. So if you want to look at the matter economically, you can, if you are one-sided, apply this concept to the painter who produces the painting; here you can give this definition. If you want to give a definition with reference to the person who bought the picture and hangs it in their room, then this economic definition of value no longer exists in reality. That is what is so incredibly important, that people today are inclined to make easy definitions if they have cribbed something from the circumstances somewhere. Then they immediately make a definition. Then it's no wonder that one person has this view and the other another. Of course, someone who takes their economic definition of a painting from Lenbach's studio will come to a completely different conclusion than someone who takes their economic definition of a painting from Mr Mendelssohn's drawing room. That way, people can also argue.

And so all the disputes that occur in social fields today are because people do not go back to the original impulses. This, however, requires a sense of reality, which only the training of spiritual science can provide. Today, you can find hundreds of definitions in the field of economics, and you will be nothing but heartbroken by the unrealistic nature of these definitions, by how terribly unrealistic these definitions are, which you can always prove because they always fit a certain area. You can say that the economic value consists of the labour that is saved—if you are talking from the point of view of the cultural worker. You can also say, the economic value consists in the labour applied if you want to speak from the point of view of the proletarian manual worker.

I have given you another example from economics. As I told you, in the field of economics there are the so-called nominalists and metallists with regard to monetary theory. Yes, they argue terribly. Some see money as a commodity, that it is worth what it is worth as gold or silver, others only as a symbol of an existing value. Some, the nominalists, others, the metallists, fight to the death, define and argue. Indeed, people know nothing of the reality. For money becomes such that nominalism is correct if you live in a time when there is a sharp decline in production; when there is hardship, then nominalism becomes correct. When there is surplus, metallism becomes correct. In reality, both are right, one time this, the other time that. Concepts, as people form them one-sidedly, can never be applied to a totality in a healthy way. Totality is always about bringing together what is complete, not making a one-sided definition, and having a sense of where you can grasp that which is instructive in reality.

The question may now arise: Where does the economic value come from? It does not arise from the crystallization of labour into the commodity, not from the saving of labour by the commodity; the economic value is not created anywhere here. The economic value is a state of tension. After all, if you have an electrical conductor here [draws], which can discharge here, and the electricity is collected here, then a state of electric tension arises between the two, between the discharger and the thing to which the discharge is transferred. It passes over with a certain strength in order to discharge itself. If the electric tension is not high enough, no discharge takes place. If the electric tension is high enough, a discharge takes place.

In a similar way, economic value is also a kind of state of tension, an economic value that can be described by saying, on the one hand there are goods, commodities, in terms of their qualities and also in relation to the place where they can be consumed; so on the one hand, the goods are at a certain place and at a certain time. On the other hand, there are human wants, which is the same as artificial or natural interest. This state of tension gives the true economic value, nothing else. The concept of labour is not in there at all. It must associate itself in a different way with the process of commodities circulating in the social organism. What is contained in the production of economic value is the peculiar tension that exists, like the tension between an electrical conductor and a receiver, between the presence of a certain qualified commodity in a certain place and at a certain time, and the human want that exists for this commodity. That alone determines the economic value. The effort that Mr Lenbach has to expend in order to complete the painting in a certain time thanks to his talent, and the work that he saves himself thanks to the painting, only determine the value of Mr Lenbach's private property. But this is also the case with all other labour and its relationship to the commodity.

None of this determines the economic value. But the economic value at any given moment is given by the demand, the want on the one hand, and the specific qualified commodity at a certain place and at a certain time on the other hand. This is what constitutes the concrete economic value of a product. You can apply this everywhere. But this is precisely how you get out of the purely economic organism, and this is where you get right into the social threefold division. For on the one hand you have the goods, the commodity that leads you to the economy, which can never be created by mere circulation, but by land and soil, by the other natural basis. This natural basis must be there. It cannot be imposed on the State. It has to be there on the one hand. On the other hand, you have the want. But this leads you towards the cultural, it leads you into the cultural world of the human being; for how different are the wants of uncultured barbarians and cultured people! Two other elements play here into the purely economic entity. That's the important thing, that's what matters: that two other elements play into it.

So that we have the social organism just like the human organism, which on the one hand has the chest, the head, in which the intellectual world plays a part, and on the other hand has the nutritional organism, where the physical side plays a part. This makes the human being a threefold being. But the social organism, too, is a threefold one, in that on the one hand everything plays into it that produces the wants themselves, which must never be produced as such by the economic process, and on the other hand that which is produced by nature. This leads to the threefold structure. In the middle is what connects the two.

You only need to consider the following and you will realize the immense fruitfulness, the social fruitfulness of what is being said here. According to what I have just said, the want must never be created by a social process of its own, by an economic process of its own, but the want must be developed from the outside by another process, be it an ethical or another cultural process. In unhealthy times, wants are developed purely for economic reasons, and the people who think in an unhealthy way are actually happy about that. At the time which has just led to our social catastrophe, at the time when the social carcinoma,[104] the social cancer, has gradually advanced, you have been able to see at every turn how the want which should not come from the social structure itself, but which should come into the social structure from other cultural tasks of humanity, how this should be produced by the social process itself.

For a while, we kept reading: Cook good soups with Maggi! Well, the want for Maggi would certainly not have arisen without this advert! This advertising stems purely from the economy. This is not a want that has arisen in a real way. To create wants in this way, to create an artificial interest in a certain product, is just as unwholesome and must lead to illness of the social organism as if you, as a doctor, for example, did not want to encourage a boy to work hard by moral means, but if you gave him a little powder so that he might experience a jolt here or there through this powder and become more industrious through his stomach. Such social bungling, which has come about because everything has been foisted on a so-called monon, a social homunculus, is what has brought about our disastrous present. For the social organism itself must not, on the one hand, produce the wants, and, on the other hand, it must not produce commodities which are only intended to serve the social organism as such. The social organism must be supplied with the commodity from the natural basis. It must be supplied with the wants, on the other hand, by the development of humanity itself.

That is also why the population question must never become a social question. And that simply means misjudging the right relationship between people and the economy, as I pointed out yesterday. This means that in our time we don't know the difference between pigs and humans, as I mentioned yesterday at the end, which means that the population problem is being turned into a social problem. Whether it is desirable to increase the number of people or to maintain the population at a certain level must never depend on economic considerations, but on other, ethical and spiritual considerations.

When discussing this question, it must be particularly borne in mind that if we artificially work towards a significant increase in the population through the economy, we will then force souls who may only have wanted to incarnate after four or five decades to come down now already so that they come down in a much worse condition in this way. This means that an increase in population may be a coercion that you exert on souls, who then have to enter their bodily incarnation in a much worse condition. This can lead to a moral quagmire.

The question of population growth or stability, or even population decline, must never be an economic question, but rather a question of ethical, moral, in short, intellectual and even spiritual views of life and the world. All these things only enter a healthy sphere if they are grasped through spiritual science. You will therefore understand the necessity of a spiritual-scientific foundation for all social thinking. If you really wanted to deal with all the dreadful things that are currently being said and written about the social question, then you would be driven to finally apply the sharp thinking that is necessary for these things by seeing the barrenness that lies in all these things alone.

Just as the successors of Plato and Aristotle had to decide to say: human beings as slaves must not be commodities, so the successors of humanity today must learn to say: under no circumstances must labour be a commodity. Instead, human beings must be driven by other impulses to serve, to work for their fellow human beings, not by the value of what they produce. The economic value of what is produced should never be regulated according to the amount of labour expended or saved, but solely according to the legitimate relationship that will discharge the tension between the commodity and such human wants. This means that neither stored nor saved labour is the deciding factor; for we do not stand in the economic process through our labour, we do not work to save labour, but merely finish goods so that they enter into a certain relationship of tension with the corresponding wants. The corresponding want may determine that a commodity on which a great deal of labour is expended must under certain circumstances be cheap; the want may determine in a sound economic process that a piece of work on which little labour is expended is even perhaps more expensive; the labour expended cannot be the deciding factor. This is the result of today's discussion. Therefore, for those who understand these things, the radical demand arises to obtain the impulse for human labour from a completely different source than from the economic value of the commodity, precisely because the latter is determined by the aforementioned relationship of tension.

Only the person who understands these things can then decide on the two important social questions at hand today: compulsory labour, compulsory work, as the Bolsheviks want it, or the right to work, as it is also called. But the person who does not delve into the depths to which we have referred today will only ever speak confused, foolish things, regardless of whether they are talking about labour law or compulsory labour in any position or for any purpose. You only have the right to talk about such questions if you delve into the depths. And today it is a serious question to earn the right to have a say in these things. More of this next time.

Tenth Lecture

DORNACH, 31 JANUARY 1919

It can be said that there is a serious tragedy hanging over humanity today. This will be clear to you from the content of the various reflections we have had recently. For the most part, these reflections covered a wide range of aspects that are relevant to the development of the social problem, the social conundrum of our time. And it is precisely with regard to this social conundrum that we can say that a certain serious tragedy hangs over contemporary humanity. We can see how the social question, which many people, especially the so-called intelligentsia, have more or less regarded as a theoretical issue, is taking on a truly meaningful, practical form across large territories of the civilized world. And what is tragic in relation to this matter is that precisely where the social conundrum comes to the surface of existence in practical life, people, one could say of all professions and all social classes, are extremely poorly prepared for the social situation of the present.

If people now find themselves in such a position in the world that they feel compelled in many places not only to make speeches about the social question, as was previously the case, but also to make judgements about this or that in relation to social organization—it is easy to see from the circumstances of the present that this must happen—then people will not find the opportunity to gain starting points for such judgements. They do not find the opportunity to develop the right thinking for such judgements, which have now become such a burning necessity.

We can see that in the course of the last few centuries the leading members of the middle classes have actually adopted certain forms of thought for the daily, and also the weekly and annual use of their thinking, which, even if it is not always obvious, derive from the scientific thinking of modern times. So people who think at all today actually think scientifically, even if they don't think about the natural sciences at all; they think the way it is good to think in the natural sciences as they have developed today. And this way of thinking doesn't really get you any further with regard to all social issues. But most people still don't want to admit this to themselves. They all want to attribute the confusion that has occurred to all sorts of other things. They do not yet want to look at the fact that they should actually be saying to themselves: we are facing social chaos in relation to a large part of the civilized world; we must have a judgement, but we actually have no points of reference for this judgement in the habits of thought that we have cultivated up to now.

If we want to visualize the full tragedy of the fact alluded to here, we must realize the following. It is important to note how, since the sixteenth and seventeenth centuries, there has been a gradual preparation for what has erupted today, and how, since the sixteenth and seventeenth centuries, leading humanity has basically done nothing to really form a judgement about what is necessary. The economic orders that have been shattered since the sixteenth and seventeenth centuries are simply no longer here today. Basically, it can be said that a kind of economic chaos, or rather economic anarchy, took their place by the middle of the nineteenth century. Since the middle of the nineteenth century, humanity has in turn been striving to organize social bodies in such a way as to get out of economic anarchy. But it strived towards this with inadequate means. Let's take a closer look at this situation, albeit just a little bit more closely.

If we look back to the time before the sixteenth or seventeenth century, we see that humanity was economically organized into more or less fixed professional associations, the inner structure of which is still little known to people today, but which were structured and arranged in such a way that they could offer a kind of satisfaction in a certain respect for the life of humanity at that time. It was above all in the professional organizations that existed as crafts, guilds and so on that individuals had the opportunity to be interested in their professional organization with the whole of their being. They were interested with all their aspirations, we might say. Anyone who joined a professional organization as an apprentice could hope to become a journeyman or even a master one day. They could hope to climb the social ladder. And these organizations were also more or less useful in other respects, in relation to the regulation of production and consumption, for certain periods in the development of humanity.

Now modern times arrived. We know from our spiritual-scientific observations how this modern time actually is inwardly in its essence. People want to consciously place themselves at the pinnacle of their own personality. They want to develop the consciousness soul. Even if it is masked by the various circumstances, this is the inner impulse of what is battling, what is developing in recent times. The old professional associations, which had [emerged] from completely different human aspirations, were no longer suitable for this endeavour to shape the personal, the individual element in people. So that we see how, from the sixteenth and seventeenth centuries onwards, a certain individualism also develops in the field of economic life, how the old associations, the old social communities are shattered. We see certain transitional phenomena during the transition to this disintegration; we see how, especially in the fifteenth and sixteenth centuries, what could be called the monopolization of various branches of production temporarily developed. But then we see how a kind of anti-monopoly movement develops under the influence of economic individualism, which basically lasts until the middle of the nineteenth century, and which then leads to the modern capitalist mode of production.

This modern capitalist mode of production takes individualism into account to a certain extent. The old professional communities were broken up, the economic initiative passed to individual people, to the capitalists who became entrepreneurs and on whose courage to take risks it depended whether economic life prospered or not. Alongside this the modern technical element developed, which completely reshaped the whole economic life, which actually created the modern proletarian class. And the consequence of this was that capitalism developed on the one hand and the proletariat on the other, and that through the hand-to-mouth existence, through the inattention and lack of interest of the leading people in economic life, a complete lack of understanding finally arose between the leading capitalists and their followers and the working proletarian population.

The great disparities which exist across the earth, especially with regard to the social condition of humanity—we have considered them—they are overlooked by a large proportion of those who today want to tinker with the social problem in one way or another. It must be remembered that the western states of Europe, with their American appendage, have in the course of modern times turned towards what can be called bourgeois democracy. This bourgeois democracy counts on certain ideals of freedom and equality, which it then transfers to economic life. But it, this bourgeois democracy, has remained backward to a certain degree, backward in that it applies the fundamentals, the principles, the programme points, so to speak, of the bourgeoisie as they existed before the actual modern machine age. So we see that in the Western countries this bourgeois democracy is developing, that it is taking on a certain social form, but is gradually being interwoven with what is the product of the modern machine age, is being interwoven with the proletariat. Now in these Western states the proletarian population is not yet being reckoned with in a radical way.

We then see how in central Europe the development of recent times has shown in a frighteningly clear way where the path is actually leading. For what was actually the basic nature of these middle States? Well, the basic nature of these middle States was that the State structure was age-old in origin. The concepts according to which the State structures in central Europe were formed, even as far as Russia, were basically age-old, traditional concepts. They had been preserved in this way—whether as a monarchy or a non-monarchy is less important here—in that the corporations were expanded into so-called modern State entities. These modern State entities in central Europe and as far as Russia are actually remnants of medieval views and sensibilities. They are also constructed in such a way that their structure corresponds to that of the Middle Ages. But life does not conform to such concepts. In the territories where such corporations were formed, the economy, the economic body, emerged from a necessity that was much stronger than that which had been transplanted from the Middle Ages. And this economic body has its own laws, it demands its own laws.

Now the thoroughly pathological situation arose in which the requirements of modern economic life turned to the old State structures and it was believed that this economic life could be penetrated by the old State structures. In a certain way, what was or is a completely new element, economic life, was to be integrated into the body politic, which had grown out of completely different conditions. That's when the modern disaster happened, this terrible disaster of recent years. And within this disaster it became evident—for what I shall now say must be understood about the course of this disaster—that it is impossible to unite modern economic life with the old concepts of the State. Now that this disaster has assumed the nature of a crisis in the last few months, it is evident as of now that because of this, these central European State structures have now been swept away. The State structures are gone, the social economic body also, and in the further course—any sensible person could already see this today—there can no longer be any coupling of the new economic demands with the old State bodies, for the reason that these old State bodies, instead of having modernized themselves in keeping with modern life, have allowed themselves to be swept away.

We are faced with a peculiar perspective here. In the Western States, the movement that must spread throughout modern humanity has been halted for the time being. It can only be arrested for as long as the old bourgeois democratic impulses, which do not yet reckon with modern economic life, are so strong that they can suppress proletarian life. The moment this proletarian life in the Western States can no longer be suppressed, the short-sighted humankind of these Western States will also realize that today it is actually gambling with life. People never want to be told that in good time. For the central and eastern European States, however, the spark has already fallen into the powder keg. It's just an anachronism if, out of sheer laziness of thought, people are still talking about concepts that no longer exist, that are no longer there. Instead of realizing that we really need to turn to new concepts, people in certain circles are still talking about Russia, Germany, even Austria, which no longer exists even externally. Some people still talk like this, while in these areas it is already clear that what has been handed down from time immemorial should simply be abandoned, even in the forms of thinking. This is what people are so unwilling to understand, that they should not just make some kind of judgement about the things that are right in front of their noses—because these judgements will never be correct—but that they have to re-educate their thinking. People in the present day find that very difficult to understand.

Well, this unwillingness to understand the necessity of relearning is mainly due to the fact that people are so firmly convinced that the way of thinking that has developed over the last few centuries and which is so extraordinarily well suited to the scientific professions is absolutely unsuitable for solving the social question. People don't want to realize that. They do not want to accept that they have developed a certain way of thinking and that the outside world has developed a certain way of life that demands a completely different way of thinking than the one they have developed themselves. This is what people find difficult to accept, even though the facts in question speak an extraordinarily significant language.

I would like to point out a fact that would be instructive in the most eminent sense if it were properly considered. Those people who were more impartially interested in the development of modern life were able to experience in a certain way a kind of, we might say, theoretical surprise at the beginning of the nineties of the last century, when German social democracy, which had always been the most advanced strand in social democracy, turned from its previous ideal to the ideal of the so-called 'Erfurt Programme'[105]—worked out at the Erfurt party conference at the beginning of the nineties. In these previous ideals, if I may simply use the term for certain propagandistic goals, there was still something, we might say, of unscientific thinking.

With the Erfurt Programme, the modern labour movement completely succumbed to the superstition about scientific thinking. From then on, the aim was to tackle the entire social question within the proletariat by using only scientifically trained thinking for this purpose. We can say that in two programme points, in two ideals, everything that constituted social democratic ideals of the working class before the Erfurt Programme came together. These two points were, firstly, the abolition of the system of wage labour and, secondly, the elimination of all socio-political inequality. So underlying these two programme points you still have, I would say, a much more general way of thinking, a way of thinking that stems from humanity's judgements, that was affective, instinctive and has become conscious in recent centuries, and that basically reckons with the human being as the centre of social endeavour. So they want to abolish wage labour, the system of wage labour. In other words, people are to be given an existence in human dignity by—this was always unclear in people's minds, the thing we are now clearly presenting from the perspective of spiritual science—no longer equating a person's labour with something that is sold as a commodity, by no longer treating labour as a commodity. They want to abolish the system of wage labour and set up a different system that no longer forces people to sell their personal labour. So this is something that still reckons with the universally human. As does the elimination of social and political inequality.

This actual basic idea of the socialist ideal of earlier times was abandoned at the beginning of the nineties of the last century with the so-called Erfurt Programme. And two other points have now become the target. These two other points are, firstly, the transformation of capitalist private ownership of the means of production into social ownership, i.e. the socialization of the means of production. Machines, land and so on should be transferred from private ownership to social ownership. That was the first point. The second point was the transformation of commodity production into socialist production, which is carried out by and for the social body. These two programme points, in the form of thinking that prevails in them, are completely adapted to the purely scientific thinking of more recent times. There is no longer any talk of people acquiring or conquering anything. There is no talk of abolishing the system of wage labour. There is no talk of any elimination of social or political inequality, but rather of an external process that is to take place entirely apart from the human being, of something that is to take place governed by the course of cause and effect, just as natural events themselves are governed by cause and effect in their course. Private ownership of the means of production is simply to be transformed into common ownership of the means of production, regardless of the transformation this entails for the human being. And the economic order should no longer be that of commodity production, but of socialist production: the community itself should produce, and what is produced should also be there for the community.

Commodity production, in other words production that the individual undertakes on their own private initiative and which is then delivered to the market to be bought by others on the market, differs from socialist production in that socialist production transfers the principle of self-production, where the person who produces something also consumes it themselves, to the whole community. Commodity production counts on the individual person. The individual person produces something and puts it on the market; the other individual person removes it from the market by buying it. Socialist production once again returns to original production, where the individual produces what they consume themselves—at least that's what people imagine once existed—but now it's not the individual who should do it, but the community. The market ceases to exist; some community produces what needs to be produced. What is produced does not become a commodity, but is distributed among those who belong to the community; those who produce it also consume it.

It is therefore a matter here of applying purely scientific concepts to the social organism. People today don't like to consider differences such as those that emerge in the socialist programme before the Erfurt party conference and in the socialist programme after the Erfurt party conference, because people today don't like to think at all, even though they have such a high opinion of their thinking.

But now there is another miserable situation. We can study this miserable situation particularly well if we look, I would say, at one of the classic writers who worked on the social conundrum when it was still a more theoretical question, for example Karl Kautsky.[106] In one of his works, Kautsky, in trying to prove that the capitalist economic order must pass over into the socialist one, says that in this transition commodity production as such must cease and that self-consumption must take its place, so that the consumer is at the same time the producer, that is, a community. But now he raises the question at the same time: What can this community be? And then he gives the answer: Of course it can only be the modern State. In other words, he gives the answer he certainly shouldn't have given. He did not realize, and people of his ilk still do not realize today, that the State they call the modern State was by no means a modern structure. Those States that have been swept away for central and eastern Europe were not modern structures, but existed from time immemorial under conditions quite different from those contained in modern economic life, and there was simply no connection evident—in the way these people thought—between modern economic life and these State structures. That is why we see that these State structures have been swept away. What remains of them are actually spectres that haunt people's minds, and that too will be swept away. Nothing will remain that is not a question in all areas of practical life; only questions will remain. And to answer these questions, which are not theoretical but are facts, we will need a thoroughly new way of thinking. This new way of thinking, as I have shown you in our reflections over the last few weeks, this new way of thinking means that people will realize that the basic laws of a human organization must be studied in the same way as the basic laws of the individual human organization are studied in spiritual science.

If we study the basic laws of the individual human organization, you know that we arrive at the threefold organization of the sensory and nervous system, the rhythmical system and the metabolic system. And only if we understand the intermeshing of these three systems in the organism can we understand what the human being is in time. This corresponds in external life to the understanding of the three parts of the social organism, which must be divided into an intellectual system, an economic system and—if we may call it that—a juridical system, in which only the external juridical system, the political juridical system, is included, but from which private law or criminal law is excluded.

Just as modern natural science does not want to know anything about this threefold organization of the human being and lumps together everything that is in the human being, so modern social thinking does not want to know anything about this threefold organization of the social body. And because it does not want to know anything about this threefold organization of the social body, it is at a loss and will remain at a loss for as long as it does not want to know anything about what has to happen in the face of the great practical demands that every day actually brings. What is therefore necessary is a regeneration of thinking. It is necessary to realize that with the modern concepts of natural science, which are of great service in a certain area, we cannot really make a single step forward in the area of the social life.

And so we see very strange phenomena occurring. We may say, after all, that it is truly no longer a strange phenomenon that people are beginning to think more or less socially, and it was also no strange phenomenon that certain people thought socially before this terrible catastrophe of recent years occured, which in part reveals the social conundrum in its original form. But then we realize, especially when we look at the leading economists and their views, their main ideas, how clueless these people actually stand before the phenomena. I will read you, for example, a definition given by a teacher of economics, Jaffé,[107] who is respected in certain circles, of what he conceives to be the desirable ideal condition of a social organism. Jaffé describes what he believes he has to describe in a way that corresponds perfectly to the concepts which modern humanity has arrived at in this field, and then summarizes how he thinks that the social condition must correspond to the demands of modern humanity, the demands also of modern industrial and other development. Look at this, I would say, thoroughly smart definition, which is truly not one of the most insignificant products of modern economic thinking. So let me read very slowly what Jaffé states as the ideal condition for the social organism that is to come. It is 'that condition of economic organization in which all constituents of the nation have grown together into an organic unity, each person assigned to their place as a serving component of a community which ultimately serves them themselves, which not only ensures an external existence in human dignity, but also lends their work the ultimate dignity, because it does not pursue individual ends, but is a service to the community'.

I believe that a large proportion of those people who develop their thinking quite in keeping with contemporary habits of thought will find this definition extraordinarily apt and witty, that they will even say it is everything, which can only be desirable. We should strive for a condition of economic organization in which each individual is properly integrated, is situated in their place, performs their work, which not only guarantees them an existence in human dignity, but also serves them by providing the corresponding service to the community through this work. To have arrived at such a definition will make the following impression on some people who believe they can think correctly today: God, how clever I am, because I have finally found out how it must be, how the matter must actually be! And yet: 'Poverty comes from *pauvreté*!'—That is also a definition of labour, and the earlier definitions are not at all different from the definition that poverty comes from *pauvreté*. Because this definition is such that it actually applies just as well to the current social organization that we have, or at least had until the war, or which individual States, such as Germany, had during the war.

But we could also say that no contemporary State fits this definition. Such a definition is the model of the most abstract vacuousness. And so we can see today that people are developing their cleverness on systems that, in the end, basically do not even faintly touch on reality with what they come up with as their clever definitions. Because let's take this Jaffé definition. He wants to portray an ideal economic condition of the future. This is to be that condition of economic organization in which all the constituents of the nation have grown together to form an organic unity. This really is the case as soon as any State, even the worst one, exists! All the constituents of the nation have nevertheless somehow grown together to form an organic unity. If a person has leprosy spread over all their limbs, all limbs are likewise afflicted with leprosy and have grown together to form an organic unity! This is because you can define a leprous body and a healthy body with exactly the same definition, if only you keep this definition appropriately general. As long as you stick with the theory, nobody will notice. But when the situation is as it is now, when the disease has broken out and needs to be cured, the concepts that people then have, the powers of judgement that people then have, turn out to be completely unsuitable.

Then he goes on to say '...where everyone is assigned to their place as a serving constituent of a community....' Well, that really was the case for most people within the German Reich, for example, with the exception of the few people who wanted absolutely nothing to do with a State, that everyone was a serving constituent in the whole, wasn't it? At minimum they cast their vote. 'Serving constituents of a community that ultimately serves them themselves' is also true, is also true of the worst State structure. 'Which not only ensures their external existence', a bit of something emerges here, but it remains a phrase-like, appended thing, because it is something that is said among the other phrases. With 'but also lends their work the ultimate dignity', it depends on what is understood by this dignity. 'Because it does not pursue individual ends, but is a service to the community', this can also be the case in the worst State!

A clever definition from a respected economics teacher is nothing other than: Poverty comes from *pauvreté*. A large part of humanity today suffers in practice from this trait of insubstantial abstraction. The reality behind the appearances barely dawns on people. Just think how far removed people are from considering something like the threefold structure, which we cite here as the basic principle, also just in practical terms! People today still think they can find some kind of formula through which, let's say for example—it's become a catchword now—'socialization' could be achieved. Indeed, it's not much better, even if the comparison is a little off, than if someone were to find a science through which digestion can take place. Digestion is something the human organism has to do in real life. To do so, it must be divided into three parts in its real life; then it will actually maintain its vital function through the correct interaction of the three constitutional elements. If you really structure the community in a threefold way, then you don't need a formula for socialization, then what wants to be socialized will socialize itself.

Just consider how infinitely complicated what happens in the human organism is. Just think if you had to work out everything that happens in the two hours after your lunch! You have eaten, what you have eaten is digested: this is a tremendously complicated process that breaks down into countless individual details. Just consider for a moment that you should think this through: of course you couldn't possibly think it through! And if everyone's digestion depended on being thought through, you wouldn't be able to live a single day; you could not live a single day. Today, committees like to get together in one place or another to find the forms how to socialize. But the thing that is the public life of humanity is also a thoroughly complicated process that can no more be intercepted in its details than the digestive process, for example, or the thinking process itself, or the breathing process can be intercepted in its details. But if you have the threefold impulses and allow them to work together, then the right thing happens. Take an example. You can hardly read a socialist or social writer today without being amazed at their extraordinary wealth of knowledge. Not so much the bourgeois ones, but especially the socialist writers have compiled a vast amount of all kinds of statistical and other historical material, right up to the present day, in order to study the necessary development of humanity up to the present. Based on past development, they now claim to recognize the need to, let's say, socialize. But this process, which takes place within the human community, is a peculiar one. They grab a phenomenon at one corner and it immediately slips away at the other! If they then socialize in the way that seems necessary to them, by grabbing one corner, the whole story slips away at the other.

Let's take a look at this by way of an example. Let's take just one fact: in 1910, an American plant that manufactured railway rails was able to produce as many rails in two and a half days as it had produced in a whole week ten years earlier. But the workers were still kept working all week! Now we can say, to obtain a view of the relationship between employer and workers, these workers produce twice as much per week as was produced in 1900. Of course, every worker works twice as much for the market! This is noticed by the worker through various conditions. What is accomplished by the worker is naturally expressed in the proletarian question. Of course, the worker knows very well that the employer earns twice as much, more than twice as much, and factors arise whereby the worker demands twice as much from the employer. But if you now hypothesize and say: Well, the worker can be paid more, even if perhaps not twice as much, because the employer naturally earns so and so much more—then you have only grasped the matter at one corner. The other corner slips out of your hand again, because the rails are getting so and so much cheaper. And this reduction in the price of the rails is reflected in turn in other phenomena of social life and corrects what appears as the proletarian question on the one side. We can say that the relationships in the social organism are so complicated that if you tackle any question from one point of view, other points of view immediately block what you have to say.

Take another example. Take the German economy. I have already explained to you in previous observations how machines are to a certain extent relieving people of human labour. It can be said of the German economy in particular that in the last few decades—it has experienced a tremendous upswing, after all—machines have done as much work as seventy or eighty million people, even if you leave aside the performance of locomotives, that is, more than the population of Germany. Of the German population only a part are in turn workers, from which it follows that in the modern German economy in the last few years before the war, one worker did what four to five workers did before the introduction of the machine. Imagine what a transformation this means for life in general! But what occurs here occurs at so many points in life that if you somehow want to socialize with regard to one point of view, you cause the greatest damage from other points of view. Because this social life is just as complicated as the life of any organic creature. And it cannot be the task to put into some formula how things should be done, but to give the social organism the structure through which it works by itself and puts things in order in the same way as the human organism puts its functions in order. That can be the only way.

So you see, the matter has to be seen from a completely different angle. It must be understood from the perspective of really penetrating into the true nature of the social organism. This is what is more important than all the talk of community and community building. It will be an extraordinarily good lesson for the central and eastern European countries that they will soon have to realize how they can no longer talk about nationalization of the means of production in the usual sense. For the time being, people are still talking about these things according to old habits of thought and are not considering that the States are no longer there, that they are gone, that something completely new has to be created in their place that has not yet arrived. First of all, people will initially be elected who still have the old concepts in their minds. They will do something in accordance with these old concepts, but it will be a human being as little as the homunculus in Wagner's retort. Then people will see that it doesn't work that way and will first have to convince themselves through practical life that all the confused concepts that the last few decades have brought to the surface are really impossible in the light of the practical situations facing humanity today.

This will make you aware that it is first and foremost a matter of examining reality in such a way that you can determine from this reality: what form can these social demands actually take in the present? There is, after all, one thing I have pointed out here again and again. Let the proletarians say today what they want; what a person says today is generally irrelevant, because what they say exists in their upper consciousness, while what they demand, what they are concerned about, is contained in their subconscious.

Today, you hardly ever learn about people through what they say. You get to learn much more about people through what dawns from their subconscious, through the way they talk, than through the content of what they say. Because the content of what they say is mostly just the propagated content of a dying or already dead time. That which sits below submerged in the soul is that which is new.

And so we see that the proletarian populace scatters categorical concepts all around, words that have been instilled in them from Marxism or other sources. And in truth, among the impulses—what isn't there among the impulses!—there is above all the impulse to no longer allow human labour to be a commodity. If you ask the modern proletarian today: what do you actually want, they will reply: I want nationalization or socialization of the means of production, I want socialization and so on. If, among the various points, all of which we can get to know in their true form, they were to place particular emphasis on the point, I want my labour henceforth not to be a commodity, but something completely different, then they would be telling the truth.

Thus in this modern thinking the very oldest is mixed with that which is unconsciously contained in human souls as the newest, the most modern demand. And again, people are not aware of this. This is why we are seeing the emergence of a demand that has already become obsolete for a large part of the educated world: the demand to replace private entrepreneurs with the old communities. It is actually bizarre for those States that have disappeared that the State should now become the entrepreneur instead of the private entrepreneur. Something that is no longer there is to become the entrepreneur! Nevertheless, people are tinkering around with this issue. This shows how this modern way of thinking and feeling has led to a dead end. And it is precisely the extent to which the State or any existing community can or cannot directly replace the private company that we intend to discuss in greater detail tomorrow.

ELEVENTH LECTURE

DORNACH, 1 FEBRUARY 1919

SOCIALISM is of the opinion that what it calls a socialist economic order is a direct and necessary causal continuation of what has gradually emerged in the economic order over the last few centuries in the development of humanity. To a certain extent, those who today hold the proletarian socialist view of life believe that the capitalist economic order must gradually transform itself into the socialist economic order, and this for the simple reason that the socialist economic order is to a certain extent already present within what has developed over the last few centuries through capitalism. Some say, in order to be able to characterize this train of thought precisely, as they believe, that every human order, every order of life, when in a sense it has reached its culmination, at the peak of its development, already contains the seed for what follows.

Well, on the face of it, I would say statistically speaking—and socialist scholars are particularly fond of statistics—what I have just described as the socialist order has a lot going for it. In certain areas, modern technology has transformed—we can summarize the process in the following way—what used to be a manageable business in the care of the human individual into a large-scale enterprise. We only have to look at the modern iron industry as an excellent example, and we will find that this modern iron industry had to combine a whole host of activities, all of which ultimately culminate in the creation of certain products, but which can only be created through the interaction of complex processes. In order to be able to operate the kind of giant enterprises that modern economic life has created, large amounts of capital are required, capital accumulations in comparison to which the economic life of earlier times would have been a laughing stock.

However, these accumulations of capital also offer individual owners or a group of owners of such giant enterprises the opportunity to employ a large labour force. The fact that the enterprises have expanded to huge proportions has brought together a large labour force within the enterprises. The commercial conditions have also meant that such huge businesses cannot stand alone because they would not be able to cope with the competition, that they have merged in a certain way, creating a connected social group of entrepreneurs and workers which is even larger in size. Thus socialist thought in more recent times holds that economic life itself has in a certain way led to socialization, and that what now accompanies this socialization must necessarily continue this whole process.

The continuation would consist in the fact that it is now no longer the individual entrepreneur who brings together a working community on a large scale, but that the communities, State, municipality, cooperatives become the entrepreneurs themselves, so that to a certain extent it is only the socialization process, which has already occurred through modern technical and economic life, which is continued in a regulated manner.

Now, basically, the idea I have just expressed has a tremendously suggestive effect on the modern proletariat. This modern proletariat must also be considered in terms of its mental state by those who really want to fully grasp the situation. And here it is really evident that such thoughts have an extraordinarily strong suggestive power on the modern proletariat. This suggestive power is indeed based on the fact that the modern worker believes themselves to be at the mercy of the entrepreneur, and that they believe they can only escape this domination in that they themselves take care of what the entrepreneur takes care of.

Now it is in the nature of modern humanity—and this is caused by the most varied of reasons—to happily give themselves over to one-sided thoughts. Healing for many a situation will only come by letting go of this tendency to indulge in one-sided thoughts and learning to look at things from all sides. Looking at the development of modern capitalist technical economic life with its culmination after socialization in this way really means nothing other than applying the modern forms of thought suitable for the natural sciences to economic life. I explained this fact to you yesterday from a different point of view.

However, if we take a purely scientific view, as the scientific way of thinking has become in recent times, then certain impulses necessarily remain absent from such a way of looking at things. Of course, when discussing such things, you have to say some things that, if misunderstood, can easily be challenged. However, you know the methods which are necessary especially in spiritual-scientific considerations, and will therefore also be certain that the following is also only an illumination from one side, but an illumination from a side that is needed.

The purely scientific approach, which views phenomena purely according to the law of cause and effect, can basically be applied to both healthy and sick organisms. You can look at the healthy organism physiologically and, if you want to stick to what modern science is particularly fond of, you will be able to see the connection between cause and effect everywhere. But you can equally well, if you stay with this abstraction—connection of cause and effect—regard the sick organism pathologically. In the sick organism, too, everything is connected by cause and effect. And if we take as a one-sided, abstract basis only a sequence of events guided by cause and effect, then the impulse, which on the one hand must be described as a healthy impulse and on the other as a sick impulse, necessarily remains absent. It falls out of view. This doesn't really matter for the scientific approach with regard to the tasks that science is initially seeking in modern times. But this does matter if we want to apply the same way of thinking to social processes, because the difference between health and sickness cannot simply be excluded from the process of human development. That cannot be done. And that is what must be mainly emphasized to begin with, that just as people today are faced with the social issues that have become so burning as a result of reality, they lack the ability to judge whether something is a healthy or sick process, whether something needs to be fostered or needs to be healed. That is why we might say that such a tragedy lies over modern humanity, because precisely this difference, which I have just roughly characterized, is absent.

If we consider the modern development of humanity over the last three or four centuries, and in particular how what is called capitalism has developed, then we must also still consider another point of view than that of the concentration of businesses into large enterprises and the like. We must, for example, rigorously ask the question: What is the actual position of the capitalist mode of production in the entire societal process of humanity? The only way to reach a judgement on this is to compare the modern capitalist mode of production with the former craftsman's mode of production with regard to a certain aspect. The former craftsman, he manufactured his products, he delivered his products to the consumer, and by being paid for his products he was able to make a living. If you follow such a craftsman's life, if you follow the productive life of earlier centuries in general, namely up to about the year 1300, you will find that people were paid, or exchanged goods if you like, for what they produced. For what they produced, they procured what was necessary for their livelihood. It was a limited economy in a sense, but it was an economy that was closely tied to the person. All production was also closely linked to personal proficiency, to personal zeal, to the honour that someone saw in making a product as good as possible and so on. Significant moral impulses were linked to the economic order in the time of simple artisan life.

All this has changed over the last three to four centuries. After a transition from the fifteenth century to around the sixteenth and seventeenth centuries, things have changed in the last three to four centuries. It was in these last three to four centuries that what we can call the capitalist mode of production really developed. If we now examine what really underlies the social question and do not focus on what people believe, the following characteristic must be considered. The essential thing for the capitalist, in so far as they are a member of the capitalist economic order, is not to earn a living like the craftsman, but to ensure that capital grows, that it increases. What capital grows by is profit. In other words, it is not working for status in life, but working for profit that is particularly characteristic of the capitalist economic order. However, this makes capital as such highly autonomous. You see, if a certain volume of capital increases over the years through the production process, if it grows, and if that is precisely the purpose of capital formation, then what is actually the main thing in the economic process is detached from everything that is personal. And that is the aspect that must be considered above all in the correct judgement of the modern social question, this detachment of the economic process from the personal.

Unfortunately, very few people in today's educated classes have any real inclination to concern themselves with these things. If they were to do so, they would be able to see how the modern human being is to a certain extent detached from everything that actually constitutes the economic process. I ask you, to what extent do people outside very narrowly defined circles enjoy the products that they produce? What was pervasive in the economic order of earlier ages, for example, that a person took great pleasure in every key they produced and had to invest their honour in making it as good as possible, that is now a thing of the past. In a sense, people are separated from the economic process as such. At most, in the artistic field and in those things that are related to the artistic field, there still takes place what used to infuse a craft like a pervasive moral moment. It cannot even be said that in intellectual life the connection between a person and their achievement has been maintained. Take a look at all the professors who work in this or that subject area and see whether they are really fully rooted as human beings in what they produce!

But in a comprehensive way, this is connected to the basic character of the capitalist economic order, which after all intervenes in everything. You can see this from yesterday's closing remarks. From this basic character of the capitalist economic order it follows that the human being is to a certain extent detached in their personal aspirations from the economic process, which is becoming more and more objective. The consequence of this is far-reaching and colours the whole socialist concept of today. This is because the belief arises that this unhealthy separation of human production from the human being themselves and what interests them really should be laid down in a new economic order. Is there anywhere today where people think of looking for a connection between a person and what they produce? On the contrary, the idea is to externalize the economic process as far as possible, to detach it from the person. And the consequence of this would be that a person would have to seek satisfaction in other areas for that which is actually connected with their personality, which is connected with all the interests of their being. This is how this preconception affects what today are called socialist ideals. Let us visualize what the socialist ideal consists of for broad circles today.

We have four points in which we can summarize everything that is, as it were, the socialist ideal in relation to the structure of the human social organism. Firstly, this socialist ideal strives for all production enterprises to become the property of the community, be this community the State or the commune or co-operatives; that, in other words, all private ownership of the means of production be abolished, that the means of production all become common property, so that all enterprises must also be managed by the community.

The second thing within the socialist ideal is that production should be regulated according to need, that is, that production should not be regulated freely according to supply and demand, that if an article is demanded here or there, a branch of production should not be opened for this article, but that it should be determined to a certain extent by the State or communally or co-operatively: people need this, so the community sets up a production plant for this article that is needed there. A third is the democratic regulation of labour and wage relations, and a fourth is that any surplus value accrues to the community. We have thus roughly placed the four components of the socialist ideal before our souls. I repeat, all production enterprises should become the property of the community, production should be regulated according to need; labour and wage relations should be regulated democratically; any added value, that is, any profit, should be handed over to the community.

These four points are in fact what millions and millions of people are striving for today. And in contrast to this, there is an absolute necessity to ask: How is it possible to make people realize that these four so-called ideals are absolutely impossible within the real human community?

You see, if thirty years ago people had shown as much zeal for the social question as some people are showing of necessity today in those countries where the old governments have been chased away—in those countries where the old governments have not been chased away, there continues to be no interest—you could even say that if people had shown some of the interest in the social question back then that they are showing today, things would have been fine, everything would have turned out differently. But where people's mouths are not yet watering, it is not yet possible to arouse any real interest in social conundrums. What the leading, so-called intelligent middle classes have failed to do in this direction over the last two to three decades is outrageous. And they are preparing to continue to fail to do the same things, only in a different area. What is necessary above all today is that people learn to understand that just as the individual organism must be understood in terms of spiritual science, the social organism must also be understood in terms of spiritual science. In this area, we must finally move beyond insubstantial abstractions. It is indeed possible to tie in here with deeper human interests, deeper human impulses, which are influencing human development right now in this era of humanity.

The current drowsiness of humanity is immense, and it is necessary to wake up in a certain direction. How often do we hear the strange judgement today wherever spiritual science is considered at all, that spiritual science is not necessary for a person who has faith and is a Christian in the good old sense, and, by the way, faith is simple and spiritual science is complicated and it is therefore not to be understood why people should exchange the simple for the complicated. But this comfortable clinging to the simple, this nefarious mere belief, this comfortable insistence, we don't need to think about it, we don't need to search for truth, we are given it by faith—this in the deeper sense of the word is to blame for the catastrophic events in which we live. And it must be emphasized again and again that this is to blame. Woe betide if there are not enough people in life who have the heart and mind for a complete dedication to serious, inwardly industrious thinking and research into the truths! For the times are over when you only had to believe in the spiritual world, when you could idle away your time here in physical existence and believe that you would be redeemed by the powers you no longer cared much about and which in turn would contribute their part to the corresponding redemption.

What matters in the progress of humanity is that the human being does not merely believe in God and the gods, but that they allow God and the gods to be active in their own being, that they allow the forces of the spiritual world to flow into what they themselves do, what they do in everyday life. What we do from morning to night must be done in such a way that there is divine-spiritual power in our actions. It will only be in our actions if it is first and foremost in our thoughts. The task of modern humanity is to embrace God actively within us, not just in terms of the content of our faith. Not just thinking about God, but thinking in such a way that God lives in our thoughts—that's what matters. If we devote ourselves to such an ideal, then we will develop the necessary interest in everything for which, unfortunately, the vast majority of modern humanity has developed no interest in recent decades.

What is important is that we find the possibility to make people realize that a change in the whole world of thought is necessary. It is high time; for after the so-called intellectuals have failed to work in this direction, the worst instincts of humanity are now awakening over almost the whole civilized world, at least over a large part of the civilized world. Do you think that when these instincts of humanity have reached a certain culmination, a certain peak, that they are then easy to banish? It will be a long, long time before they in turn consume themselves. Teaching only works to a certain point in time; setting an example to calm, to restrain the instincts of humanity only works to a certain point in time. The animal in humanity strives towards the surface because there has been a failure to encourage what is nobler in the human being.

And here we are at the point where we need to talk about the moral side of the modern social question. I said that what I called the last characteristic of the capitalist economic order, the increase of capital as such, the growth of capital, which strives not for output but for profit, detaches the human being from their product. And in this detachment of the human being from their product lies an essential characteristic of the whole of modern development. But in the world it is the case that one phenomenon does not usually occur without the other, but that phenomena belong together in a variety of ways. You cannot walk on soft ground without your footprints being imprinted on the ground at the same time. This is an example that you can apply anywhere to see how in the real world one always belongs with the other. The thing that has driven the modern world towards the growth of capital that lies within modern capitalism, the growth of capital, has on the other hand—not one-sidedly logically, but in the logic of reality—linked the rise of capitalism with the lack of interest that we find in modern humanity precisely for the deepest impulses of the human soul. On the one hand, the peeling away of the human personality from the economic process; on the other hand, the desiccation of this personality, which has detached itself from the economic process, specifically with regard to the most intimate characteristics of a person's spiritual and soul being. The two things belong together. The two things have brought about that terrible hustle of the modern metropolises in which capitalism has set up its special headquarters, where on the one hand capitalism is at work and on the other hand there prevails a lack of interest in the most intimate questions of the innermost human being.

These things are often veiled in the way they appear outwardly, and only a more detailed examination reveals them. Of course, you can say that there are a large number of people who are not involved in the modern capitalist process. Certainly, it is only a few who are directly involved, but the whole of modern humanity, especially educated modern humanity, is indirectly involved in the capitalist process. Involved in that their livelihoods depend on the capitalist economic order. Someone may be an artist: just as they used to produce for the prince or the pope, today they produce for the capitalist. And if you draw such strands as loop from art to capitalism today over the most diverse areas of life, then you will see how capitalism has spread its tentacles in all directions, especially over intellectual life. However, there are a lot of unconscious things at work in these things that, if you just look at the surface of life, don't reveal themselves straight away.

I will now have to characterize an unconscious or subconscious process. This objectification of the production process, this detachment of the production process from human aspirations, as it takes place in modern capitalism, requires justification in a certain sense. People always need a justification for what they do, and it is not important to them, if they want to justify themselves, to investigate the truth, but it is only important to them to say something that justifies them. Take an obvious example. The Entente[108] has won; this victory has to be justified. That's why people say what the Entente is saying today, not because it's the truth, but because the victory has to be justified. It is the same in individual human life. What do most people care about really finding out the truth! They are concerned about justifying what they do. That is what capitalism wants: to justify its existence above all else. It can only justify it if it observes the most extreme material process, the most material economic process in its mirror image, in the growth of capital. But then, if the capitalist economic order is to be justified in this physical world, everything that is of a spiritual and soul nature must be eliminated. It has to go to a special area. Let the pastor speak on his pulpit about the things of faith as he pleases—I can believe it, someone else can believe it, I can stop believing it, someone else can stop believing it—he is talking about a completely different world. In the world we have to live in, things can't happen in the way the pastor says from the pulpit, of course not, things have to be done in a capitalist way.

Thus, on the one hand, extreme capitalism has given rise to this terribly abstract moral and spiritual life, which seeks to separate itself completely from all external realities of existence. Just as bad in modern life as material capitalism on the one hand, has been the attitude on the other, which says: Oh, what do I care about Ahriman! Let Ahriman remain Ahriman, I dedicate myself to the impulses in the innermost part of my soul, I surrender to the spiritual world, I seek the spiritual world as I can find it within myself; it is the affairs of the soul that interest me. What do I care about this ahrimanic credit, money, wealth and property system! What do I care about the difference between annuity and interest, between gross income and net profit and so on. I take care of the affairs of my soul! But just as the human being is a unity of body, soul and spirit, and just as body, soul and spirit are bound together between birth and death, so those impulses that we can find through the innermost structure of our soul and those impulses that lie in the external economic order are bound together in our external physical existence.

And just as guilty of the modern catastrophe as the materialistic capitalists are on the one hand with their way of thinking and attitude, just as guilty are those who, on the other hand, only want to be pious, only want to be spiritual scientific, abstractly restrict this spiritual science in their sense and do not get involved in the penetration of everyday reality with an engaged way of thinking. This is what has prompted me again and again to speak to you about the fact that you should not take this anthroposophical spiritual movement as an opportunity to listen to mere Sunday afternoon sermons that do you good in your soul because they tell you that life is eternal and so on, but that you should take this anthroposophical movement as the way to really tackle the modern tasks of existence, which are coming towards us with such urgency, in a meaningful way. And one of the first necessities is this: to understand where to start and that nothing will help if people do not gain access to unbiased thinking.

And here, at the end of today's reflections, I would like to say something that will be taken up tomorrow in practical and social observations. What I am going to say will appear to be very far removed from all socialist thinking or thinking about the social question, but tomorrow you will see how close that which appears to be far away is, and how, precisely through these observations, we will be able to correct the four points that I have indicated to you as the components of the socialist ideal. People so often say in life: opinions are different, convictions are different, one person believes this, another believes that. Doesn't it look as if, when we indulge in our thinking, one person can have these thoughts, the other those, and these and those thoughts can then be justified? It looks like that, and yet it is not. Taking into account the fact that every characterization of a thing is in a higher sense always a photograph from one side, that is, that there are observations from the most diverse sides—always assuming that this is taken into account—all people have the same opinion about one and the same matter in their deepest inner being. There are no two people in the world who do not have the same opinion about one and the same matter—as I said, always under the given condition. There aren't. So why do people still talk about different opinions? Because their emotions interfere in the truth and what people hear in their innermost being, their egoistic prejudices interfere and distort and caricature the matter. People are only truly different in terms of their emotions, not in terms of their concepts and ideas.

Once you have gained access to a real concept, you cannot have an opinion about this concept that differs from another person who has also gained access to this concept. And it is the greatest frivolity of the soul to believe that we have some right to subjective opinions. We do not have this right to subjective opinions, but as human beings we have the obligation to go beyond our subjectivity to the objective. However, in order to see this point correctly, it is very necessary to consider all the sources of error that result from human emotions. A person believes that they can be convinced of a matter. Often the reason they believe they are convinced of some matter is none other than that they are too lazy to really consider the concept. Well, it is indeed necessary to point to this inner moral side of human nature if we want to draw attention to what is needed today.

This present age is, after all, primarily full of arrogance, full of emotions even in what is called objective science, and not at all inclined to seek access to the judgement that lies in real ideas and real concepts. But where are we heading if the burning social conundrums that are now on our doorstep are solved out of people's emotions? As you know, there are imaginations, there are inspirations, there are intuitions. In truth, everything that needs to be explored with regard to economic relationships and economic legislation lies in imaginations; everything that needs to be investigated in the economic organism lies in imaginations.

For most people, these imaginations may only dawn from the unconscious in hunches. But then, these hunches are better than the concepts that have been acquired by study, many of which figure in humanity. Everything that lives in what can be called the intellectual and cultural life, which we have characterized in the way we have characterized the intellectual and cultural life as a component of the future social order, is based on inspirations: the intellectual and cultural organism. And everything that is really allowed to exist detached from the human being, indeed must exist detached from the human being, that in which human beings must be equal, equal, as they say, before the law, can only be based on intuitions. What we might call the political organism is based on this. Imagination: economic organism—inspiration: intellectual and cultural organism—intuition: political organism.

In this way, inspiration, intuition and imagination must really work together in shaping the conditions of life. This is something we have to consider, that this is so. And then we will also realize how the social questions that are not only on the doorstep today, but are burning it down, can basically only be directed towards their solution by using methods of spiritual science. This is what matters, discarding all laxity, all complacency in thinking, and really going for that which connects the human soul with reality. Ultimately, only this can bring us to where we need to be in the present. From this perspective, we will then characterize and critically discuss the four elements of the so-called socialist ideal tomorrow.

Twelfth Lecture

DORNACH, 2 FEBRUARY 1919

YESTERDAY I listed the four main elements of the current socialist programme. They are, as you will remember, firstly, that the production enterprises must be socialized. Secondly, production must be geared to demand. Thirdly, labour and wage relations should be regulated democratically. Fourthly, any added value should go to the community. Yesterday we already had to point out some things that showed us that within those currents of judgement and sentiment that led to this fourfold programme, there is more that is completely detached from the human being than just facts as derived by social-democratic attitudes today from what we have come to know as the materialist conception of history and the doctrine of economic class struggle. Spiritual forces, spiritual impulses play into the things that have developed today, that have specifically become established as the views and aspirations of the proletariat. And it will be disastrous if we do not try to gain sufficient insight into how strong the spiritual impulses are that play into the course of socialist thinking and socialist intentions in recent times. It can be said that the most striking aspect of such socialist thinking and socialist intentions is the absolute mistrust of any involvement of human morality, of human ethics in the organization of the social organism. It is simply like a sediment in proletarian thinking and intentions not to believe that any moral impulses or even only intellectual impulses among the ruling classes could contribute anything to the solution of the social problem.

Don't be fooled by these things, especially not by the words that can sometimes be heard from socialists. To be sure, these words will be used particularly where criticism is made, where the faults of the ruling classes are discussed in such a way that many things in the ruling classes are morally condemned. But where the socialist proletariat consciously reflects on what it hopes for in modern times, it only says: even if the ruling classes were to undertake to endeavour to improve the social situation of the proletariat out of moral impulses, they would not be able to do so. An improvement can only result from the real class struggle, from the struggle of economic interests and economic forces as such. It is extremely important to fully realize this. Because what may still exist today as a remnant of faith and trust in the moral power of the ruling classes will also disappear.

We must realize that the so-called intelligentsia, the intellectual leaders of today's humanity, have themselves gradually come to disbelieve the power of moral or even spiritual impulses in the widest possible circles on the basis of those preconditions of capitalism that I spoke of yesterday. Bourgeois circles, too, in the depths of their hearts, do not think much of the effective power of moral impulses. Certainly, they talk a lot about such moral impulses, but compared to the way these things then occur, this talk often seems like a more or less conscious or unconscious untruthfulness. For let us never forget one of the most disastrous facts in the development of humanity today, a fact that we have already touched on from the most diverse points of view; we can characterize it something like this: today, on the one hand, we have a certain trust in a pure, one might say morality-free, spirit-free knowledge of external things of nature. Just consider how much the present time endeavours to shape the knowledge of nature in such a way that there is no relationship between the thoughts we have about the way nature is and the thoughts we have about the moral world order. A characteristic fact is that, for example, the Roman Catholic Church, which has among its priests people who truly are thoroughly learned, points out that the learned people who are in its ranks should just stick to the external sensory facts and should never try to mix anything relating to the spiritual or moral into what is said to be purely causal knowledge with reference to the external facts. At most, this should be done in parables.

And on the other hand, take the things that are written today about moral, ethical and spiritual questions by the various authorities and people who are considered to have the right qualifications. Certainly, there are a number of ethical impulses and ideals that are more or less unctuous, more or less melodramatic, aspiring to compassion or seeking to arouse disgust. But see for yourself and really pick up such writings: ask yourself what you can gain today from these ethics books or spiritual books of the present in relation to the burning questions of the present time, which are called the social questions, the social conundrums. Nothing, but nothing at all! Ethical thinking has to a certain extent withdrawn from what is directly effective in everyday social life. You can find over and over again in ethical books such terms as benevolence; love, love is especially popular; nobility; right, right is again especially popular, and similar things. But the way people talk, it has no power to have an effect on people. There is no moral momentum in what is addressed to people in abstract moral terms. So on the one hand we have rhetoric that plays over into the ethical, into the moral sphere, which is incapable of really taking hold of people; and equally we have what takes hold of people, the economic order, which no longer cares at all about these merely rhetorical ethics, but only wants to build just on the thoughts of natural causality, and only wants to bring this natural causality into the economic order of humanity.

When people who have come from the so-called intelligent circles want to speak ethically, or when people want to write ethically, where do you hear today or where do you read today something that really reaches people in such a way that the ethical demands immediately become socio-economic demands? That would be what is essential today, that a straight path leads from ethics, religion and spirituality to the most mundane economic and social issues. Knowledge of this path must not be overlooked if even greater misfortune is not to befall humanity than has already occurred in recent times. For with regard to these things, the socialist proletarian party of the present day, from its most right wing to its centre to its most left wing, goes along with everything that it has inherited from the capitalist bourgeoisie as it has developed over the past centuries. That is the peculiarity of this bourgeoisie, that on the one hand it has completely objectified, detached the process of capital formation, the economy, from the personal aspirations of the human being; and that on the other hand this bourgeoisie—no matter whether it leans towards this or that traditional religious community or towards some newer sectarian grouping—that this bourgeoisie, because it considers it to be high-minded and right, wants to keep the life of the soul separate from everyday life and thus loses all overview of life, the overview that would be so necessary for people today.

I have met members of this Anthroposophical Society who, for example, asked a question like this: So, should we accept a person into the Society who works in a brewery, that is, who contributes to people drinking beer? I don't here want to speak either for or against drinking beer; but people's starting point was precisely that they were against drinking beer. In such a case, the only thing to say is: Well, you see, your judgement goes about as far as the tip of your nose; because, you see, your judgement extends just far enough to see a member or non-member who has a relatively unimportant position in a brewery. But I'm talking about facts. You have shares, you also have all kinds of securities; do you know how much beer you brew with your shares, with your securities? You don't care about that at all; you only pay attention to what is right in front of your nose.

It's not about criticizing someone because they think one way or another, but about pointing out the inconsistency, the incoherence, the confusion of this way of thinking. For that is the greatest misfortune in our time, that people, out of convenience, remain and want to remain with this disjointed, incoherent thinking, with this inner inconsistency, because they do not want to build the bridge from ethics, religion, spirituality on the one side to the other side, to direct real life, which today in the form of social and economic demands, the social conundrums in general, confronts humanity.

In this respect, there is still a lot to be learnt. Just remember how I have emphasized again and again that in dealing with the social question in the present, the most important thing is to look at intellectual and cultural matters. The school questions, the questions of intellectual and cultural life in general, these are the most important. If we look deeper into things, we can even say: as long as you allow the intellectual and cultural life to be dependent on the political community, as long as you allow the intellectual and cultural community, the intellectual and cultural life to be dependent, to be absorbed by just the political community, you can do what you want, you will not manage. What matters is that the school system should be made independent, that the way in which intellectual and cultural matters are dealt with should be made independent. And basically, humanity doesn't have much time to do this, because it could very soon be too late. Because there is only enough time for as long as there is still any possibility of getting through to the inner being of people despite their wildly raging instincts. Try preaching to people today who have already developed their angry instincts in the social chaos of the present, try preaching to them; you will be laughed at. That is why we want to appeal again and again to hearts and souls, so that people listen to what is actually necessary. Just as the development of capitalism in recent centuries has driven engagement with the spirit and thus engagement with the world in general into complete confusion, so anthroposophically orientated spiritual science wants to bring clarity to these things.

Let's take a look at the first point in the fourfold socialist ideal: the transfer of production enterprises into common ownership, into social ownership. Well, what this involves depends precisely on questions of the spirit, on a clear insight into certain answers to spiritual questions. For what will spiritual science, if it is not merely taken as dry theory, actually bring to human souls? This spiritual science will bring three things to human souls: firstly, not just a belief in some spiritual divine entity, but a perception of the spiritual worlds, even if perhaps only a perception mediated by concepts, but one that can be grasped by common sense.

In contrast to the blurred, often pantheistic or vaguely defined way of speaking about the spiritual world, anthroposophically orientated spiritual science provides perceptions of this spiritual world, speaks of a very specific structure of spiritual beings, of a structure of hierarchical orders within the spiritual world, provides perceptions of the spiritual world that are just as concrete as the perceptions of the mineral, plant and animal kingdoms within the physical world. These perceptions have been completely brushed aside by the developments of the last few centuries. Just consider how people today insist on faith without perception! That is the characteristic of anthroposophically orientated spiritual science, that it wants to give an insight into the spiritual world.

A second thing that this spiritual science gives to those who do not take it merely as sober, dry theory, but who allow it to take hold of their heart and soul, is a real, immeasurably far-reaching respect and appreciation of the human being. Can a spiritual view of life, which manifests itself as has been attempted in my *Occult Science. An Outline*, for example, lead to anything other than a real appreciation of the human being, if it is embraced by the whole soul, not just by theoretical reason? Consider, the whole cosmos is looked at insofar as the human being is placed in this cosmos. By not just speaking about earth evolution, but also about Moon, Sun and Saturn evolution, it is, after all, basically always the human being who is looked at. Compare in this respect anthroposophically orientated spiritual science with the ordinary natural science of the present day. The latter can lead to such hypotheses as the Kant Laplace hypothesis. It does not go back very far compared to what we go back to in the perception of the moon, sun and Saturn; it goes back to a certain state of the earth.

In the philosophical and scientific lunacy known as the Kant Laplace theory alone, human beings have long since been lost. They are no longer in it; there is a grey, primordial fog that this lunatic theory, which today is perceived as scientific, speaks of. This loss of the human being already within the earthly itself is contrasted with the observations of spiritual science, which seek out the human being in the entire cosmos. Certainly, this can be done by merely applying clever thoughts to the matter, by merely pursuing the matter theoretically. But for those who do not merely pursue this theoretically, but for whom the pursuit of this matter is the innermost content of their entire human being, such a view of the world leads to an immeasurably broad appreciation of the human being, an appreciation of the human being as such.

The appreciation of the human being as such—this is lacking in the modern view, which only focuses on the outwardly sensory sphere. Spiritual science remains in reality; it precisely sees the external sensory sphere as an illusion. But if we stop at external reality, we have no corrective, no such corrective as spiritual science has by looking at the cosmic human being and thereby arriving at an appreciation of the human being, in contrast to what sensory perception sometimes says about the human being. This materialistic view cannot arrive at any appreciation of the human being; it would have to be untrue. It would have to value the individual empirical person, the everyday person, that is, what it knows about this person. Well, that's not exactly possible!

Thus spiritual science is, firstly, the path to a spiritual perception as opposed to mere belief; it is the path to a genuine appreciation of human beings as opposed to the indifference to human beings that necessarily follows from a merely materialistic perception. And a third thing. There are, of course, things and processes in the cosmos outside the human being. How does spiritual science view these things and processes outside the human being? All in relation to the human being! Nothing is considered except in relation to the human being. The mineral, vegetable and animal kingdoms are considered in relation to the human being by spiritual science. This gives a certain appreciation of what is present in the outer physical world alongside the human being, or we could also say, below the human being.

Take the sentiment which is a genuinely spiritual-scientific one, and which Christian Morgenstern[109] took from out of spiritual science and recast in poetic form: human beings feel themselves to be at the top of the physical kingdoms of earth. Below them is the animal, vegetable and mineral kingdom. But if this vegetable kingdom could reflect emotionally on the mineral kingdom, what would it have to say to itself? I bow in reverence to you, thou mineral, for to you I owe my existence. If you did not give me the ground, even though you are lower than me in the hierarchical order of nature, if you did not give me the ground, I could not be. Similarly, the animal must bow in reverence to the plant and say: I thank you for my existence. And so on upwards. Every higher realm bows in reverence to the lower realm.

In this way, spiritual science finds the means to look also at the other world in relation to the human being, to bring it into a correct relationship. Spiritual science intervenes in three directions when it is able to intervene in spiritual life, but also in the life of the material in the present: firstly through spiritual perception; secondly, through appreciation of the human being; thirdly, through correctly valuing all things in the world in relation to the human being. Without these things happening, any demand for the socialization of production enterprises remains an empty demand. For as long as the three afore-mentioned preconditions in the human being's attitude to the world, to other human beings and to spirituality are not present, it is impossible for the right impulses to prevail in community life, which is supposed to pursue something in a socialist manner.

Nor is it possible to realize the second point in any way: regulating production according to need. After all, need is not just something that can be statistically recorded and used to regulate other things. Needs in real life are constantly changing, constantly metamorphosing. I ask you, let someone establish how great the demand for electric railways was in 1840! This need is conjured up by the cultural process itself, is transformed by the cultural process itself. If you want to regulate production according to an existing need, if you do not want to give production the initiative, you will cause need to stagnate. You can only establish the right relationship between need and production if you organize the social organism in a threefold way. Then, in living collaboration, the regulation between production and need is there by itself, as between the other impulses of the social organism.

Labour and wage relations should be regulated democratically. Well, the point here is that democracy is of no help at all if it is not based on the correct appreciation of the human being, the appreciation of the human being that can really only be thoroughly inscribed in the human soul through spiritual science. Democracy always contains the ferment of its own downfall if it does not at the same time contain the seed of real appreciation of the human being.

Added value—that is the fourth point—should be handed over to the community. My dear friends, allow me to say that in such a matter you catch the absolutely impossible thinking of such a course. What is added value? Added value is the very thing that the Marxist proletariat criticizes as impossible, as something to be abolished. A socialist order is to be established so that there is no more added value. In this socialist order, one essential aspect is that there would no longer be any added value. But one of their ideal points is that this added value should be passed on to the community! This indeed figures as one of the special points. Why does it figure? Well, because there will indeed be added value, and because the fact that there will be added value casts a shadow over the programme. But that is the shadow that definitely falls on the programme. This in turn throws all its blackness back on the whole theory.

And so humanity today lives reeling in a terrible blackness that can only be illuminated if we overcome the inconvenience of moving from faith to perception, from the mere empirically given position of one human being in relation to another to real appreciation of the human being, from the mere eating of things and the like to that appreciation of things in the world that are external to the human being, which is given when we know anthroposophically how to relate all things to the human being.

This is how closely the fate of spiritual-scientific endeavours is linked to the social conundrums of the present. And more than the desire to disseminate spiritual science in general, those who are serious about spiritual science have the desire in their souls to evoke a feeling in people of how necessary it is to disseminate those ideas, feelings and impulses of will that can only come from spiritual science, especially with regard to the most important and justified needs of the present. Well, these are things we will also continue to talk about.

NOTES

Textual basis: The lectures were recorded in shorthand by the professional stenographer Helene Finckh (1883–1960) and transcribed into plain text. The present edition is based on this transcript. During the review for the new edition, some passages were compared with the original shorthand, which gave rise to minor text corrections, and some unclear passages were also made more readable; this is the reason for occasional text deviations from the previous edition.

Works by Rudolf Steiner which are part of the Complete Works (CW—Gesamtausgabe GA) are indicated in the notes with their bibliography number. See also the overview at the end of the volume.

[1] Walther Rathenau, 1867–1922, industrialist, writer, politician. Foreign Minister in 1922, assassinated by right-wing radicals.
See Rudolf Steiner 'Experiences of the Old Year and Outlook over the New Year', lectures of 31 December 1918 and 1 January 1919, in *How Can Mankind Find the Christ Again? The Threefold Shadow-Existence of Our Time and the New Light of Christ*, CW 187.

[2] Could not be determined for lack of more detailed information.

[3] Ernst Haeckel, 1834–1919.

[4] Rudolf Eucken, 1846–1929, philosopher, Nobel Prize for Literature in 1908.

[5] Henri Bergson, 1859–1941, French philosopher.

[6] Otto Willmann, 1839–1920. Catholic educator and philosopher based on the modernized Aristotelian-Thomistic worldview.

[7] Arthur Drews, 1865–1935. *'Hat Jesus gelebt?' Berliner Religionsgespräch, Reden über die Christusmythe*, Berlin 1910.

[8] Erich Wasmann, 1859–1931. A Jesuit since 1875. He studied the life of ants and wrote, among other things, *Menschen- und Tierseele*, Cologne 1904.

[9] The name of this person could not be determined.

[10] Carl Vogt, 1817–1895. Zoologist, author of anthropological pamphlets, advocate of materialism.

[11] Jakob Moleschott, 1822–1893. Dutch physiologist, leading exponent of materialism.

[12] WK Clifford, 1845–1879, English mathematician.

[13] Herbert Spencer, 1820–1903, English philosopher.

[14] See Rudolf Steiner, *Knowledge of the Higher Worlds. How is it Achieved?*, CW 10.

[15] Cf. *Founding a Science of the Spirit*, CW 95, lecture 9; as well as *Universe, Earth, Human Being*, CW 105, lecture 4.

[16] 'He calls it reason—to use not least,/More animal to be than any beast.' *Faust I*, 'Prologue in Heaven'.

[17] 'If only in the grass he were still homely!/Instead he sniffs out any old baloney.' *Faust I*, 'Prologue in Heaven'.

[18] See 'Experiences of the Old Year and Outlook over the New Year' (cf. Note 1).

[19] See *Spiritual Beings in the Heavenly Bodies and in the Kingdoms of Nature*, lecture of 13 April 1912, CW 136.

[20] 'Luziferisches und Ahrimanisches in ihrem Verhältnis zum Menschen', in *Philosophie und Anthroposophie. Gesammelte Aufsätze 1904 –1918*. GA 35.

[21] See Hegel, *Enzyklopädie der philosophischen Wissenschaften*, 3. 'Gattung und Individuum', § 371.

[22] See Rudolf Steiner *From Symptom to Reality In Modern History*, CW 185.

[23] In *Stimmen der Zeit*, Volume 48, 1918, Issue 10 and 11.

[24] *Knowledge of the Higher Worlds. How it is Achieved?* (1904/05), CW 10.

[25] Juan de la Cruz, 1542–1591, Spanish mystic, disciple of Saint Teresa of Avila.

[26] This passage, which is unclear in the shorthand, was printed in the wrong rendering in the earlier editions.

[27] Copernicus' work was removed from the Index of Forbidden Books as early as 1757, but official permission to print and publish those works explaining the stationary position of the sun and the movement of the earth was not decided upon in Rome until 1822.

[28] In the eight and ninth lecture of *From Symptom to Reality In Modern History*, CW 185.

²⁹ The so-called St John's Masonry, which is most widespread in Central Europe, knows only three degrees. The masonry with high degrees is predominantly found in Western countries. Political and occult Freemasonry are practised by the Order with high degrees.

³⁰ Cf. in particular Rudolf Steiner, *The Temple Legend*, CW 93.

³¹ Spartacus, slave leader 73–71 BC. A newspaper edited by Karl Liebknecht was named after him in 1916, and the forces furthest to the left in the German revolution of 1918/19 were called 'Spartacists'.

³² See i.a. 'Sprüche in Prosa', Section 4 'Naturwissenschaft', in *Goethes Naturwissenschaftlichen Schriften*, edited with a commentary by Rudolf Steiner in Kürschners Deutsche National Litteratur, Volume 117, Section 2. Reprint Dornach 1975, GA 1 a-e.

³³ In the fourth Mystery Drama *The Souls' Awakening*, Scene 6. *Four Mystery Dramas* (1910–13), CW 14.

³⁴ No peace agreement had yet been reached (Armistice 11 November 1918, Peace of Versailles June 1919).

³⁵ Jean-Jacques Rousseau, 1712–1778.

³⁶ *Philosophy of Freedom* (1894), CW 4.

³⁷ *Occult Science. An Outline.* (1910), CW 13.

³⁸ Shortly after these lectures, Rudolf Steiner's fundamental work *Towards Social Renewal*, CW 23, was published.

³⁹ Karl Marx, 1818–1883.

⁴⁰ Gustav Schmöller, 1838–1883, political scientist, historian, economist.

⁴¹ Wilhelm Roscher, 1817–1894, historian of national economics.

⁴² Immanuel Kant, 1724–1804, see *Die Religion innerhalb der Grenzen der bloßen Vernunft* (1793), 1. Stück, 'Von der Einwohnung des bösen Prinzips neben dem Guten; oder über das radikale Böse in der menschlichen Natur'.

⁴³ At the time, a widely read Chinese author of works on cultural history. See the fourth lecture in *Innere Entwickelungsimpulse der Menschheit. Goethe und die Krisis des 19. Jahrhunderts*, GA 171 and the seventh lecture in *The Karma of Vocation*, CW 172.

⁴⁴ From 1902–1913 Rudolf Steiner was general secretary of the German section of the Theosophical Society, whose headquarters were in Adyar (India). The split took place in 1913. Cf. The *Anthroposophic Movement.*

The History and Conditions of the Anthroposophical Movement in Relation to the Anthroposophical Society: An Encouragement for Self-Examination, CW 258.

45 See *Cosmic Memory,* (1904–08), CW 11, offprint from the journal *Lucifer-Gnosis,* July 1904 to May 1908.

46 *Theosophie. An Introduction to the Spiritual Processes in Human Life and in the Cosmos* (1904), CW 9.

47 1 Corinthians 15:14.

48 *Christianity as a Mystical Fact and the Mysteries of Antiquity* (1902), CW 8.

49 Followers of Arius, died 336, presbyter in Alexandria. Arianism, to which the Germanic peoples in particular turned, was declared a heresy and eradicated after centuries of conflict.

50 Plato, 427–347 BC.

51 This view of Plato is expressed, among other things, in the *Timaeus.*

52 *Dichtung and Wahrheit,* Part 1, Book 1 (end).

53 'Die Natur' (aphoristic), c. 1780. *Goethes Naturwissenschaftliche Schriften,* edited with a commentary by Rudolf Steiner, vol. 2, pp. 5–9, see Note 32.

54 There were words of remembrance for Ms Leyh at the beginning of the lecture; they have been published in a different context.

55 Matthew 28:20.

56 Cf. in this respect the volumes *The Mystery of Death. The Nature and Significance of Central Europe and the European Folk-Spirits,* CW 159; *The Karma of Untruthfulness,* Volume 1, CW 173, Volume 2, CW 174; *The Spiritual Background to the First World War,* CW 174b.

57 President Wilson's Fourteen Points.

58 1825–1900, professor of literature at the Technical University in Vienna.

59 'Versuch einer Darstellung der deutschen Mundarten des ungarischen Berglands' in *Sitzungsberichte der k. Akademie der Wissenschaften* XLIV (1863), as well as XLV (1864).

60 In 1867, at the end of long disputes, a settlement was reached between Austria and Hungary based on dualism; Hungary became an independent half of the empire.

61 See Note 1.

62 To Eckermann, 12 March 1828: 'Meanwhile, let us have hope and expectation as to how things will look with us Germans in a century or so, and whether we will then have managed to become human beings rather than abstract scholars and philosophers.'

63 Herman Grimm, 1828–1902.

64 *Die Geheimnisse*, Fragment (1784), Sophien-Ausgabe, Weimar, Volume 16.

65 *Pandora. Ein Festspiel* (Pandorens Wiederkunft) (1807), Sophien-Ausgabe, Weimar, Volume 50. *Prometheus*, Dramatisches Fragment (1795), Sophien-Ausgabe Weimar, Volume 39.

66 *Die Natürliche Tochter, ein Trauerspiel* (1803), Sophien-Ausgabe Weimar, Volume 10.

67 *Goethes Geistesart in ihrer Offenbarung durch seinen 'Faust' und durch das Märchen von der Schlange und der Lilie* (1918), GA 22. *Goethe's Standard of the Soul*, Anth. Publ. Co. 1925.

68 Johann Kaspar Lavater, 1741–1801, writer and Protestant clergyman. Founder of physiognomics.

69 Johann Bernhard Basedow, 1723–1790, director of the Philantropinum in Dessau.

70 In the poem 'Between Lavater and Basedow'.

71 William Shakespeare, 1564–1616.

72 Goethe, *Italian Journey*.

73 Baruch Spinoza, 1632–1677.

74 Carl von Linné, 1707–1778.

75 *Italian Journey*, 6 September 1787.

76 See Note 67.

77 On 16 January, a performance of the scene 'Aegean Sea' from *Faust* Part 2 had taken place.

78 Earl of Shaftesbury, 1671–1713, English philosopher.

79 Frans Hemsterhuis, 1721–1790, Dutch philosopher.

80 In *Fragmente*, Stuttgart 1902, second and last part, page 40.

81 Martin Luther, 1483–1546.

82 Frederick the Great, 1712–1786, King of Prussia from 1740.

83 Otto, Prince von Bismarck, 1815–1898. Founder of the German Empire in 1871, of which he became the chancellor.

84 Friedrich Schiller, 1759–1805. *On the Aesthetic Education of Man, in a Series of Letters* (1793–1795).

85 'Duty! thou sublime and mighty name that dost embrace nothing charming or insinuating, but requirest submission ...'. *Critique of Practical Reason*, 1788, Part 1, Chapter III, 'Of the Motives of Pure Practical Reason'.

86   From the *Xenien*: 'Gewissensskrupel'.

87   See Note 58.

88   H Grimm on the Kant Laplace theory of the origin of the world in *Goethe*, lectures, held in Berlin, 2 vols, 8th edition, Stuttgart and Berlin 1903, 2nd volume, 23rd lecture, p. 171 f.

89   *Von Seelenrätseln* (1917), GA 21.

90   Pepsin, ptyalin: substances contained in human gastric juice or saliva.

91   Oneness, unstructured whole.

92   *Faust* Part 2, Act 2 (Classic Walpurgis Night). Cf. also Rudolf Steiner, 17 January 1919 in *Goethe's Faust in the Light of Anthroposophy*, CW 273. as well as Dornach, 21 December 1923 in *Mystery Knowledge and Mystery Centres*, CW 232.

93   'There probably the eighth is living, to whom no one yet a thought has given,' Faust op. cit.

94   In *Four Mystery Dramas* (1910–1913), CW 14.

95   *The Soul's Probation*, ibid.

96   Ferdinand Lassalle, 1825–1864, socialist leader. *Die Wissenschaft und die Arbeiter. Eine Verteidigungsrede vor dem Berliner Kriminalgericht gegen die Anklage, die besitzlosen Klassen zum Hass und zur Verachtung gegen die Besitzenden öffentlich aufgereizt zu haben.* Zürich 1863 (Science and the Workingmen: An argument in his own defence before the Criminal Court of Berlin on the charge of having publicly incited the unpropertied classes to hatred and contempt of the propertied classes.) A Translation of 'Die Wissenschaft und die Arbeiter' (January 1863) by Thorstein Veblen. With a Prefatory Note by Eduard Bernstein. New York:The International Library Publishing Co.,1901.

97   1818–1883. *The Communist Manifesto* (1848), *Capital* (3 volumes, 1867–1894).

98   *Wissen und Leben*, Volume XII, Issue 8/9 (15 January and 1 February 1919), p. 248: 'Für das deutsche Volk', by Hermann Fernau.

99   Cf. i.a. *Christ and the Spiritual World. The Quest for the Holy Grail* (1913/14), CW 149; *Unifying Humanity Spiritually Through the Christ Impulse* (1915/16), CW 165; *Materialism and the Task of Anthroposophy* (1921), CW 204.

100 On 25 December 1918 in *How Can Mankind Find the Christ Again?*, CW 187.

101 The human being created from the retort in Goethe's *Faust*, Part 2, Act 2 'Laboratory'.

[102] From March 1919 onwards, Rudolf Steiner devoted himself to the task of representing threefolding in public and publicizing the ideas summarized in the book *The Key Points of the Social Question* (see Note 38). See H Wiesberger, 'Chronik. 50 Jahre Die Kernpunkte der sozialen Frage 1919–1969' in Issue 24/25, and '1919, das Jahr der Dreigliederungsbewegung' in Issue 27/28 of *Beiträge zur Rudolf Steiner-Gesamtausgabe*, Dornach 1969.

[103] See Rudolf Steiner, *Rethinking Economics*, CW 340.

[104] The production of goods without a real need, i.e. for 'purely economically' generated needs, was first called a 'social carcinoma' by Rudolf Steiner in Vienna in 1914. See the lecture of 14 April in *The Inner Nature of Man and our Life between Death and Rebirth*, CW 153.

[105] Programme of the Social Democratic Party of Germany drawn up in 1891.

[106] 1854 –1939, social democratic theorist and historian. The Erfurt Programme is mainly due to him.

[107] Edgar Jaffé, professor of economics. The quote is from his brochure *Volkswirtschaft und Krieg*, Tübingen 1915, page 28.

[108] The victorious powers in the First World War.

[109] Christian Morgenstern (1871–1914) in his poem 'Fusswaschung' in the collection *Wir fanden einen Pfad*.

Rudolf Steiner's Collected Works

The German Edition of Rudolf Steiner's Collected Works (the *Gesamtausgabe* [GA], published by Rudolf Steiner Verlag, Dornach, Switzerland) will be completed in the year 2025. The works are organized either by type of work (written, spoken, artistic creations), chronology, audience (public or other), or subject (education, art, etc.). For ease of comparison, the Collected Works in English (CW), listed below, follows the German organization and numbering.

The volumes that have so far been published in the English Collected Works edition appear *in italics with their published titles*; all other volumes, including those that have appeared in editions other than the CW, are set in Roman type with *literal translations* of the German titles. Published English titles are not necessarily the same as the German.

This list is current as of the date of this volume's publication.

A. Written Works

I. Writings 1884–1925

CW 1	Introductions and Selected Commentary on Goethe's Natural-scientific Writings
CW 1a–e	Goethe's Natural-scientific Writings
CW 1f	Editorial Afterwords to Goethe's Natural-scientific Writings in the Weimar Edition (1891–1896)
CW 2	*Goethe's Theory of Knowledge: An Outline of the Epistemology of His Worldview*
CW 3	Truth and Science
CW 4	The Philosophy of Freedom
CW 4a	Documents to "The Philosophy of Freedom"
CW 5	Friedrich Nietzsche, A Fighter against His Own Time

CW 6   Goethe's Worldview
CW 7   Mysticism at the Dawn of Modern Spiritual Life and Its Relation-
            ship with Modern Worldviews
CW 8   *Christianity as Mystical Fact and the Mysteries of Antiquity*
CW 9   Theosophy: An Introduction into Supersensible World Knowl-
            edge and Human Purpose
CW 10   How Does One Attain Knowledge of Higher Worlds?
CW 11   From the Akasha-Chronicle
CW 12   Levels of Higher Knowledge
CW 13   Occult Science in Outline
CW 14   *Four Modern Mystery Dramas*
CW 15   The Spiritual Guidance of the Individual and Humanity
CW 16/17   *A Way of Self-Knowledge & The Threshold of the Spiritual World*
CW 18   The Riddles of Philosophy in Their History, Presented as an
            Outline
CW 18a   Views of the World and of Life in the Nineteenth Century
CW 19   Thoughts during the Time of War (1915) and Further Texts on
            the Events of the World War (1917–1921)
CW 20   The Riddles of the Human Being: Articulated and Unarticulated
            in the Thinking, Views and Opinions of a Series of German and
            Austrian Personalities
CW 21   The Riddles of the Soul
CW 22   Goethe's Spiritual Nature and Its Revelation in "Faust" and
            through the "Fairy Tale of the Snake and the Lily"
CW 23   The Central Points of the Social Question in the Necessities of
            Life in the Present and the Future
CW 24   Essays Concerning the Threefold Division of the Social Organ-
            ism and the Period 1915–1921
CW 25   Three Steps of Anthroposophy. Philosophy – Cosmology – Religion
CW 26   Anthroposophical Leading Thoughts
CW 27   Fundamentals for Expansion of the Art of Healing according to
            Spiritual-Scientific Insights
CW 28   *Autobiography: Chapters in the Course of My Life: 1861–1907*

II. Collected Essays

CW 29   Collected Essays on Dramaturgy, 1889–1900
CW 30   Methodical Foundations of Anthroposophy: Collected Essays on
            Philosophy, Natural Science, Aesthetics and Psychology, 1884–
            1901
CW 31   Collected Essays on Culture and Current Events, 1887–1901
CW 32   Collected Essays on Literature, 1884–1902
CW 33   Biographies and Biographical Sketches, 1894–1905

CW 34   Lucifer-Gnosis: Foundational Essays on Anthroposophy and Reports from the Periodicals "Luzifer" and "Lucifer-Gnosis," 1903–1908
CW 35   Philosophy and Anthroposophy: Collected Essays, 1904–1923
CW 36   The Goetheanum-Idea in the Middle of the Cultural Crisis of the Present: Collected Essays from the Periodical "Das Goetheanum," 1921–1925
CW 37   Writings on the History of the Anthroposophical Movement and Society 1902–1925

III. Publications from the Literary Estate

CW 38/1   Complete Letters, Vol. 1: Weimar Period 1879–1890
CW 38/2   Complete Letters, Vol. 2: Weimar Period 1890–1897
CW 38/3   Complete Letters, Vol. 3: Early Berlin Period 1897–1905 [forthcoming]
CW 38/4   Complete Letters, Vol. 4: Activity within the Theosophical Society 1905–1912 [forthcoming]
CW 38/5   Complete Letters, Vol. 5: From the Founding of the Anthroposophical Society to the Opening of the Goetheanum 1913–1920 [forthcoming]
CW 38/6   Compelte Letters, Vol. 6: The Last Years 1920–1925 [forthcoming]
CW 40   Truth-Wrought Words
CW 40a   Sayings, Poems and Mantras; Supplementary Volume
CW 41a   Translations and Free Renderings from the Old and New Testaments
CW 41b   Translations and Free Renderings of Various Works
CW 42   Stage Adaptations I: Dramas by Edouard Schuré
CW 43   Stage Adaptations II: The Oberufer Christmas Plays
CW 44   Sketches, Fragments and Paralipomena on the Four Mystery Dramas
CW 45   Anthroposophy: A Fragment from the Year 1910
CW 46   Posthumous Essays and Fragments 1879–1924
CW 47/48   Notebooks and Notepads (digital edition)
CW 49   Notes for and about Helmuth and Eliza von Moltke and Relatives, 1904–1924 [forthcoming]
CW 50   [Blank number]

B. Lectures

I. Public Lectures

CW 51   *On Philosophy, History, and Literature: Lectures at the Worker Education School and the Independent College, Berlin, 1901–1905*
CW 52   Spiritual Teachings Concerning the Soul and Observation of the World

II. Lectures to the Members of the Anthroposophical Society

The Theosophy in the Gospel of John

III. Lectures and Courses on Specific Realms of Life Lectures on Art

Lectures on Education

Lectures on Medicine

Lectures on Natural Science

CW 320   Spiritual-Scientific Impulses for the Development of Physics 1: The First Natural-Scientific Course: Light, Colour, Tone, Mass, Electricity, Magnetism

CW 321   Spiritual-Scientific Impulses for the Development of Physics 2: The Second Natural-Scientific Course: Warmth at the Border of Positive and Negative Materiality

CW 322   The Borders of the Knowledge of Nature

CW 323   *Interdisciplinary Astronomy: Third Scientific Course*

CW 324   Nature Observation, Mathematics, and Scientific Experimentation and Results from the Viewpoint of Anthroposophy

CW 324a   The Fourth Dimension in Mathematics and Reality

CW 325   Natural Science and the World-Historical Development of Humanity since Ancient Times

CW 326   The Moment of the Coming Into Being of Natural Science in World History and Its Development Since Then

CW 327   *Agriculture: Spiritual-Scientific Foundations for Agricultural Renewal*

Lectures on Social Life and the Threefold Arrangement of the Social Organism

CW 328   The Social Question

CW 329   The Liberation of the Human Being as the Foundation for a New Social Form

CW 330   The Renewal of the Social Organism

CW 331   Work-Council and Socialization

CW 332a   The Social Future

CW 332b   Lectures and Speeches on Social and Economic Issues

CW 333   *Freedom of Thought and Societal Forces: Implementing the Demands of Modern Society*

CW 334   From the Unified State to the Threefold Social Organism

CW 335   The Crisis of the Present and the Path to Healthy Thinking

CW 336   The Great Questions of the Times and Anthroposophical Spiritual Knowledge

CW 337a   Social Ideas, Social Realities, Social Practice, Vol. 1: Question-and-Answer Evenings and Study Evenings of the Alliance for the Threefold Social Organism in Stuttgart, 1919–1920

CW 337b   Social Ideas, Social Realities, Social Practice, Vol. 2: Discussion Evenings of the Swiss Alliance for the Threefold Social Organism

CW 338   *Communicating Anthroposophy: The Course for Speakers to Promote the Idea of Threefolding*

CW 339   Anthroposophy, Threefold Social Organism, and the Art of Public Speaking

CW 340/41   *Rethinking Economics: Lectures and Seminars on World Economics*

Lectures and Courses on Christian Religious Work

CW 342   *First Steps in Christian Religious Renewal: Preparing the Ground for The Christian Community*

CW 343   Lectures and Courses on Christian Religious Work, Vol. 2: Spiritual Knowledge – Religious Feeling – Cultic Doing

CW 344   Lectures and Courses on Christian Religious Work, Vol. 3: Lectures at the Founding of The Christian Community

CW 345   Lectures and Courses on Christian Religious Work, Vol. 4: Concerning the Nature of the Working Word

CW 346   Lectures and Courses on Christian Religious Work, Vol. 5: The Apocalypse and the Work of the Priest

Lectures for Workers at the Goetheanum

CW 347   The Knowledge of the Nature of the Human Being According to Body, Soul and Spirit. On Earlier Conditions of the Earth

CW 348   On Health and Illness. Foundations of a Spiritual-Scientific Doctrine of the Senses

CW 349   On the Life of the Human Being and of the Earth. On the Nature of Christianity

CW 350   Rhythms in the Cosmos and in the Human Being. How Does One Come To See the Spiritual World?

CW 351   The Human Being and the World. The Influence of the Spirit in Nature. On the Nature of Bees

CW 352   Nature and the Human Being Observed Spiritual-Scientifically

CW 353   The History of Humanity and the World-Views of the Folk Cultures

CW 354   The Creation of the World and the Human Being. Life on Earth and the Influence of the Stars

<h3 style="text-align:center">C. Artistic Works</h3>

CW A 1–10; 57 The Architectural Work I: The Goetheanum and Its Predecessors

CW A 11   The Sculptural Work

CW A 12   The Goetheanum Windows. The Speech of Light. Sketches and Studies

CW A 13–16;
52–56   Painting Work
CW A 14   Sketches for the Painting of the Small Dome of the First Goethe-
                 anum
CW A 27–43 The Architectural Work II: Commercial and Residential Buildings
                 in Dornach and Other Places [forthcoming]
CW A 45   The Graphic Work
CW A 48   The Drawing Work
CW A 51   The Art of Jewellry as a Goethean Language of Form
CW A 54.0   A Path of Training in Painting. Pastel Sketches and Watercolours
CW A 54.1   Nature Moods. Nine Training Sketches for Painters

Eurythmy Figures

CW A 26   Skectches of the Eurythmy Figures
CW A 26a   The Eurythmy Figures of Rudolf Steiner, Artistically Executed by
                 Annemarie Bäschlin
CW A 26b   Eurythmy Figures from the Time When They Were Created

Eurythmy Forms

CW A 23/1   Volume I: Eurythmy Forms for Poems by Rudolf Steiner
CW A 23/2   Volume II: Eurythmy Forms for the Calendar of the Soul by
                 Rudolf Steiner
CW A 23/3   Volume III: Euythmy Forms for Poems by J. W. von Goethe
CW A 23/4   Volume IV: Eurythmy Forms for Poems by Christian Morgen-
                 stern
CW A 23/5   Volume V: Eurythmy Forms for Poems by Albert Steffen
CW A 23/6   Volume VI: Eurythmy Forms for German Poems by Fercher von
                 Steinwand, Hamerling, Hebbel, C. F. Meyer, Nietzsche, among oth-
                 ers
CW A 23/7   Volume VII: Eurythmy Forms for English Poems
CW A 23/8   Volume VIII: Eurythmy Forms for French and Russian Poems
CW A 24   Volume IX: Eurythmy Forms for Tone Eurythmy

Blackboard Drawings from Lectures

CW A 58/1   Volume I: 20 Plates from Public Lectures 1920–1924 in CWs 73a,
                 74, 76, and 84
CW A 58/2   Volume II: 38 Plates from Lectures in 1919 in CWs 191 and 194
CW A 58/3   Volume III: 34 Plates from Lectures in 1920 in CWs 196 and 198
CW A 58/4   Volume IV: 33 Plates from Lectures in 1920 in CWs 199 and 200
CW A 58/5   Volume V: 31 Plates from Lectures in 1920 in CW 201
CW A 58/6   Volume VI: 46 Plates from Lectures 1920–1921 in CWs 202–204

CW A 58/7   Volume VII: 38 Plates from Lectures in 1921 in CWs 205 and 206
CW A 58/8   Volume VIII: 42 Plates from Lectures in 1921 in CWs 207–209
CW A 58/9   Volume IX: 40 Plates from Lectures in 1922 in CWs 210–212
CW A 58/10   Volume X: 35 Plates from Lectures in 1922 in CWs 213–215
CW A 58/11   Volume XI: 41 Plates from Lectures 1922–1923 in CWs 216, 218–220
CW A 58/12   Volume XII: 37 Plates from Lectures in 1923 in CWs 221–225
CW A 58/13   Volume XIII: 38 Plates from Lectures in 1923 in CWs 227–230
CW A 58/14   Volume XIV: 36 Plates from Lectures in 1923 in CWs 232 and 233
CW A 58/15   Volume XV: 37 Plates from Lectures in 1924 in CWs 233a, 234, and 243
CW A 58/16   Volume XVI: 56 Plates from the "Karma Lectures" in CWs 235–238 and 240
CW A 58/17   Volume XVII: 21 Plates from Lectures on the History of the Anthroposophical Society in CWs 257, 258, 260, and 260a
CW A 58/18   Volume XVIII: 33 Plates from Lectures on Art in CWs 271, 276, 283, 288–290, and 291
CW A 58/19   Volume XIX: 41 Plates from Lectures on Eurythmy in CWs 278, 279, and 315
CW A 58/20   Volume XX: 27 Plates from Lectures on Speech Formation in CWs 281 and 282
CW A 58/21   Volume XXI: 42 Plates from Lectures on Education in CWs 296, 303, 304, 306, and 311
CW A 58/22   Volume XXII: 46 Plates from Lectures on Medicine in CWs 312–315
CW A 58/23   Volume XXIII: 48 Plates from Lectures in 1924 in CWs 316–318
CW A 58/24   Volume XXIV: 39 Plates from Lectures on Natural Science and the Social Question in CWs 322, 326, 327, 339, and 340
CW A 58/25   Volume XXV: 33 Plates from the "Workers Lectures" (Volumes 1 and 2) in CWs 347 and 348
CW A 58/26   Volume XXVI: 51 Plates from the "Workers Lectures" (Volumes 3 and 4) in CWs 349 and 350
CW A 58/27   Volume XXVII: 35 Plates from the "Workers Lectures" (Volumes 5 and 6) in CWs 351 and 352
CW A 58/28   Volume XXVIII: 42 Plates from the "Workers Lectures" (Volumes 7 and 8) in CWs 353 and 354
CW A 58/29   Volume XXIX: 43 Plates from Lectures and Courses on Christian Religious Activity in CWs 342–344 and 346
CW A 58/30   Volume XXX: 27 Plates from CWs 255b, 324a, 337b, and 340, Corrigenda, Plates without CW Assignment, Copies

SIGNIFICANT EVENTS IN THE LIFE OF
RUDOLF STEINER

1829:	June 23: birth of Johann Steiner (1829–1910)—Rudolf Steiner's father—in Geras, Lower Austria.
1834:	May 8: birth of Franciska Blie (1834–1918)—Rudolf Steiner's mother—in Horn, Lower Austria. 'My father and mother were both children of the glorious Lower Austrian forest district north of the Danube.'
1860:	May 16: marriage of Johann Steiner and Franciska Blie.
1861:	February 25: birth of *Rudolf Joseph Lorenz Steiner* in Kraljevec, Croatia, near the border with Hungary, where Johann Steiner works as a telegrapher for the South Austria Railroad. Rudolf Steiner is baptized two days later, February 27, the date usually given as his birthday.
1862:	Summer: the family moves to Mödling, Lower Austria.
1863:	The family moves to Pottschach, Lower Austria, near the Styrian border, where Johann Steiner becomes stationmaster. 'The view stretched to the mountains . . . majestic peaks in the distance and the sweet charm of nature in the immediate surroundings.'
1864:	November 15: birth of Rudolf Steiner's sister, Leopoldine (d. November 1, 1927). She will become a seamstress and live with her parents for the rest of her life.
1866:	July 28: birth of Rudolf Steiner's deaf-mute brother, Gustav (d. May 1, 1941).
1867:	Rudolf Steiner enters the village school. Following a disagreement between his father and the schoolmaster, whose wife falsely accused the boy of causing a commotion, Rudolf Steiner is taken out of school and taught at home.
1868:	A critical experience. Unknown to the family, an aunt dies in a distant town. Sitting in the station waiting room, Rudolf Steiner sees her 'form', which speaks to him, asking for help. 'Beginning with this

experience, a new soul life began in the boy, one in which not only the outer trees and mountains spoke to him, but also the worlds that lay behind them. From this moment on, the boy began to live with the spirits of nature . . .'

1869: The family moves to the peaceful, rural village of Neudorfl, near Wiener Neustadt in present-day Austria. Rudolf Steiner attends the village school. Because of the 'unorthodoxy' of his writing and spelling, he has to do 'extra lessons'.

1870: Through a book lent to him by his tutor, he discovers geometry: 'To grasp something purely in the spirit brought me inner happiness. I know that I first learned happiness through geometry.' The same tutor allows him to draw, while other students still struggle with their reading and writing. 'An artistic element' thus enters his education.

1871: Though his parents are not religious, Rudolf Steiner becomes a 'church child', a favourite of the priest, who was 'an exceptional character'. 'Up to the age of ten or eleven, among those I came to know, he was far and away the most significant.' Among other things, he introduces Steiner to Copernican, heliocentric cosmology. As an altar boy, Rudolf Steiner serves at Masses, funerals, and Corpus Christi processions. At year's end, after an incident in which he escapes a thrashing, his father forbids him to go to church.

1872: Rudolf Steiner transfers to grammar school in Wiener-Neustadt, a five-mile walk from home, which must be done in all weathers.

1873–75: Through his teachers and on his own, Rudolf Steiner has many wonderful experiences with science and mathematics. Outside school, he teaches himself analytic geometry, trigonometry, differential equations, and calculus.

1876: Rudolf Steiner begins tutoring other students. He learns bookbinding from his father. He also teaches himself stenography.

1877: Rudolf Steiner discovers Kant's *Critique of Pure Reason,* which he reads and rereads. He also discovers and reads von Rotteck's *World History.*

1878: He studies extensively in contemporary psychology and philosophy.

1879: Rudolf Steiner graduates from high school with honours. His father is transferred to Inzersdorf, near Vienna. He uses his first visit to Vienna 'to purchase a great number of philosophy books'—Kant, Fichte, Schelling, and Hegel, as well as numerous histories of philosophy. His aim: to find a path from the 'I' to nature.

October
1879–1883: Rudolf Steiner attends the Technical College in Vienna—to study mathematics, chemistry, physics, mineralogy, botany, zoology,

biology, geology, and mechanics—with a scholarship. He also attends lectures in history and literature, while avidly reading philosophy on his own. His two favourite professors are Karl Julius Schröer (German language and literature) and Edmund Reitlinger (physics). He also audits lectures by Robert Zimmermann on aesthetics and Franz Brentano on philosophy. During this year he begins his friendship with Moritz Zitter (1861–1921), who will help support him financially when he is in Berlin.

1880: Rudolf Steiner attends lectures on Schiller and Goethe by Karl Julius Schröer, who becomes his mentor. Also 'through a remarkable combination of circumstances', he meets Felix Koguzki, a 'herb gatherer' and healer, who could 'see deeply into the secrets of nature'. Rudolf Steiner will meet and study with this 'emissary of the Master' throughout his time in Vienna.

1881: January: '... I didn't sleep a wink. I was busy with philosophical problems until about 12:30 a.m. Then, finally, I threw myself down on my couch. All my striving during the previous year had been to research whether the following statement by Schelling was true or not: *Within everyone dwells a secret, marvellous capacity to draw back from the stream of time—out of the self clothed in all that comes to us from outside—into our innermost being and there, in the immutable form of the Eternal, to look into ourselves.* I believe, and I am still quite certain of it, that I discovered this capacity in myself; I had long had an inkling of it. Now the whole of idealist philosophy stood before me in modified form. What's a sleepless night compared to that!'
Rudolf Steiner begins communicating with leading thinkers of the day, who send him books in return, which he reads eagerly.

July: 'I am not one of those who dives into the day like an animal in human form. I pursue a quite specific goal, an idealistic aim—knowledge of the truth! This cannot be done offhandedly. It requires the greatest striving in the world, free of all egotism, and equally of all resignation.'

August: Steiner puts down on paper for the first time thoughts for a 'Philosophy of Freedom'. 'The striving for the absolute: this human yearning is freedom.' He also seeks to outline a 'peasant philosophy', describing what the worldview of a 'peasant'—one who lives close to the earth and the old ways—really is.

1881–1882: Felix Koguzki, the herb gatherer, reveals himself to be the envoy of another, higher initiatory personality, who instructs Rudolf Steiner to penetrate Fichte's philosophy and to master modern scientific thinking as a preparation for right entry into the spirit. This 'Master' also teaches him the double (evolutionary and involutionary) nature of time.

1882:   Through the offices of Karl Julius Schröer, Rudolf Steiner is asked by Joseph Kürschner to edit Goethe's scientific works for the *Deutsche National-Literatur* edition. He writes 'A Possible Critique of Atomistic Concepts' and sends it to Friedrich Theodor Vischer.

1883:   Rudolf Steiner completes his college studies and begins work on the Goethe project.

1884:   First volume of Goethe's *Scientific Writings* (CW 1) appears (March). He lectures on Goethe and Lessing, and Goethe's approach to science. In July, he enters the household of Ladislaus and Pauline Specht as tutor to the four Specht boys. He will live there until 1890. At this time, he meets Josef Breuer (1842–1925), the co-author with Sigmund Freud of *Studies in Hysteria,* who is the Specht family doctor.

1885:   While continuing to edit Goethe's writings, Rudolf Steiner reads deeply in contemporary philosophy (Eduard von Hartmann, Johannes Volkelt, and Richard Wahle, among others).

1886:   May: Rudolf Steiner sends Kürschner the manuscript of *Outlines of Goethe's Theory of Knowledge* (CW 2), which appears in October, and which he sends out widely. He also meets the poet Marie Eugenie Delle Grazie and writes 'Nature and Our Ideals' for her. He attends her salon, where he meets many priests, theologians, and philosophers, who will become his friends. Meanwhile, the director of the Goethe Archive in Weimar requests his collaboration with the *Sophien* edition of Goethe's works, particularly the writings on colour.

1887:   At the beginning of the year, Rudolf Steiner is very sick. As the year progresses and his health improves, he becomes increasingly 'a man of letters', lecturing, writing essays, and taking part in Austrian cultural life. In August–September, the second volume of Goethe's *Scientific Writings* appears.

1888:   January–July: Rudolf Steiner assumes editorship of the 'German Weekly' *(Deutsche Wochenschrift).* He begins lecturing more intensively, giving, for example, a lecture titled 'Goethe as Father of a New Aesthetics'. He meets and becomes soul friends with Friedrich Eckstein (1861–1939), a vegetarian, philosopher of symbolism, alchemist, and musician, who will introduce him to various spiritual currents (including Theosophy) and with whom he will meditate and interpret esoteric and alchemical texts.

1889:   Rudolf Steiner first reads Nietzsche *(Beyond Good and Evil).* He encounters Theosophy again and learns of Madame Blavatsky in the theosophical circle around Marie Lang (1858–1934). Here he also meets well-known figures of Austrian life, as well as esoteric figures like the occultist Franz Hartmann and Karl Leinigen-Billigen (translator of C.G. Harrison's *The Transcendental Universe*). During this period, Steiner first reads A.P. Sinnett's *Esoteric Buddhism* and Mabel Collins's *Light on the Path*. He also begins travelling, visiting Budapest, Weimar, and Berlin (where he meets philosopher Eduard von Hartmann).

1890:   Rudolf Steiner finishes Volume 3 of Goethe's scientific writings. He begins his doctoral dissertation, which will become *Truth and Science* (CW 3). He also meets the poet and feminist Rosa Mayreder (1858–1938), with whom he can exchange his most intimate thoughts. In September, Rudolf Steiner moves to Weimar to work in the Goethe-Schiller Archive.

1891:   Volume 3 of the Kürschner edition of Goethe appears. Meanwhile, Rudolf Steiner edits Goethe's studies in mineralogy and scientific writings for the *Sophien* edition. He meets Ludwig Laistner of the Cotta Publishing Company, who asks for a book on the basic question of metaphysics. From this will result, ultimately, *The Philosophy of Freedom* (CW 4), which will be published not by Cotta but by Emil Felber. In October, Rudolf Steiner takes the oral exam for a doctorate in philosophy, mathematics, and mechanics at Rostock University, receiving his doctorate on the twenty-sixth. In November, he gives his first lecture on Goethe's 'Fairy Tale' in Vienna.

1892:   Rudolf Steiner continues work at the Goethe-Schiller Archive and on his *Philosophy of Freedom. Truth and Science,* his doctoral dissertation, is published. Steiner undertakes to write Introductions to books on Schopenhauer and Jean Paul for Cotta. At year's end, he finds lodging with Anna Eunike, née Schulz (1853–1911), a widow with four daughters and a son. He also develops a friendship with Otto Erich Hartleben (1864–1905) with whom he shares literary interests.

1893:   Rudolf Steiner begins his habit of producing many reviews and articles. In March, he gives a lecture titled 'Hypnotism, with Reference to Spiritism'. In September, volume 4 of the Kürschner edition is completed. In November, *The Philosophy of Freedom* appears. This year, too, he meets John Henry Mackay (1864–1933), the anarchist, and Max Stirner, a scholar and biographer.

1894:   Rudolf Steiner meets Elisabeth Fürster Nietzsche, the philosopher's sister, and begins to read Nietzsche in earnest, beginning with the as yet unpublished *Antichrist.* He also meets Ernst Haeckel (1834–1919). In the fall, he begins to write *Nietzsche, A Fighter against His Time* (CW 5).

1895:   May, *Nietzsche, A Fighter against His Time* appears.

1896:   January 22: Rudolf Steiner sees Friedrich Nietzsche for the first and only time. Moves between the Nietzsche and the Goethe-Schiller

Archives, where he completes his work before year's end. He falls out with Elisabeth Förster Nietzsche, thus ending his association with the Nietzsche Archive.

1897:   Rudolf Steiner finishes the manuscript of *Goethe's Worldview* (CW 6). He moves to Berlin with Anna Eunike and begins editorship of the *Magazin für Literatur*. From now on, Steiner will write countless reviews, literary and philosophical articles, and so on. He begins lecturing at the 'Free Literary Society'. In September, he attends the Zionist Congress in Basel. He sides with Dreyfus in the Dreyfus affair.

1898:   Rudolf Steiner is very active as an editor in the political, artistic, and theatrical life of Berlin. He becomes friendly with John Henry Mackay and poet Ludwig Jacobowski (1868–1900). He joins Jacobowski's circle of writers, artists, and scientists—'The Coming Ones' (*Die Kommenden*)—and contributes lectures to the group until 1903. He also lectures at the 'League for College Pedagogy'. He writes an article for Goethe's sesquicentennial, 'Goethe's Secret Revelation', on the 'Fairy Tale of the Green Snake and the Beautiful Lily'.

1898–99:   'This was a trying time for my soul as I looked at Christianity. . . . I was able to progress only by contemplating, by means of spiritual perception, the evolution of Christianity. . . . Conscious knowledge of real Christianity began to dawn in me around the turn of the century. This seed continued to develop. My soul trial occurred shortly before the beginning of the twentieth century. It was decisive for my soul's development that I stood spiritually before the Mystery of Golgotha in a deep and solemn celebration of knowledge.'

1899:   Rudolf Steiner begins teaching and giving lectures and lecture cycles at the Workers' College, founded by Wilhelm Liebknecht (1826–1900). He will continue to do so until 1904. Writes: *Literature and Spiritual Life in the Nineteenth Century; Individualism in Philosophy; Haeckel and His Opponents; Poetry in the Present;* and begins what will become (fifteen years later) *The Riddles of Philosophy* (CW 18). He also meets many artists and writers, including Käthe Kollwitz, Stefan Zweig, and Rainer Maria Rilke. On October 31, he marries Anna Eunike.

1900:   'I thought that the turn of the century must bring humanity a new light. It seemed to me that the separation of human thinking and willing from the spirit had peaked. A turn or reversal of direction in human evolution seemed to me a necessity.' Rudolf Steiner finishes *World and Life Views in the Nineteenth Century* (the second part of what will become *The Riddles of Philosophy*) and dedicates it to

Ernst Haeckel. It is published in March. He continues lecturing at *Die Kommenden,* whose leadership he assumes after the death of Jacobowski. Also, he gives the Gutenberg Jubilee lecture before 7,000 typesetters and printers. In September, Rudolf Steiner is invited by Count and Countess Brockdorff to lecture in the Theosophical Library. His first lecture is on Nietzsche. His second lecture is titled 'Goethe's Secret Revelation.' October 6, he begins a lecture cycle on the mystics that will become *Mystics after Modernism* (CW 7). November–December: 'Marie von Sivers appears in the audience. . . .' Also in November, Steiner gives his first lecture at the Giordano Bruno Bund (where he will continue to lecture until May, 1905). He speaks on Bruno and modern Rome, focusing on the importance of the philosophy of Thomas Aquinas as monism.

1901: In continual financial straits, Rudolf Steiner's early friends Moritz Zitter and Rosa Mayreder help support him. In October, he begins the lecture cycle *Christianity as Mystical Fact* (CW 8) at the Theosophical Library. In November, he gives his first 'theosophical lecture' on Goethe's 'Fairy Tale' in Hamburg at the invitation of Wilhelm Hubbe-Schleiden. He also attends a gathering to celebrate the founding of the Theosophical Society at Count and Countess Brockdorff's. He gives a lecture cycle, 'From Buddha to Christ,' for the circle of the *Kommenden.* November 17, Marie von Sivers asks Rudolf Steiner if Theosophy needs a Western–Christian spiritual movement (to complement Theosophy's Eastern emphasis). 'The question was posed. Now, following spiritual laws, I could begin to give an answer. . . .' In December, Rudolf Steiner writes his first article for a theosophical publication. At year's end, the Brockdorffs and possibly Wilhelm Hubbe-Schleiden ask Rudolf Steiner to join the Theosophical Society and undertake the leadership of the German section. Rudolf Steiner agrees, on the condition that Marie von Sivers (then in Italy) work with him.

1902: Beginning in January, Rudolf Steiner attends the opening of the Workers' School in Spandau with Rosa Luxemberg (1870–1919). January 17, Rudolf Steiner joins the Theosophical Society. In April, he is asked to become general secretary of the German Section of the Theosophical Society, and works on preparations for its founding. In July, he visits London for a theosophical congress. He meets Bertram Keightly, G.R.S. Mead, A.P. Sinnett, and Annie Besant, among others. In September, *Christianity as Mystical Fact* appears. In October, Rudolf Steiner gives his first public lecture on Theosophy ('Monism and Theosophy') to about three hundred people at the Giordano Bruno Bund. On October 19–21, the

German Section of the Theosophical Society has its first meeting; Rudolf Steiner is the general secretary, and Annie Besant attends. Steiner lectures on practical karma studies. On October 23, Annie Besant inducts Rudolf Steiner into the Esoteric School of the Theosophical Society. On October 25, Steiner begins a weekly series of lectures: 'The Field of Theosophy'. During this year, Rudolf Steiner also first meets Ita Wegman (1876–1943), who will become his close collaborator in his final years.

1903:   Rudolf Steiner holds about 300 lectures and seminars. In May, the first issue of the periodical *Luzifer* appears. In June, Rudolf Steiner visits London for the first meeting of the Federation of the European Sections of the Theosophical Society, where he meets Colonel Olcott. He begins to write *Theosophy* (CW 9).

1904:   Rudolf Steiner continues lecturing at the Workers' College and elsewhere (about 90 lectures), while lecturing intensively all over Germany among theosophists (about 140 lectures). In February, he meets Carl Unger (1878–1929), who will become a member of the board of the Anthroposophical Society (1913). In March, he meets Michael Bauer (1871–1929), a Christian mystic, who will also be on the board. In May, *Theosophy* appears, with the dedication: 'To the spirit of Giordano Bruno'. Rudolf Steiner and Marie von Sivers visit London for meetings with Annie Besant. June: Rudolf Steiner and Marie von Sivers attend the meeting of the Federation of European Sections of the Theosophical Society in Amsterdam. In July, Steiner begins the articles in *Luzifer-Gnosis* that will become *How to Know Higher Worlds* (CW 10) and *Cosmic Memory* (CW 11). In September, Annie Besant visits Germany. In December, Steiner lectures on Freemasonry. He mentions the High Grade Masonry derived from John Yarker and represented by Theodore Reuss and Karl Kellner as a blank slate 'into which a good image could be placed'.

1905:   This year, Steiner ends his non-theosophical lecturing activity. Supported by Marie von Sivers, his theosophical lecturing—both in public and in the Theosophical Society—increases significantly: 'The German Theosophical Movement is of exceptional importance.' Steiner recommends reading, among others, Fichte, Jacob Boehme, and Angelus Silesius. He begins to introduce Christian themes into Theosophy. He also begins to work with doctors (Felix Peipers and Ludwig Noll). In July, he is in London for the Federation of European Sections, where he attends a lecture by Annie Besant: 'I have seldom seen Mrs Besant speak in so inward and heartfelt a manner... Through Mrs Besant I have found the way to H.P. Blavatsky.' September to October, he gives a course of 31 lectures for a small group of esoteric students. In October, the annual meeting of the German Section of the Theosophical Society, which still remains very small, takes place. Rudolf Steiner reports membership has risen from 121 to 377 members. In November, seeking to establish esoteric 'continuity', Rudolf Steiner and Marie von Sivers participate in a 'Memphis-Misraim' Masonic ceremony. They pay 45 marks for membership. 'Yesterday, you saw how little remains of former esoteric institutions.' 'We are dealing only with a "framework" … for the present, nothing lies behind it. The occult powers have completely withdrawn.'

1906:   Expansion of theosophical work. Rudolf Steiner gives about 245 lectures, only 44 of which take place in Berlin. Cycles are given in Paris, Leipzig, Stuttgart, and Munich. Esoteric work also intensifies. Rudolf Steiner begins writing *An Outline of Esoteric Science* (CW 13). In January, Rudolf Steiner receives permission (a patent) from the Great Orient of the Scottish A & A Thirty-Three Degree Rite of the Order of the Ancient Freemasons of the Memphis-Misraim Rite to direct a chapter under the name 'Mystica Aeterna.' This will become the 'Cognitive-Ritual Section' (also called 'Misraim Service') of the Esoteric School. (See: *Freemasonry and Ritual Work: The Misraim Service,* CW 265.) During this time, Steiner also meets Albert Schweitzer. In May, he is in Paris, where he visits Édouard Schuré. Many Russians attend his lectures (including Konstantin Balmont, Dimitri Mereszkovski, Zinaida Hippius, and Maximilian Woloshin). He attends the General Meeting of the European Federation of the Theosophical Society, at which Col Olcott is present for the last time. He spends the year's end in Venice and Rome, where he writes and works on his translation of H.P. Blavatsky's *Key to Theosophy.*

1907:   Further expansion of the German Theosophical Movement according to the Rosicrucian directive to 'introduce spirit into the world'—in education, in social questions, in art, and in science. In February, Col Olcott dies in Adyar. Before he dies, Olcott indicates that 'the Masters' wish Annie Besant to succeed him: much politicking ensues. Rudolf Steiner supports Besant's candidacy. April–May: preparations for the Congress of the Federation of European Sections of the Theosophical Society—the great, watershed Whitsun 'Munich Congress,' attended by Annie Besant and others. Steiner decides to separate Eastern and Western (Christian–Rosicrucian) esoteric schools. He takes his esoteric school out of the Theosophical Society (Besant and Rudolf Steiner are 'in harmony' on this). Steiner makes his first lecture tours to Austria and

Hungary. That summer, he is in Italy. In September, he visits Édouard Schuré, who will write the Introduction to the French edition of *Christianity as Mystical Fact* in Barr, Alsace. Rudolf Steiner writes the autobiographical statement known as the 'Barr Document.' In *Luzifer-Gnosis*, 'The Education of the Child' appears.

1908: The movement grows (membership: 1,150). Lecturing expands. Steiner makes his first extended lecture tour to Holland and Scandinavia, as well as visits to Naples and Sicily. Themes: St John's Gospel, the Apocalypse, Egypt, science, philosophy, and logic. *Luzifer-Gnosis* ceases publication. In Berlin, Marie von Sivers (with Johanna Mücke (1864–1949) forms the *Philosophisch-Theosophisch* (after 1915 *Philosophisch-Anthroposophisch) Verlag* to publish Steiner's work. Steiner gives lecture cycles titled *The Gospel of St John* (CW 103) and *The Apocalypse* (104).

1909: *An Outline of Esoteric Science* appears. Lecturing and travel continues. Rudolf Steiner's spiritual research expands to include the polarity of Lucifer and Ahriman; the work of great individualities in history; the Maitreya Buddha and the Bodhisattvas; spiritual economy (CW 109); the work of the spiritual hierarchies in heaven and on earth (CW 110). He also deepens and intensifies his research into the Gospels, giving lectures on the Gospel of St Luke (CW 114) with the first mention of two Jesus children. Meets and becomes friends with Christian Morgenstern (1871–1914). In April, he lays the foundation stone for the Malsch model—the building that will lead to the first Goetheanum. In May, the International Congress of the Federation of European Sections of the Theosophical Society takes place in Budapest. Rudolf Steiner receives the Subba Row medal for *How to Know Higher Worlds*. During this time, Charles W. Leadbeater discovers Jiddu Krishnamurti (1895–1986) and proclaims him the future 'world teacher,' the bearer of the Maitreya Buddha and the 'reappearing Christ.' In October, Steiner delivers seminal lectures on 'anthroposophy,' which he will try, unsuccessfully, to rework over the next years into the unfinished work, *Anthroposophy (A Fragment)* (CW 45).

1910: New themes: *The Reappearance of Christ in the Etheric* (CW 118); *The Fifth Gospel; The Mission of Folk Souls* (CW 121); *Occult History* (CW 126); the evolving development of etheric cognitive capacities. Rudolf Steiner continues his Gospel research with *The Gospel of St Matthew* (CW 123). In January, his father dies. In April, he takes a month-long trip to Italy, including Rome, Monte Cassino, and Sicily. He also visits Scandinavia again. July–August, he writes the first Mystery Drama, *The Portal of Initiation* (CW 14). In November, he gives 'psychosophy' lectures. In December, he submits 'On the

1911: Psychological Foundations and Epistemological Framework of Theosophy' to the International Philosophical Congress in Bologna. The crisis in the Theosophical Society deepens. In January, 'The Order of the Rising Sun,' which will soon become 'The Order of the Star in the East,' is founded for the coming world teacher, Krishnamurti. At the same time, Marie von Sivers, Rudolf Steiner's co-worker, falls ill. Fewer lectures are given, but important new ground is broken. In Prague, in March, Steiner meets Franz Kafka (1883–1924) and Hugo Bergmann (1883–1975). In April, he delivers his paper to the Philosophical Congress. He writes the second Mystery Drama, *The Soul's Probation* (CW 14). Also, while Marie von Sivers is convalescing, Rudolf Steiner begins work on *Calendar 1912/1913*, which will contain the 'Calendar of the Soul' meditations. On March 19, Anna (Eunike) Steiner dies. In September, Rudolf Steiner visits Einsiedeln, birthplace of Paracelsus. In December, Friedrich Rittelmeyer, future founder of The Christian Community, meets Rudolf Steiner. The *Johannes-Bauverein,* the 'building committee,' which would lead to the first Goetheanum (first planned for Munich), is also founded, and a preliminary committee for the founding of an independent association is created that, in the following year, will become the Anthroposophical Society. Important lecture cycles include *Occult Physiology* (CW 128); *Wonders of the World* (CW 129); *From Jesus to Christ* (CW 131). Other themes: esoteric Christianity; Christian Rosenkreutz; the spiritual guidance of humanity; the sense world and the world of the spirit.

1912: Despite the ongoing, now increasing crisis in the Theosophical Society, much is accomplished: *Calendar 1912/1913* is published; eurythmy is created; both the third Mystery Drama, *The Guardian of the Threshold* (CW 14) and *A Way of Self-Knowledge* (CW 16) are written. New (or renewed) themes included life between death and rebirth and karma and reincarnation. Other lecture cycles: *Spiritual Beings in the Heavenly Bodies and in the Kingdoms of Nature* (CW 136); *The Human Being in the Light of Occultism, Theosophy, and Philosophy* (CW 137); *The Gospel of St Mark* (CW 139); and *The Bhagavad Gita and the Epistles of Paul* (CW 142). On May 8, Rudolf Steiner celebrates White Lotus Day, H.P. Blavatsky's death day, which he had faithfully observed for the past decade, for the last time. In August, Rudolf Steiner suggests the 'independent association' be called the 'Anthroposophical Society.' In September, the first eurythmy course takes place. In October, Rudolf Steiner declines recognition of a Theosophical Society lodge dedicated to the Star of the East and decides to expel all Theosophical Society members belonging to the order.

Also, with Marie von Sivers, he first visits Dornach, near Basel, Switzerland, and they stand on the hill where the Goetheanum will be built. In November, a Theosophical Society lodge is opened by direct mandate from Adyar (Annie Besant). In December, a meeting of the German section occurs at which it is decided that belonging to the Order of the Star of the East is incompatible with membership in the Theosophical Society. December 28: informal founding of the Anthroposophical Society in Berlin.

1913:   Expulsion of the German section from the Theosophical Society. February 2–3: Foundation meeting of the Anthroposophical Society. Board members include: Marie von Sivers, Michael Bauer, and Carl Unger. September 20: Laying of the foundation stone for the *Johannes Bau* (Goetheanum) in Dornach. Building begins immediately. The fourth Mystery Drama, *The Soul's Awakening* (CW 14), is completed. Also: *The Threshold of the Spiritual World* (CW 147). Lecture cycles include: *The Bhagavad Gita and the Epistles of Paul* and *The Esoteric Meaning of the Bhagavad Gita* (CW 146), which the Russian philosopher Nikolai Berdyaev attends; *The Mysteries of the East and of Christianity* (CW 144); *The Effects of Esoteric Development* (CW 145); and *The Fifth Gospel* (CW 148). In May, Rudolf Steiner is in London and Paris, where anthroposophical work continues.

1914:   Building continues on the *Johannes Bau* (Goetheanum) in Dornach, with artists and co-workers from seventeen nations. The general assembly of the Anthroposophical Society takes place. In May, Rudolf Steiner visits Paris, as well as Chartres Cathedral. June 28: assassination in Sarajevo ('Now the catastrophe has happened!'). August 1: War is declared. Rudolf Steiner returns to Germany from Dornach—he will travel back and forth. He writes the last chapter of *The Riddles of Philosophy*. Lecture cycles include: *Human and Cosmic Thought* (CW 151); *Inner Being of Humanity between Death and a New Birth* (CW 153); *Occult Reading and Occult Hearing* (CW 156). December 24: marriage of Rudolf Steiner and Marie von Sivers.

1915:   Building continues. Life after death becomes a major theme, also art. Writes: *Thoughts during a Time of War* (CW 24). Lectures include: *The Secret of Death* (CW 159); *The Uniting of Humanity through the Christ Impulse* (CW 165).

1916:   Rudolf Steiner begins work with Edith Maryon (1872–1924) on the sculpture 'The Representative of Humanity' ('The Group'—Christ, Lucifer, and Ahriman). He also works with the alchemist Alexander von Bernus on the quarterly *Das Reich*. He writes *The Riddle of Humanity* (CW 20). Lectures include: *Necessity and Freedom in World History and Human Action* (CW 166); *Past and Present in the*

Human Spirit (CW 167); *The Karma of Vocation* (CW 172); *The Karma of Untruthfulness* (CW 173).

1917:   Russian Revolution. The U.S. enters the war. Building continues. Rudolf Steiner delineates the idea of the 'threefold nature of the human being' (in a public lecture March 15) and the 'threefold nature of the social organism' (hammered out in May–June with the help of Otto von Lerchenfeld and Ludwig Polzer-Hoditz in the form of two documents titled *Memoranda,* which were distributed in high places). August–September: Rudolf Steiner writes *The Riddles of the Soul* (CW 20). Also: commentary on 'The Chymical Wedding of Christian Rosenkreutz' for Alexander Bernus (Das *Reich*). Lectures include: *The Karma of Materialism* (CW 176); *The Spiritual Background of the Outer World: The Fall of the Spirits of Darkness* (CW 177).

1918:   March 18: peace treaty of Brest-Litovsk—'Now everything will truly enter chaos! What is needed is cultural renewal.' June: Rudolf Steiner visits Karlstein (Grail) Castle outside Prague. Lecture cycle: *From Symptom to Reality in Modern History* (CW 185). In mid-November, Emil Molt, of the Waldorf-Astoria Cigarette Company, has the idea of founding a school for his workers' children.

1919:   Focus on the threefold social organism: tireless travel, countless lectures, meetings, and publications. At the same time, a new public stage of Anthroposophy emerges as cultural renewal begins. The coming years will see initiatives in pedagogy, medicine, pharmacology, and agriculture. January 27: threefold meeting: 'We must first of all, with the money we have, found free schools that can bring people what they need.' February: first public eurythmy performance in Zurich. Also: 'Appeal to the German People' (CW 24), circulated March 6 as a newspaper insert. In April, *Towards Social Renewal* (CW 23) appears—'perhaps the most widely read of all books on politics appearing since the war'. Rudolf Steiner is asked to undertake the 'direction and leadership' of the school founded by the Waldorf-Astoria Company. Rudolf Steiner begins to talk about the 'renewal' of education. May 30: a building is selected and purchased for the future Waldorf School. August–September, Rudolf Steiner gives a lecture course for Waldorf teachers, *The Foundations of Human Experience (Study of Man)* (CW 293). September 7: Opening of the first Waldorf School. December (into January): first science course, the *Light Course* (CW 320).

1920:   The Waldorf School flourishes. New threefold initiatives. Founding of limited companies *Der Kommende Tag* and *Futurum A.G.* to infuse spiritual values into the economic realm. Rudolf Steiner also focuses on the sciences. Lectures: *Introducing Anthroposophical*

Medicine (CW 312); *The Warmth Course* (CW 321); *The Boundaries of Natural Science* (CW 322); *The Redemption of Thinking* (CW 74). February: Johannes Werner Klein—later a co-founder of The Christian Community—asks Rudolf Steiner about the possibility of a 'religious renewal,' a 'Johannine church.' In March, Rudolf Steiner gives the first course for doctors and medical students. In April, a divinity student asks Rudolf Steiner a second time about the possibility of religious renewal. September 27–October 16: anthroposophical 'university course.' December: lectures titled *The Search for the New Isis* (CW 202).

1921:   Rudolf Steiner continues his intensive work on cultural renewal, including the uphill battle for the threefold social order. 'University' arts, scientific, theological, and medical courses include: *The Astronomy Course* (CW 323); *Observation, Mathematics, and Scientific Experiment* (CW 324); the *Second Medical Course* (CW 313); *Colour.* In June and September–October, Rudolf Steiner also gives the first two 'priests' courses' (CW 342 and 343). The 'youth movement' gains momentum. Magazines are founded: *Die Drei* (January), and—under the editorship of Albert Steffen (1884–1963)—the weekly, *Das Goetheanum* (August). In February–March, Rudolf Steiner takes his first trip outside Germany since the war (Holland). On April 7, Steiner receives a letter regarding 'religious renewal,' and May 22–23, he agrees to address the question in a practical way. In June, the Klinical-Therapeutic Institute opens in Arlesheim under the direction of Dr Ita Wegman. In August, the Chemical-Pharmaceutical Laboratory opens in Arlesheim (Oskar Schmiedel and Ita Wegman are directors). The Clinical Therapeutic Institute is inaugurated in Stuttgart (Dr Ludwig Noll is director); also the Research Laboratory in Dornach (Ehrenfried Pfeiffer and Gunther Wachsmuth are directors). In November–December, Rudolf Steiner visits Norway.

1922:   The first half of the year involves very active public lecturing (thousands attend); in the second half, Rudolf Steiner begins to withdraw and turn toward the Society—'The Society is asleep.' It is 'too weak' to do what is asked of it. The businesses—*Der Kommende Tag* and *Futurum A.G.*—fail. In January, with the help of an agent, Steiner undertakes a twelve-city German lecture tour, accompanied by eurythmy performances. In two weeks he speaks to more than 2,000 people. In April, he gives a 'university course' in The Hague. He also visits England. In June, he is in Vienna for the East–West Congress. In August–September, he is back in England for the Oxford Conference on Education. Returning to Dornach, he gives the lectures *Philosophy, Cosmology, and*

Religion (CW 215), and gives the third priests' course (CW 344). On September 16, The Christian Community is founded. In October–November, Steiner is in Holland and England. He also speaks to the youth: *The Youth Course* (CW 217). In December, Steiner gives lectures titled *The Origins of Natural Science* (CW 326), and *Humanity and the World of Stars: The Spiritual Communion of Humanity* (CW 219). December 31: Fire at the Goetheanum, which is destroyed.

1923: Despite the fire, Rudolf Steiner continues his work unabated. A very hard year. Internal dispersion, dissension, and apathy abound. There is conflict—between old and new visions—within the Society. A wake-up call is needed, and Rudolf Steiner responds with renewed lecturing vitality. His focus: the spiritual context of human life; initiation science; the course of the year; and community building. As a foundation for an artistic school, he creates a series of pastel sketches. Lecture cycles: *The Anthroposophical Movement; Initiation Science* (CW 227) (in Wales at the Penmaenmawr Summer School); *The Four Seasons and the Archangels* (CW 229); *Harmony of the Creative Word* (CW 230); *The Supersensible Human* (CW 231), given in Holland for the founding of the Dutch Society. On November 10, in response to the failed Hitler-Ludendorff putsch in Munich, Steiner closes his Berlin residence and moves the *Philosophisch-Anthroposophisch Verlag* (Press) to Dornach. On December 9, Steiner begins the serialization of his *Autobiography: The Course of My Life* (CW 28) in *Das Goetheanum.* It will continue to appear weekly, without a break, until his death. Late December–early January: Rudolf Steiner re-founds the Anthroposophical Society (about 12,000 members internationally) and takes over its leadership. The new board members are: Marie Steiner, Ita Wegman, Albert Steffen, Elisabeth Vreede, and Gunther Wachsmuth. (See *The Christmas Meeting for the Founding of the General Anthroposophical Society, CW 260.)* Accompanying lectures: *Mystery Knowledge and Mystery Centres* (CW 232); *World History in the Light of Anthroposophy* (CW 233). December 25: the Foundation Stone is laid (in the hearts of members) in the form of the 'Foundation Stone Meditation.'

1924: January 1: having founded the Anthroposophical Society and taken over its leadership, Rudolf Steiner has the task of 'reforming' it. The process begins with a weekly newssheet ('What's Happening in the Anthroposophical Society') in which Rudolf Steiner's 'Letters to Members' and 'Anthroposophical Leading Thoughts' appear (CW 26). The next step is the creation of a new esoteric class, the 'first class' of the 'University of Spiritual Science' (which was to have been followed, had Rudolf Steiner lived longer, by two more advanced classes). Then comes a new language for

Anthroposophy—practical, phenomenological, and direct; and Rudolf Steiner creates the model for the second Goetheanum. He begins the series of extensive 'karma' lectures (CW 235–40); and finally, responding to needs, he creates two new initiatives: biodynamic agriculture and curative education. After the middle of the year, rumours begin to circulate regarding Steiner's health. Lectures: January–February, *Anthroposophy* (CW 234); February: *Tone Eurythmy* (CW 278); June: *The Agriculture Course* (CW 327); June–July: *Speech Eurythmy* (CW 279); *Curative Education* (CW 317); August: (England, 'Second International Summer School'), *Initiation Consciousness: True and False Paths in Spiritual Investigation* (CW 243); September: *Pastoral Medicine* (CW 318). On September 26, for the first time, Rudolf Steiner cancels a lecture. On September 28, he gives his last lecture. On September 29, he withdraws to his studio in the carpenter's shop; now he is definitively ill. Cared for by Ita Wegman, he continues working, however, and writing the weekly instalments of his *Autobiography* and *Letters to the Members/Leading Thoughts* (CW 26).

1925:   Rudolf Steiner, while continuing to work, continues to weaken. He finishes *Extending Practical Medicine* (CW 27) with Ita Wegman. On March 30, around ten in the morning, Rudolf Steiner dies.

Index